Stella Möhrle

Case-Based Decision Support for Disaster Management

Case-Based Decision Support for Disaster Management

by
Stella Möhrle

KIT Scientific Publishing

Karlsruher Institut für Technologie
Institut für Thermische Energietechnik und Sicherheit (ITES)
(früher: Institut für Kern- und Energietechnik (IKET))
Institut für Angewandte Informatik und Formale Beschreibungsverfahren (AIFB)
Center for Disaster Management and Risk Reduction Technology (CEDIM)

Case-Based Decision Support for Disaster Management

Zur Erlangung des akademischen Grades eines Doktors der Ingenieurwissenschaften von der KIT-Fakultät für Wirtschaftswissenschaften des Karlsruher Instituts für Technologie (KIT) genehmigte Dissertation

von Dipl.-Math. oec. Stella Möhrle

Tag der mündlichen Prüfung: 10. Oktober 2019
Erster Gutachter: Prof. Dr. Andreas Oberweis
Zweiter Gutachter: Prof. Dr. Frank Schultmann

Impressum

KIT Scientific Publishing

Karlsruher Institut für Technologie (KIT)
KIT Scientific Publishing
Straße am Forum 2
D-76131 Karlsruhe

www.ksp.kit.edu

Print on Demand 2020 – Gedruckt auf FSC-zertifiziertem Papier

ISBN 978-3-7315-0992-9
DOI 10.5445/KSP/1000099369

Vorwort

Diese Arbeit entstand im Rahmen meiner Tätigkeiten am Institut für Kern- und Energietechnik (IKET), mittlerweile Institut für Thermische Energietechnik und Sicherheit (ITES), am Institut für Angewandte Informatik und Formale Beschreibungsverfahren (AIFB) und am Center for Disaster Management and Risk Reduction Technology (CEDIM) des Karlsruher Instituts für Technologie (KIT). Die Ergebnisse dieser Arbeit resultierten unter anderem aus einem Forschungsprojekt zum nuklearen Katastrophenmanagement, das von der Europäischen Atomgemeinschaft im 7. Rahmenprogramm unter dem Förderkennzeichen 323287 gefördert wurde.

Mit Freude möchte ich mich an dieser Stelle bei den Menschen bedanken, die mich bei der Erstellung dieser Arbeit maßgeblich unterstützt haben. Besonderer Dank gilt meinem Doktorvater Herrn Prof. Dr. Andreas Oberweis für die hervorragende und engagierte Betreuung der Arbeit. Des Weiteren danke ich herzlich Herrn Prof. Dr. Frank Schultmann für die Übernahme des Korreferats, Herrn Prof. Dr. Hartmut Schmeck für die hilfreichen Anregungen und Herrn Prof. Dr. Hagen Lindstädt für die Übernahme des Prüfungsvorsitzes.

Mein besonderer Dank gilt Wolfgang Raskob für die uneingeschränkte Unterstützung meines Promotionsvorhabens, die zahlreichen fachlichen Diskussionen sowie wertvollen Impulse und Ratschläge. Mein Dank gilt ebenfalls Ruth Petters-Raskob, die mich stets mit ihrer Begeisterung für das Thema unterstützt und meine Arbeit Korrektur gelesen hat. Dr. Tim Oliver Müller danke ich für die vielen Gedankenanstöße, konstruktive Kritik und motivierenden Worte. Mein herzlicher Dank gilt ebenfalls Elvira Munz für die gemeinsame Entwicklung des Prototyps.

Die kollegiale Zusammenarbeit und gute Arbeitsatmosphäre haben ebenfalls zum Gelingen der Arbeit beigetragen. Daher gilt mein herzlicher Dank allen aktuellen und ehemaligen Kolleginnen und Kollegen der Gruppe Unfallfolgen des ITES, des Lehrstuhls für Betriebliche Informationssysteme des Instituts AIFB und des CEDIM. Mein besonderer Dank gilt allen Projektpartnern aus verschiedenen europäischen Institutionen für ihre aufschlussreichen Beiträge und engagierte Unterstützung. Für die vielen fachlichen Diskussionen, persönliche Unterstützung und Freundschaften danke ich besonders Meike Ullrich, Dr. Andreas Schoknecht, Dr. Shan Bai, Dima Trybushnyi, Dr. Thomas Münzberg, Irmgard Hasemann, Dr. Thomas Schichtel, Gerhard Benz, Susan Mickel und Annemarie Wengert.

Schließlich danke ich meiner Familie und meinen Freunden, die mir stets mit Enthusiasmus und Hilfsbereitschaft zur Seite stehen. Meinem Partner Jeremy Hofmann und unserer Tochter Matilda danke ich für ihre vielseitige und liebevolle Unterstützung sowie ihre Geduld und ihr Verständnis in arbeitsintensiven Phasen. Besonderer Dank gilt meinen Schwiegereltern Isabella und Udo Hermann, die mir stets den Rücken gestärkt und zeitliche Freiräume ermöglicht haben. Weiterhin danke ich Dr. Jessica Koch, die mich seit vielen Jahren stärkt und inspiriert. Von Herzen danke ich meinen Großeltern, Wanse und Karl Peter Möhrle, die mir diesen Weg ermöglicht und immer an mich geglaubt haben.

Karlsruhe, im November 2019 Stella Möhrle

Kurzfassung

Katastrophen beeinträchtigen das Funktionieren einer Gemeinschaft oder Gesellschaft schwerwiegend, führen zu menschlichen, materiellen, ökonomischen und ökologischen Verlusten großen Ausmaßes und erfordern nationale oder internationale Hilfe zur Bewältigung. Die Ursachen können technischen, menschlichen oder natürlichen Ursprungs sein. Kerntechnische Unfälle stellen erhöhte Anforderungen an die Entscheider, da die Freisetzung von radioaktiven Substanzen zu langfristigen und auch grenzüberschreitenden gesundheitlichen Risiken für den Mensch und zur Kontamination der Umwelt führen kann. Ein kerntechnischer Unfall kann in mehrere Phasen eingeteilt werden, die durch unterschiedliche Maßnahmen zum Schutz der Bevölkerung charakterisiert sind. Entscheidungen über geeignete Maßnahmen in der Frühphase werden durch eine sehr hohe Unsicherheit in entscheidungsrelevanten Informationen erschwert. In den späteren Phasen eines Unfalls liegt die Schwierigkeit in der Vielzahl möglicher Maßnahmen und sich teilweise widersprechenden Interessen der zu berücksichtigenden Akteure.

Entscheidungsunterstützende Methoden und Systeme können bei der Auswahl geeigneter Maßnahmen helfen. Deren Entwicklung ist Teil der Vorsorgeforschung, um die Bewältigung einer Katastrophe und die Wiederherstellung normaler Lebensbedingungen zu unterstützen. Die Unfälle in Tschernobyl und Fukushima haben die Wichtigkeit einer guten Vorbereitung und Bereitstellung notwendiger Werkzeuge aufgezeigt, insbesondere, um dann im Ereignisfall schnell und umfassend reagieren zu können.

Im Rahmen dieser Arbeit wird eine Entscheidungsunterstützungsmethode vorgestellt, um geeignete Maßnahmen zum Schutz der Bevölkerung zu identifizieren. Die Arbeit ist Teil der Vorsorgeforschung mit dem Fokus auf kerntechnische Unfälle. Die entwickelte Methode berücksichtigt (i) das Problem der Unsicherheit in der Entscheidungsfindung, (ii) die Einzigartigkeit der betrachteten Ereignisse, (iii) die strukturierte Integration von Erfahrung und Expertenwissen, (iv) die Durchführungsreihenfolge der Maßnahmen, (v) die Integration von Akteuren mit unterschiedlichen Präferenzen und (vi) die Möglichkeiten der Anwendung mit Hilfe eines computergestützten Werkzeugs.

Den Kern dieser Methode bildet das Fallbasierte Schließen (CBR), ein Paradigma zur Problemlösung, welches auf der Annahme basiert, dass ähnliche Probleme ähnliche Lösungen besitzen. CBR löst Probleme mit Hilfe von Erfahrungswissen und orientiert sich an der Entscheidungsfindung von Experten in unsicheren und zeitkritischen Situationen. CBR beruht auf dem Prinzip, in einem aktuellen Ereignis auf ähnliche Ereignisse und deren Maßnahmen zurückzugreifen, um Lösungen für den aktuellen Problemfall zu erarbeiten. Aufgrund der geringen Anzahl historischer Ereignisse wird dieser Ansatz durch die Entwicklung geeigneter Szenarien erweitert, um ein breites Spektrum an möglichen Ereignissen abzudecken. Ferner wird auf Basis von Petri-Netzen ein Modell entwickelt, um die Durchführungsreihenfolge von Maßnahmen festzuhalten. Die abschließende Bewertung mehrerer Handlungsalternativen erfolgt multikriteriell, um insbesondere viele Akteure mit unterschiedlichen Präferenzen anzusprechen. Die Arbeit wird durch eine prototypische Implementierung abgerundet und zeigt damit die Anwendbarkeit der entwickelten Methode auf.

Abstract

Disasters are characterized by severe disruptions of the society's functionality and adverse impacts on humans, the environment, and economy that cannot be coped with by society using its own resources. Their causes can be of technical, human, or natural origin. Nuclear disasters pose greater demands on decision-makers, since the release of radioactive substances may lead to long-term and transnational health risks for humans and environmental contamination. A nuclear disaster can be divided into several phases that are characterized by different measures for protecting the public. During the early phase, decision-making is challenged by a great uncertainty in decisive information, whereas during the later phase, the difficulties lie in a multitude of possible measures and stakeholders with partially competing objectives that need to be taken into account.

Decision support methods and systems can help determine measures for responding to and recovering from nuclear disasters. The accidents in Chernobyl and Fukushima particularly emphasized the need for a better preparedness and development of tools to react quickly and comprehensively in case of an incident.

This thesis presents a decision support method that identifies appropriate measures for protecting the public in the course of a nuclear accident. The method takes into account (i) the issue of uncertainty in decision-making, (ii) the exceptionality of this type of disaster, (iii) the structured integration of experience and expert knowledge, (iv) the implementation order of measures, (v) the integration of stakeholders with different preferences, and (vi) the applicability by means of a prototype.

The core of the method is case-based reasoning, a problem-solving paradigm that utilizes knowledge from previously experienced problematic situations, which particularly corresponds to the decision-making behavior of experts under time pressure and uncertainty. The idea is to reuse measures of similar accidents and to combine them in an appropriate way to cope with a current disaster event. Due to few events in the past, the approach is enhanced by the development of scenarios to cover a wide range of possible kinds of accidents. Furthermore, combinations of measures are modeled with the help of Petri nets to take their order of implementation into account. A subsequent multi-criteria assessment of different decision alternatives particularly addresses the issue of various preferences that need to be respected in the final decision. A prototype demonstrates the applicability of the method presented.

Contents

List of Figures

List of Tables

1 Introduction

Large-scale disasters are characterized by severe disruptions of the society's functionality and adverse impacts on humans, the environment, and economy that cannot be coped with by society using its own resources (UNDRR, 2017). Disaster management deals with "the organization, planning and application of measures preparing for, responding to and recovering from disasters" (UNDRR, 2017). Decision-making concerning appropriate measures during and in the aftermath of disasters can be demanding and complex owed to a highly dynamic environment, a limited time frame, uncertainty, and presence of multiple stakeholders with possibly competing objectives (Paton & Flin, 1999; van Borkulo, Scholten, Zlatanova, & van den Brink, 2005). Decisions can be made fast and intuitive, by remembering an appropriate procedure, which can be more time-consuming, or analytically where several possible courses of action need to be evaluated to select the best option (Paton & Flin, 1999). All three decision styles may be applied in the framework of disasters depending on the time and information available. Research on the behavior of experts in such situations emphasizes the importance of experience and solutions of known situations and particularly their reuse for tackling a current problem (Klein, 2008; Klein, Calderwood, & Clinton-Cirocco, 2010; Meso, Troutt, & Rudnicka, 2002; Paton & Flin, 1999). Being part of disaster management and especially preparedness, the development of decision supporting methods and systems can help identifying appropriate measures to respond to and recover from disasters.

This thesis develops a decision support method built upon an experience-based decision-making style which is enhanced by analytical approaches. This method is particularly elaborated by means of nuclear accidents. These types of disasters pose greater demands on decision-makers, since the release of radioactive substances may lead to long-term and transnational health risks for humans and environmental contamination. In the framework of nuclear accidents, disaster management is divided into *on-site* and *off-site* nuclear emergency management. This thesis particularly focuses on the latter and on measures outside a nuclear power plant that concern the population being potentially affected.

1.1 Decision-Making in Nuclear Emergency Management

The Chernobyl accident in 1986 initiated many developments towards a coherent, harmonized, and sensitive response to nuclear emergencies to counter confusion in the public, support an effective implementation of measures, and reduce stress levels of the affected population, that, besides radiation impacts, may have negative health effects as well (Papamichail & French, 2013). In off-site emergency management, a

> *measure* is an *action intended to reduce or avert contamination (deposition of radioactive material) or likelihood of contamination of a specific target.*[1]

Decision-making concerns the identification of a

> *management strategy* or *strategy* in short, which comprises several measures taking into account their order of implementation. A strategy aims at reducing the level of radiation exposure to human and, especially in the longer term, returning to normal living conditions.
>
> A *decision* is a choice of a measure or of several measures including their combination to a strategy out of a set of possible measures, in consideration of the objectives defined in nuclear emergency management.

The specific measures and objectives are explained in more detail in Chapter 3. The term 'strategy' is a common notion in nuclear emergency management and concerns short- as well as long-term decisions. Since short-term measures intend to protect people from long-term consequences as well, a strategy always takes long-term objectives into account. As an example and which is explained more in detail in Chapter 3, an objective in nuclear emergency management is to protect people from radiation-induced health effects (somatic and hereditary) such as cancer induction. Decision-makers aim at balancing health risks against the gravity of intervening in people's lives. For example, they decide between evacuation and advising people

---

[1] This definition is based on the definition of 'management option' of (Nisbet et al., 2010). For clarity, the notion 'measure' is chosen throughout this thesis, which is a common notion in the field of application as well.

to stay indoors. Evacuation is the most effective but also very disruptive measure. Hence, a strategy containing evacuation or staying indoors, determines the fundamental procedure of protecting the public. A plan would then present concrete steps for implementing the strategy. In case of evacuation, a schedule which groups are to be evacuated at which time would be specified more in detail. For example, the evacuation of hospital patients is in general complicated and requires a detailed preparation and a plan, respectively, in advance of an accident. Also, for the later phases of a nuclear accident when the focus is on decontamination, for example, the strategy would specify the measures to enable the affected population to return to their homes and particularly to normal living (see also Chapter 3). The concrete implementation of the measures and which parts of the affected areas should be regarded first, would be part of a plan. The strategy would rather state to clean up the playgrounds first, for example.

Decision support systems for off-site emergency management were built to predict the evolution and impact of a release (of radioactive material), the effectiveness of measures, and to support decision-making on recovery strategies. In particular, the early stages of such an accident demand fast decisions and reliable information whereas decisions on later recovery actions involve heterogeneous groups of stakeholders and various decisive factors that need to be taken into account (Bertsch, Treitz, Geldermann, & Rentz, 2007). Particularly, stakeholder involvement and public participation have emerged as important research topics (Papamichail & French, 2013). Despite the constant work on the issues pointed out so far, the Fukushima Daiichi nuclear power plant accident in 2011 revealed new problems, such as long-lasting releases and a foregoing tsunami that destroyed infrastructure and communities and caused a high death toll (Papamichail & French, 2013). Hence, learning and applying lessons learned may be limited without suitable adaptation mechanisms or by focusing too much on the specifics of the incident to be learned of (Papamichail & French, 2013).

Numerous papers focusing on different aspects of the Fukushima Daiichi nuclear power plant accident have been published since 2011. For instance, they investigate lessons that have been learned so far (Labib & Harris, 2015; Nakamura & Kikuchi, 2011; Omoto, 2013), focus on resilience engineering (Hollnagel & Fujita, 2013) or policy (Aoki & Rothwell, 2013), integrate social and technological aspects

(Pfotenhauer, Jones, Saha, & Jasanoff, 2012), or discuss the contribution of information behavior to the disaster (Thatcher, Vasconcelos, & Ellis, 2015). Furthermore, the accident is compared to former nuclear accidents (Aoki & Rothwell, 2013; Konoplev et al., 2016; Mousseau & Møller, 2014; Steinhauser, Brandl, & Johnson, 2014) and safety goals for reducing seismic and tsunami risks are subjects of research as well (Saji, 2014). Also, assessments of environmental impacts are reviewed or presented (Song, 2018; Strand, Sundell-Bergman, Brown, & Dowdall, 2017) or monitoring results were summarized (Matsuda, Mikami, Sato, & Saito, 2017; Wada et al., 2016). In addition to retrospective analyses, the status of remediation (Hardie & McKinley, 2014) and findings concerning decontamination (Shiba et al., 2013) are presented. The overall objective of existing work is to understand causes and consequences of the disaster and to learn from this experience to be better prepared for possible nuclear accidents in the future.

With regard to emergency management, response during the Fukushima Daiichi nuclear power plant accident was impaired by the foregoing earthquake and tsunami that caused a lack of electricity supply and extensive damage of transport infrastructure. Furthermore, inter alia, missing detailed pre-planned arrangements concerning protective actions as well as inconsistent information and some uncoordinated decisions of the local and national governments contributed to the confusion and uncertainty of the public emphasizing the need to enhance emergency preparedness (Callen & Homma, 2017; International Atomic Energy Agency (IAEA), 2015b; Sihver & Yasuda, 2018). The latter particularly calls attention on severe accidents also possibly linked to natural disasters. Furthermore, a lack of experience concerning decontamination challenged decision-making on appropriate strategies (Hardie & McKinley, 2014). Further issues that arose during the Fukushima Daiichi nuclear power plant accident were lack of cooperation at the European level and diverging as well as non-harmonized response in Europe, which lead to confusion amongst the public (ENCO for European Commission DG ENER, 2014; Investigation Committee on the Accident at Fukushima Nuclear Power Stations of Tokyo Electric Power Company, 2012). In summary, the complexity of the disaster, a lack of preparedness, missing experience, time pressure, and various stakeholders and decision criteria to be taken into account, complicated decision-making on appropriate strategies for response and recovery within Japan as well as worldwide.

This thesis focus on developing a method that supports decision-making on appropriate response and recovery strategies in the course of nuclear accidents.

Most decision support tools and methods for nuclear emergency management so far emerged from the Chernobyl accident and are mainly simulation-based or pursue other approaches such as multi-criteria methods. In the following, decision support systems as well as decision support methods and concepts in respect of selecting appropriate measures are presented.

1.1.1 Decision Support Systems and Methods in Nuclear Emergency Management

Several comprehensive computerized systems for off-site nuclear emergency management resulted from projects partly financed by the European Commission, where several institutions from different European countries participated. These systems particularly account for the choice of measures and their effectiveness. Pure dispersion models and monitoring systems for situation awareness have not been regarded in this overview.

The Real-time On-line Decision Support System for Off-Site Emergency Management in Europe JRodos (Ehrhardt & Weis, 2000; Ievdin, Trybushnyi, Zheleznyak, & Raskob, 2010) provides support for all stages of a nuclear accident. The system determines the dispersion and deposition of material released and models the transfer of radioactive material to feed- and foodstuff and to man. Furthermore, decision support concerning the choice of measures is provided. ARGOS (Hoe et al., 2009) is the equivalent to JRodos and both systems are installed throughout Europe and in some countries outside Europe. MOIRA (A Model-Based Computerised System for Management Support to Identify Optimal Remedial Strategies for Restoring Radionuclide Contaminated Aquatic Ecosystems and Drainage Areas) (Gallego et al., 2000) supports decision-making on radionuclide contaminated aquatic ecosystems. Apart from supra-regional decision support systems, local systems, such as SPEEDI for Japan, which has a worldwide version WSPEEDI (Chino, Ishikawa, & Yamazawa, 1993), or the NARAC system developed at the National Atmospheric

Release Advisory Center in the United States (Bradley, 2007), are in use. Comprehensive decision support systems such as JRodos particularly take into account recommendations of national and international commissions (ICRP, 2007).

Besides simulation-based systems, decision support by means of measure assessment is a subject of research. The focus is on multi-criteria methods (Geldermann et al., 2009; Kiker, Bridges, Varghese, Seager, & Linkov, 2005; Papamichail & French, 2000, 2013; Ríos-Insua, Gallego, Jiménez, & Mateos, 2006; Zeevaert, Bousher, Brendler, Hedemann Jensen, & Nordlinder, 2001), secondary effects of measure application (Rafferty, 2001), or optimization algorithms to find response actions (Georgiadou, Papazoglou, Kiranoudis, & Markatos, 2010; Yumashev & Johnson, 2017). Especially multi-criteria approaches are useful in the aftermath of a disaster or to be applied for preparedness to support decision-making. Multi-criteria decision analysis in general comprises several methods to support decision-making taking into account a variety of possibly conflicting objectives (Belton & Stewart, 2002), which is particularly the case when deciding on long-term decontamination strategies.

A further branch of research is the development of scenarios (French, Argyris, Haywood, Hort, & Smith, 2017), also in combination with multi-criteria methods (T. Comes, Wijngaards, & Van de Walle, 2015). The notion of 'scenario' is defined in Chapter 2.4 more in detail. However, the general idea is to allow a variety of possible event developments to be investigated during preparedness instead of focusing on a reasonable worst case scenario (French et al., 2017).

Furthermore, handbooks for assisting the management of contaminated inhabited areas, food production systems, and drinking water in Europe following a radiological emergency (J. Brown, Hammond, & Kwakman, 2009; Nisbet et al., 2010, 2009) resulted from the project EURANOS (European approach to nuclear radiological emergency management and rehabilitation strategies) with updated versions for United Kingdom (J. Brown, Watson, Nisbet, 2015; Nisbet & Watson, 2015a, 2015b) and corresponding tools (Public Health England, 2015). They serve as guidelines for planning, response as well as training purposes and assist the strategy construction process. The handbooks are generic and comprehensive and the contained knowledge is used in this thesis as well.

To particularly counter the harmonization issues in Europe in the course of the Fukushima Daiichi nuclear power plant accident, the heads of the national nuclear and radiation safety regulators in Europe published a new approach which respects national arrangements but promotes the alignment of decisions across borders (HERCA & WENRA, 2014). In order to handle uncertainty in the early stages of an accident, a scheme referred to as the 'HERCA-WENRA approach', was presented. Recommendations concerning protective actions (evacuation, sheltering, and iodine thyroid blocking – further explanations in Chapter 3.1.1), were made keeping in mind four criteria, namely, 'risk of core melt', 'containment integrity', 'wind direction', and 'time of release'. The HERCA-WENRA approach provides an outline on protective actions and particularly looks at severe accident scenarios from a more general point of view. Especially during the Fukushima Daiichi nuclear power plant accident, estimations on the source term could not be made due to the loss of on-site power. Hence, the local decision support system for protective actions could not be run. Another example to counter the above mentioned cooperation and harmonization issue is NERIS - an European platform on preparedness for nuclear and emergency response and recovery, involving amongst others, authorities, operators, technical support organizations, non-governmental organizations, and research institutes (NERIS, 2014). Objectives are to share the knowledge throughout Europe, to achieve a better harmonization, and to support the development of tools and methods.

Open issues

The decision support systems and methods listed so far, help in selecting appropriate measures and constructing a strategy. However, there is no system that directly identifies a strategy that can be further discussed. Hence, strategies need to be constructed with each new event by hand with the help of, for example decision support systems such as JRodos, to determine effectiveness values for chosen combinations of measures.

In general,

> an *event* is an *occurrence of an incident that triggers the necessity of constructing and implementing a strategy*. The term comprises historical and fictitious nuclear accidents.

The method of this thesis aims at automating strategy construction by identifying appropriate strategies directly serving as discussion basis. This solution particularly counters the lack of experience on the choice and combination of measures, which has shown in Japan in respect of long-term decontamination strategies.

Furthermore, uncertainty is still a crucial issue in nuclear emergency management where the key uncertainties relate to the source term and the weather prognosis (French et al., 2017), which are mandatory for the simulation systems. Current research focuses on constructing scenarios or improving simulation systems and multi-criteria decision analysis tools. Within the frame of this thesis, these ideas are, amongst others, taken up and integrated into a comprehensive decision support method. In addition to uncertainty and as has shown in Japan, decision-making in the beginning of such an accident is complicated by time pressure and a highly dynamic environment. This thesis particularly addresses these issues by taking a new direction through rough accident classifications and hence complements existing simulation-based decision support systems that require source term estimations and weather prognosis and hence numerical input data.

Another open issue is the structured and automated reuse of experience and expert knowledge. As could be seen in Japan, experience concerning decontamination was sparse and demonstration projects to test certain measures, reports on former nuclear accidents, and handbooks provided the basis for decisions on strategies. This thesis particularly presents a solution that automatically reuse already existing knowledge for the right purpose.

Addressed users

The organization of emergency management is country-specific, differs in terms of whether decisions are made locally or nationally and at which level technical support is provided (Carter & French, 2005). Although the main activities ('Monitoring', 'Technical support and advice', 'Decision-making', 'Implementation of Measures', Communication') seem to be the same, a national decision-making center tends to have structured advice including a technical evaluation group and possibly a social and economic advisory group giving advice to decision-makers. Local decision-making centers seem to be more variable with regard to advisory groups, strategic meetings and smaller ad hoc groups (Carter & French, 2005). The users addressed by the work of this thesis are experts of radiation protection and nuclear safety providing technical support and advice of responsible authorities in decision-making.

1.2 Objectives of the Thesis

The **research question** of this thesis is: How can decision-making in nuclear emergency management be supported taking into account the issues of time pressure, uncertainty, multiple stakeholders as well as the exceptionality of the underlying events?

This thesis aims at developing a decision support method that addresses the issues in emergency management that came up during and after the Fukushima Daiichi nuclear power plant accident. In particular, the **objective** of this thesis is to develop a **decision support method**, which

- **Identifies appropriate strategies**: Measures as well as their implementation order are to be identified.
- **Provides support during all phases of a nuclear accident**: Important information for decision-making as well as strategies differ in the course of an accident. The decision-support method needs to take the different phases and their specialties into account.
- **Handles uncertainty:** A key problem is uncertainty, especially in the beginning of an accident and before any radioactive material is released, respectively.
- **Integrates experience and expert knowledge**: Knowledge on historical events and of experts should be the core of the method.
- **Takes into account multiple stakeholders**: Especially in the later phases of an accident, the different objectives need to be respected in the decisions on strategies.

- **Supports the harmonization work in Europe and interaction with existing tools**: As mentioned before, the Fukushima accident revealed some difficulties concerning response in Europe. Parts of this work resulted from the European project PREPARE[2] where a close cooperation with experts from different European countries took place. In particular, this thesis aims at complementing and building upon existing tools.
- **Is applicable in the context of emergency management**. A prototype particularly should demonstrate the applicability of the presented method.

To answer the overarching question, case-based reasoning (CBR), a problem-solving paradigm, which utilizes knowledge of previously experienced problematic situations (Aamodt & Plaza, 1994) is combined with the development of scenarios. The experience-based decision-making style is particularly new in nuclear emergency management and corresponds to the behavior of experts under time pressure and uncertainty (Klein, 2008; Meso et al., 2002; Paton & Flin, 1999; Riesbeck & Schank, 1989). The notion of 'scenario' is not consistent in the literature resulting in diverse typologies and scenario construction techniques (Börjeson, Höjer, Dreborg, Ekvall, & Finnveden, 2006). In context of this work, a scenario is understood as a fictitious event underlying the same structure as a historical event (see Chapter 2.4). The idea is to determine possible accidents and appropriate strategies in advance to promote preparedness. Furthermore, the similarity concept and the adaptation mechanism of CBR allow for handling situations, which are not completely anticipated. The modeling of strategies is realized with the help of Petri Nets (Peterson, 1981) taking into account the implementation order of measures. A multi-criteria assessment (Belton & Stewart, 2002) additionally supports the users in their final decision. The latter particularly addresses the issue of multiple stakeholders to be involved in decision-making.

The decision support method identifies appropriate and comprehensive strategies during all phases of a nuclear accident (accident phases are defined in Chapter 3.1)

---

2 PREPARE – Innovative integrated tools and platforms for radiological emergency preparedness and post-accident response in Europe. https://resy5.iket.kit.edu/PREPARE/

with the help of some outline data and on the basis of expert knowledge and experience. Also with reference to the problems that arose in Japan, this work aims at complementing existing decision support systems at times source term estimations are not available, providing first brief estimations on the area size where protective actions, based on pre-calculated scenarios, are to be implemented, and first suggestions on strategies for the recovery phase.

As mentioned in the introductory words, most decision support tools are simulation-based or assist the construction of a strategy. This work takes a new direction and appeals to figuring out possible scenarios in advance to reuse them in future. This thesis provides a basic configuration of the set of attributes describing an accident as well as the similarity function and adaptation mechanism. Thus following **limitations** need to be clarified:

- **Flexibility is maintained deliberately**: As can be seen in the course of this work, decision-making during nuclear emergencies is not only complex but also demands flexible integration and adjustments of decisive parameters. Hence, the rather common attribute-value based case representation and the local-global principle for the similarity assessment are central for this work. Other different and more complicated approaches are used in CBR at the expense of flexibility and understanding of the results which hence would be counterproductive.

- **Implementation is prototypical**: As mentioned above, one objective of this work is the implementation of the presented method to show the principle applicability. Other issues, such as computational performance could be considered more in detail but are beyond the scope of this work.

- **Decisions are made by humans**: This method should support the decision-making process by identifying possible strategies serving as discussion basis. It is not intended to have the final say or making human decision or opinion redundant.

- **Decision support method represents an important building block**: This work considers a part of the decision-making procedures and steps that need

> to be taken in case of a nuclear emergency. The focus of this work is on decisions on measures to protect the public or mitigate the radiological consequences to the affected people in conjunction with re-establishing their normal lives.

The decision space during crisis response can be divided according to the extent how cause and effect are discernable and understood (French & Niculae, 2005). Recognizing patterns and particularly recognition-primed decision-making (Klein, 1993) to which CBR can be associated to, is assigned to the known space where cause and effect are known and predictions can be made. The events this thesis is dealing with leave the known space and particularly issues such as social or political impacts need to be taken into account (French & Niculae, 2005). However, more and more knowledge on nuclear accidents is gained over the last years and despite the exceptionality of each event, one may not be completely left beyond the known space. Particularly scenario-building helps to be prepared for future events by thinking of possible accidents and event developments that might happen. In general, CBR is considered as beneficial, if domain knowledge is incomplete (Leake, 1996b) and decision-making during crises by those who are experienced are characterized by recognition-primed decision-making (Klein & Clinton-Cirocco, 2010). Since crucial aspects such as public perception or public reassurance can be implicitly considered in the scenario-building, CBR in combination with scenarios is not regarded as to be associated to the known space only. Furthermore, the resulting CBR application is one component of a larger platform that tackles issues discussed for crisis management decision support systems, namely they focus primarily on short-term consequences and very detailed modeling neglecting collaboration, judgment building, and public communication (French & Niculae, 2005). Hence, the results of this thesis should not be seen as a complete decision support system that answer all the needs at hand but provide a discussion basis for measures that are gained with the help of models developed in close collaboration with experts.

1.3 Publications within the Scope of the Thesis

Several articles were published in conference proceedings and journals addressing parts of the research proposal. The early publications are associated to the non-nuclear field and resulted from the KRITIS project[3] supported by the Center for Disaster Management and Risk Reduction Technology (CEDIM), the RiKoV[4] project, and CEDIMs Forensic Disaster Analysis (FDA)[5]. These publications discuss mainly CBR related questions and present results with regard to the modeling and assessing of strategies. However, experience and results gained in the non-nuclear field contributed to the final outcome presented in this thesis. The research leading to these results has received funding from the European Atomic Energy Community Seventh Framework Programme FP7/2012-2013 under grant agreement 323287. Research is particularly conducted in the frame of the European project PREPARE (Innovative integrated tools and platforms for radiological emergency preparedness and post-accident response in Europe) that aimed at closing gaps that have been identified in nuclear and radiological preparedness following the first evaluation of the Fukushima Daiichi nuclear power plant accident. The project was headed by the Karlsruhe Institute of Technology (KIT) and 46 institutions participated. The author of this thesis participated in a work package that aimed at developing methods to be integrated in an emergency management tool of European dimension for collecting, sharing, and exchanging information about an on-going nuclear or radiological event, and analyzing potential consequences. Part of the results, especially the decision supporting component of the emergency management tool, is presented in this thesis. The author particularly created this thesis as part of the work at the Institute for Thermal Energy Technology and Safety of KIT.

In the following, the publications are listed according to their type. Publications marked with * include self-given presentations.

Journal articles

Raskob, W., Möhrle, S., & Bai, S. (2016). Knowledge Database and Case-Based Reasoning. *Radioprotection, 51(HS2),* S185–S186.

[3] http://www.cedim.de/english/1959.php

[4] http://www.rikov.de/

[5] https://www.cedim.de/english/2863.php

Raskob, W., Möhrle, S., Bai, S., & Müller, T. (2016). Overview and Applicability of the Analytical Platform. *Radioprotection, 51(HS2)*, S179–S180.

Moehrle, S., & Raskob, W. (2015). Structuring and Reusing Knowledge from Historical Events for Supporting Nuclear Emergency and Remediation Management. *Engineering Applications of Artificial Intelligence, 46, Pt. B*, 303–311.

Conference articles and presentations

Moehrle, S., Bai, S., Mueller, T., Munz, E., Trybushnyi, D., & Raskob, W. (2019). Triggering Events and Distributed Responsibilities, Capabilities of Web-based Decision Support in Nuclear Emergency Management. In *4th NERIS Workshop, Adapting nuclear and radiological emergency preparedness, response and recovery to a changing world*. Dublin, Ireland. (pp. 122-130).

Lin, L., Moehrle, S., Muenzberg, T., & Raskob, W. (2014). A Decision Support Approach: Evaluating the Effectiveness of Security Measures by Scenario-Based Multi-Criteria Analysis. In K. Thoma, I. Häring, & T. Leismann (Eds.), *Future Security 2014: 9th Security Research Conference.* Berlin, Germany (pp. 266–273).

Raskob, W., & Möhrle, S. (2014). Knowledge Databases as Instrument for a Fast Assessment in Nuclear Emergency Management. *3rd International Conference on Radioecology & Environmental Radioactivity (ICRER 2014)*. Barcelona, Spain.

*Moehrle, S. (2014). On the Assessment of Disaster Management Strategies. In S.R. Hiltz, M.S. Pfaff, L. Plotnick, & P.C. Shih (Eds.), *11th International Conference on Information Systems for Crisis Response and Management (ISCRAM 2014).* Pennsylvania State University, USA.

Münzberg, T., Müller, T., Möhrle, S., Comes, T., & Schultmann, F. (2013). An Integrated Multi-Criteria Approach on Vulnerability Analysis in the Context of Load Reduction. In T. Comes et al. (Eds.), *10th International Conference on Information Systems for Crisis Response and Management (ISCRAM 2013).* Baden-Baden, Germany.

*Moehrle, S. (2013a). Modeling of Countermeasures for Large-Scale Disasters Using High-Level Petri Nets. In T. Comes et al. (Eds.), *10th International Conference on Information Systems for Crisis Response and Management (ISRAM 2013).* Baden-Baden, Germany.

*Moehrle, S. (2013b). Towards a Decision Support System for Disaster Management. In R. D. J. M. Steenbergen et al. (Eds.), *Safety, Reliability and Risk Analysis: Beyond the Horizon - Proceedings of the European Safety and Reliability Conference, ESREL 2013.* Amsterdam, The Netherlands (pp. 239–246).

Lin, L., Brauner, F., Münzberg, T., Meng, S., & Moehrle, S. (2013). Prioritization of Security Measures Against Terrorist Threats to Public Rail Transport Systems Using a Scenario-Based Multi-Criteria Method and a Knowledge Database. In M. Lauster (Ed.), *Future Security 2013: 8th Security Research Conference.* Berlin, Germany (pp. 195–204).

*Moehrle, S. (2012). Generic Self-Learning Decision Support System for Large-Scale Disasters. In L. Rothkrantz, J. Ristvej and Z. Franco (Eds.), *9th International Conference on Information Systems for Crisis Response and Management (ISCRAM 2012).* Vancouver, Canada.

Invited talks

*Raskob, W., & Möhrle, S. (2017). Nuclear Emergency Response and Big Data Technologies. *Invited talk on BDE Workshop on Big Data in Climate Action, Environment, Resource Efficiency and Raw Materials.* Brussels, Belgium.

Book articles

Moehrle, S. & Raskob, W. (2019). Reusing Strategies for Decision Support in Disaster Management – A Case-based High-level Petri Net Approach. In S. Y. Yurish (Ed.) *Advances in Artificial Intelligence: Reviews, Book Series, Vol. 1.* IFSA Publishing, S.L. (Barcelona, Spain).

Posters

Moehrle, S., Bai, S., Mueller, T., Munz, E., Trybushnyi, D., & Raskob, W. (2018). Web-based decision support system for emergency management – System architecture and enhancement possibilities. In *4th NERIS Workshop, Adapting nuclear and radiological emergency preparedness, response and recovery to a changing world*. Dublin, Ireland.

Raskob, W., Müller, T., Möhrle, S., & Bai, S. (2016). The Analytical Platform of the PREPARE project. In *14th Congress of the International Radiation Protection Association (IRPA)*. Cape Town, South Africa.

*Möhrle, S., Schoknecht, A., Raskob, W., & Oberweis, A. (2015). Ontology-Based Retrieval for Cased-Based Decision Support in Nuclear Emergency Management. In *12th International Conference on Information Systems for Crisis Response and Management (ISCRAM 2015)*. Kristiansand, Norway.

Möhrle, S., & Mühr, B. (2015). Case-Based Damage Assessment of Storm Events in Near Real-Time. In *Geophysical Research Abstracts, EGU2015-12293, General Assembly European Geosciences Union 2015* (Vol. 17). Vienna, Austria.

Möhrle, S., & Raskob, W. (2014). Case-Based Analytical Support for Rapidly Assessing Natural Disasters. In *14. Forum Katastrophenvorsorge*. Leipzig, Germany.

1.4 Structure of the Thesis

This thesis is structured as follows: Chapter 2 introduces the foundations of the decision support method, which basically combines several methods. The integrated approach comprises the core method CBR, the development of scenarios, multi-criteria decision analysis, and Petri nets. Each topic presented in this chapter includes overviews of related work. The following chapters present the key results of this thesis. At first, an overview of the developed decision support method of this thesis is given in Chapter 3. Assumptions made are clarified and the novelty of the approach is emphasized. The following chapters particularly present the components of the decision support method more in detail. Chapter 4 explains the development of the structure of the case base and especially expert participation as well as the development of the case model. This chapter closes with data collection. Chapter 5 presents how the similarity between two accidents is determined. The reuse step of solutions of similar cases is explained in more detail in Chapter 6. Here, the merging of several Petri nets as well as a subsequent multi-criteria assessment of several strategies is presented. Chapter 7 is dedicated to the implementation of the developed method and shows the achievement of the objectives in the framework of an evaluation. Chapter 8 concludes this thesis with a summary of the main results, evinces some limitations, and discusses future research topics and how open issues could be solved.

2 Foundations and Related Work

The first part of this chapter motivates the usage of case-based reasoning (CBR) as core method of the decision support method developed in this thesis. This section gives an overview of the main aspects of CBR and introduces some concepts that are relevant for the work of this thesis. As an adjacent research field, Case-base planning (CBP) is shortly introduced as well. The application of CBR and CBP in disaster management is discussed, respectively. Thereafter, the notion of a scenario is clarified and their development in the framework of this thesis is motivated. Furthermore, the purpose and use of multi-criteria decision analysis in disaster management is explained. Afterwards, modeling languages for strategies, particularly Petri Nets, are introduced. The foundation chapter concludes with a summary and discusses the methods chosen for handling the issues discussed in Chapter 1.

2.1 Case-Based Reasoning

CBR, which has its origins in cognitive science, is a problem-solving paradigm that utilizes specific knowledge of previously experienced problem situations to solve a new problem. The main assumption of CBR is that *similar problems have similar solutions*. Specific knowledge that might be reused in similar situations contrasts with generalized knowledge to be applied by humans via inference. In general, a *case* is an experience of a solved problem and particularly contains the specific knowledge to be reused. Typically, a case consists of a problem and corresponding solution part. The problem part contains information to decide whether a case is reusable. The solution part contains information useful for reusing a case (Richter & Weber, 2013). CBR can be described by a cycle of solving a problem and learning from this experience (Figure 2.1). Learning is an inherent by-product since the experience made in the course of problem-solving is retained (Aamodt & Plaza, 1994).

At first, the problem to be solved needs to be identified and described. This description represents a *new case* or *query* for CBR. The first step of the cycle is to retrieve the most similar case or *cases*. Subsequently, the knowledge captured in the retrieved cases are reused to solve the new problem. Afterwards, the solution proposed is revised and possibly tested or repaired. Finally, the *case base,* which is a collection of stored cases, is updated by retaining the new experience and the confirmed solution, respectively.

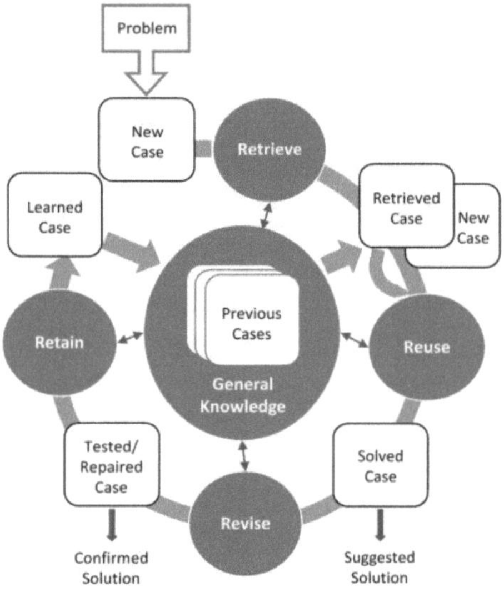

Figure 2.1: CBR Cycle (Aamodt & Plaza, 1994, Figure 1)

Each step can be viewed as a task to be achieved, which in turn involves several sub-tasks, which yet have various methods to be realized (Figure 2.2). Tasks are in bold letters, methods in normal letters. Plain lines denote task decompositions, which are complete. The top-level task is problem-solving and learning from experience. CBR is the way to accomplish this task and the four major tasks correspond to the steps illustrated in the cycle. The method set is incomplete and suggests alternative solutions to fulfill the tasks.

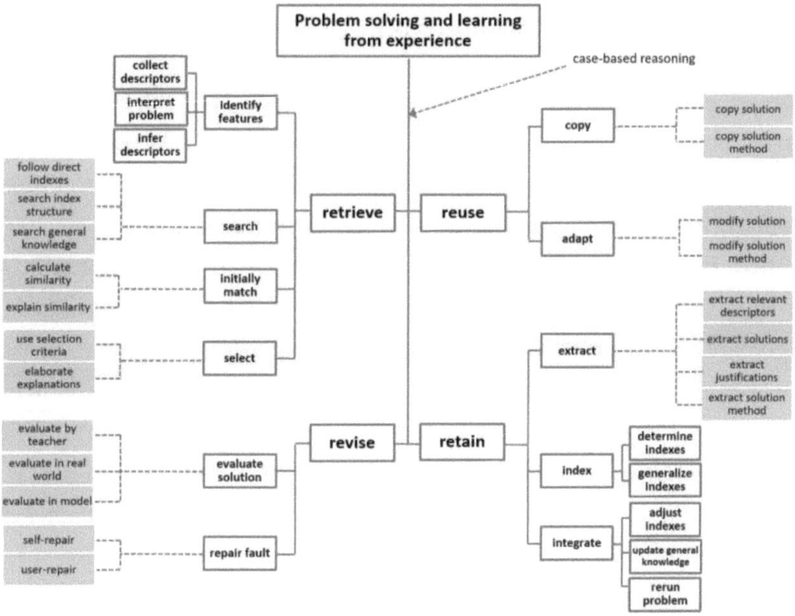

Figure 2.2: Task-method decomposition of CBR (Aamodt & Plaza, 1994, Figure 2)

Besides previous cases, a CBR system includes knowledge in terms of vocabulary and in particular knowledge representation, similarity measures, and adaptation knowledge (Richter, 1995). The vocabulary provides means to communicate the domain knowledge and is central for all commonly called 'knowledge containers' (Figure 2.3). Indicated by the arrows, the knowledge is distributed over the containers and they depend on each other to solve the tasks (Richter, 1995). In the following, the knowledge containers are introduced in more detail.

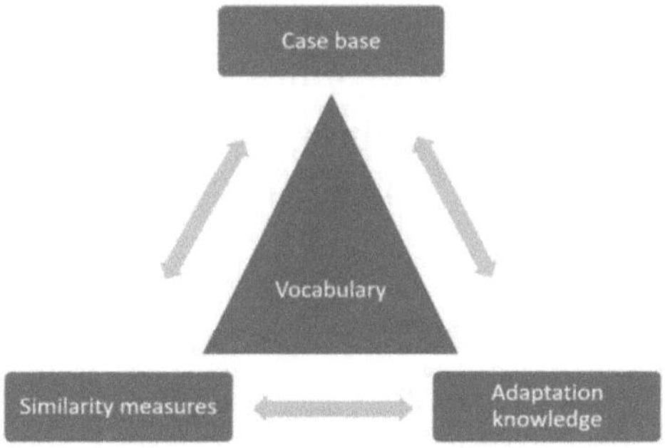

Figure 2.3: Knowledge containers in case-based reasoning (Richter, 1995)

2.1.1 Vocabulary and Knowledge Representation

The *vocabulary* chosen is the basis for describing the current problem and previous cases as well as for implementing similarity measures and adaptation mechanisms that means *representing knowledge in a CBR system*. The notion of knowledge is linked to experience and learning and is hence of dynamic nature (McInerney, 2002), being distinguished from data and information (Davenport & Prusak, 1998). Whereas data are objective facts that become information when a meaning is added, knowledge can be understood as expertise and assumptions gained from experience to be applied for evaluation and creation of more experience, practices, or values (Davenport & Prusak, 1998). Knowledge being more tacit (Polanyi, 1958) can be made explicit by sharing, explaining, recording, or documenting and hence creating a knowledge artifact (McInerney, 2002). With respect to CBR, the *knowledge representation* refers to the content and structure of the case base and the appropriate organization and indexing for later retrieval and reuse, however in line with the general domain knowledge that may be useful for adaptation (Aamodt & Plaza, 1994). Cases in form of texts, images, speeches, sensor data, or conversations are found in CBR systems whereas most commonly the attribute-value representation is used, to which the other representations may also be reduced to (Richter & Weber, 2013):

Definition 2.1 Attribute/Attribute-value representation

> For a given set of objects U, an *attribute* A assigns to each object $u \in U$ some value taken from $dom(A)$, which is the domain of A. An *attribute-value representation* depicts a finite vector of attributes.

Attribute domains can be numerical, textual, or an enumeration of symbols. The attribute types may also be classified according to different scales of measure: nominal, ordinal, interval, and real and their corresponding operation possibilities (Table 2.1). Furthermore, attributes may be single-valued or many-valued.

Table 2.1: Attribute types categorized according to different scales of measure

Attribute type	Description	Mathematical operation	Example
Nominal	Enumerable values	$=, \neq$	Seasons
Ordinal	Ordered values	$=, \neq, \geq, \leq$	School grades
Interval	Degree of difference between values determinable, arbitrary zero value	$=, \neq, \geq, \leq, +, -$	Temperature on Celsius scale
Ratio	As interval with unique zero value	$=, \neq, \geq, \leq, +, -, /, \cdot$	Speed

The foundation for the attribute-value representation of cases is the local-global principle (Richter & Weber, 2013):

Definition 2.2 Local-global principle

> The *local-global principle* says that each object O is globally described by some construction operator $\tilde{C}$ from the local elements: $O = \tilde{C}(A_i | i \in I)$, with I being an index set for the local elements A_i.

According to this principle, objects can be described by elementary or local description elements, which can be assumed to be the attributes. In respect of similarity calculation, according to this principle it is possible to decompose the entire similarity computation in local parts as well (Richter & Weber, 2013; Stahl, 2003). Hence, in the framework of similarity calculation, the local-global principle is very useful for complex case representations that consist of various attributes with different attribute types.

An overview of different case representations can be found in the literature (Bergmann, Kolodner, & Plaza, 2006; Richter & Weber, 2013) as well as specialized applications (Bergmann, Wilke, Vollrath, & Wess, 1996; El-Sappagh & Elmogy, 2015; B. Sun, Xu, Pei, & Li, 2003; Tran & Schönwälder, 2007).

As mentioned before, a case is typically divided into a *problem* and *solution part*. The distinction is not mandatory but useful for the purpose of this thesis. Hence, the description of a case comprises the description of a problem and its solution.

The corresponding case base may be organized flat, object-oriented, by trees and graphs, hierarchies and taxonomies, or set-oriented. Except for the flat representation, the cases are linked through case features and all of these examples use attribute-values (Richter & Weber, 2013).

In the context of vocabulary and knowledge representation, completeness and efficiency are of major importance (Richter & Weber, 2013). Completeness refers to the coverage of all relevant properties and inclusion of all important concepts. Efficiency refers to the effort of formulating knowledge with the given representation formalism and how efficient retrieval and computing similarity is. When introducing the results of this research (Chapter 3 and following), these two requirements are discussed more in detail.

2.1.2 Similarity Measures

Before introducing the notion of similarity and similarity measures mathematically, the meaning and purpose of 'similarity' need to be clarified. In general, two objects of interest are similar in a certain respect depending on what the focus is on, which can be appearance, content, or where they are physically located. Hence, one may always ask for the dimension in focus making similarity a subjective and application dependent concept. Furthermore, gradiations are possible, that means one object A is at least similar to an object B as A to C is. This particularly defines a partial order relation where objects can be ranked due to their similarity to a certain object A. Hence, the nearest neighbors to A can be found on the top of the list, the objects, which are most similar to A. The nearest neighbor concept is particularly used widely in CBR applications following the intuition that closer means always better and, in the context of problem-solving, more useful (Richter & Weber, 2013). Relational models are independent of the representation of the objects to be analyzed. This changes when similarity needs to be expressed quantitatively in order to distinguish subtler between the similar objects. Usually, similarity measures are introduced returning a number between 0 and 1 to express the similarity between two objects. The maximal similarity value is 1 which, in respect of problem-solving, hints to the highest usefulness of the solution returned back. This does not necessarily mean, that the two problems to be analyzed are identical, but rather being the same in context of the questioning or with regard to the information available. An object being represented by certain features may lack information when searching for similar objects. In this case one would add the basis on which similarity is assessed instead of solely the similarity value. Also with regard to problem-solving, in addition to the information situation, the task to be fulfilled may be referenced to when announcing the similarity value of two problem descriptions:

> Denote d_1 and d_2 two problem descriptions where l_1 denotes the solution description of d_1 and d_2 has an empty solution part. The *similarity value* of d_1 and d_2 is $x \in [0,1]$ means it is assessed on the basis of information available and with the objective to find a solution to solve problem d_2. The value x indicates the usefulness of l_1 to solve d_2.

Similarity measures are used for implementing the retrieve step of CBR. They operate on problem descriptions. Thus a variety of possibilities exist for definition. Since the attribute-value representation is central for this thesis, attribute-based similarity concepts are regarded only. Representing similarity with the help of functions particularly includes similarity and distance measures where distance-based similarity measures may be defined. They can typically be specified with the help of base functions that are monotonic increasing and decreasing for negative and positive distance, respectively (Stahl, 2003). Here, a subtraction of query features from the case features is assumed, for instance. In order to be a metric, distance measures need to fulfill several properties which could be discussed for similarity measures as well but which are not fulfilled in general. For this purpose, let P denote the set of problem descriptions.

Definition 2.3 Similarity measure

> A *similarity measure* for P is a function
>
> $$f: P \times P \rightarrow [0,1].$$

A value of 1 means maximal similarity whereas 0 means there is no similarity between the two problem descriptions. Typical properties investigated are:

Reflexivity: f is reflexive: $\Leftrightarrow \forall\, x \in P : f(x,x) = 1$. If it holds $f(x,y) = 1 \Rightarrow x = y$, the similarity measure is called strong reflexive.

Symmetry: f is symmetric: $\Leftrightarrow \forall x, y \in P: f(x,y) = f(y,x)$.

As mentioned before, similarity refers to the solutions of the cases, of which the most suitable are searched for. If the case base contains cases whose solutions are actually not useful for solving the corresponding problem, the reflexivity is violated. However, these cases might be valuable experiences in terms of indicating potential pitfalls. The strong reflexivity would exclude alternative solutions and hence might not be reasonable. Whether the symmetry property is valid depends on the application domain and if the problem description of the query has the same meaning as the problem description of the case used for comparison (Stahl, 2003). For example, lessons learned in the first situation may be useful for a second situation but lessons learned in a second situation may not be useful for the first one (Bergmann, 2002). The fulfillment of the strong reflexivity, symmetry as well as the triangle inequality is demanded for distance measures to be a metric. Distance measures and similarity measures can be treated mathematically equivalently by applying bijective order-inverting mappings g (Burkhard & Richter, 2001). The translation of the triangle inequality of distance metrics to similarity measures would be

$$g\big(f(x,y)\big) + g\big(f(y,z)\big) \geq g(f(x,z))$$

with order-inverting functions g. For example, $g(x) = 1 - x$ leads to

Triangle inequality: f fulfills the triangle equality: $\Leftrightarrow \forall x, y, z \in P: f(x,y) + f(y,z) \leq 1 + f(x,z)$.

Nevertheless, the metric property is not mandatory for distance or similarity measures (Burkhard & Richter, 2001)

In case of more complex case representations where different attribute types are involved, the local-global principle facilitates the modeling of similarity measures by decomposing the similarity assessment. Local similarities between attribute values are considered and then composed to a global similarity for the entire cases. Hereby, the linear independence of the attributes is presumed, particularly since the global similarity measure only access the local similarity values but not to the actual attribute values. If two attributes are linear dependent, the similarity only changes in one direction, due to a change of a certain attribute value, if the dependent attribute changes its value, too. In order to dissolve linear dependency, virtual attributes may be introduced that explicitly describe the dependency (Richter & Weber, 2013).

Definition 2.4 Local similarity function

A *local similarity function* for an attribute A is a function

$$f_A: dom(A) \times dom(A) \rightarrow [0,1].$$

In order to express the individual importance of attributes, weights can be introduced:

Definition 2.5 Attribute weight vector

For attributes $A_1, \dots, A_n$ describing the problems,

$$\vec{w} = (w_1, \dots, w_n) \text{ with } w_i \in [0,1] \text{ and } \sum_{i=1}^{n} w_i = 1$$

denotes the *attribute weight vector*, where each w_i is called the *attribute weight* for A_i.

There are different weight models such as globally valid, case specific, or user specific that can be combined, if required (Stahl, 2003). Attribute weights play a crucial role in the retrieval step. Furthermore, they are also used to compensate imperfect attribute choices to describe the problems at hand where several methods exist to assign weights automatically with little or no domain knowledge (Wettschereck & Aha, 1995). Weights and particularly retrieval can be improved through learning (Bonzano, Cunningham, & Smyth, 1997; S. W. Lin & Chen, 2011) or optimization (Ahn, Kim, & Han, 2006; Z. Liao, Mao, Hannam, & Zhao, 2012; Shin & Han, 1999; Wu, Li, & Liang, 2013; A. Yan, Shao, & Guo, 2014; Zhang, Coenen, & Leng, 2002). Moreover, weights can also be determined systematically with the help of domain experts (Park & Han, 2002). The overall objective here is to improve similarity assessment, also by considering similarity functions locally and globally (Stahl, 2003; Stahl & Gabel, 2006). In contrast to modeling similarity functions directly, learning methods that incorporate qualitative feedback, establish an order between the cases without determining exact distances between them (Cheng & Hüllermeier, 2008).

Definition 2.6 Global similarity function

> Assuming the problems are described by attributes $A_1, \dots, A_n$, a *global similarity function* for $A_1, \dots, A_n$ is a function
>
> $$f: P \times P \to [0,1]$$
>
> which is represented by some *aggregation function* $\sigma: [0,1]^{2n} \to [0,1]$ that aggregates the local similarities:
>
> $$f(x,y) = \sigma(f_{A_1}(x_1, y_1), \dots, f_{A_n}(x_n, y_n), \vec{w}),$$
>
> where x_i denotes the value of x for attribute A_i, f_{A_i} the local similarity measure for A_i, and $\vec{w}$ the attribute weight vector.

The local-global principle gives rise to an axiom for composite measures, which is the *global monotonicity axiom* that states that a higher global similarity results by at least one higher local similarity (Burkhard & Richter, 2001):

$$f(x,y) > f(x,z) \Rightarrow \exists i \in \{1, \dots, n\} : sim_i(x_i, y_i) > sim_i(x_i, z_i).$$

As mentioned before, distance measures can be transformed to similarity measures by appropriate functions. This can be done for local as well as global similarity measures. However, transformation and aggregation do not commute in general.

The representation formalism for local and global similarity measures depends on the respective attribute types and case representation (Boriah, Chandola, & Kumar, 2008; T. W. Liao, Zhang, & Claude, 1998; Richter & Weber, 2013). Furthermore, there are global measures that handle numerical and nominal input values at the same time which are called heterogeneous distance functions (Wilson & Martinez, 1997).

Often, domain knowledge is structured and made explicit with the help of ontologies. An ontology specifies a conceptualization of knowledge (Gruber, 1993) containing the objects of interest and their relationships. Retrieval mechanisms differ, such as focusing on the path length for similarity calculation (Zhao, Cui, Zhao, Qiu, & Chen, 2009), combining hierarchical and path-based approaches (Y. Guo, Peng, & Hu, 2013), or concentrating on concept-based approaches (Recio-García, Díaz-Agudo, González-Calero, & Sánchez-Ruiz-Granados, 2007) with the addition of fillers of common attributes (Assali, Lenne, & Debray, 2009). Some CBR systems are enhanced by Fuzzy Set Theory (Zadeh, 1965) and particularly use fuzzy retrieval and fuzzy integral, respectively, to account for the interactiveness of features and improve the commonly used weighted average model to determine the overall similarity (Lee, Barcia, & Khator, 1995; X. Z. Wang & Yeung, 2000). Fuzzy set theory is particularly interesting with regard to uncertainty issues concerning attribute values. Another example is a hybrid similarity measure taking into account crisp symbols, crisp numbers, interval numbers, fuzzy linguistic variables, and random variables (Fan, Li, Wang, & Liu, 2014).

The knowledge contained in similarity measures strongly depends on the vocabulary chosen and if semantics of the attributes is taken into account. The local measures consider the knowledge each attribute contains whereas the aggregation function controls their influences on the overall solution. Local and global similarity measures together need to reflect the meaning of a useful solution in the application domain and for the user, respectively. However, the adaptation knowledge is responsible as well to improve the solution of an already solved problem.

2.1.3 Adaptation Knowledge

As shown in Figure 2.2, two possibilities exist for reusing the solution of the already solved problem: either the retrieved problem is the same under the conditions discussed in Chapter 2.1.2 to the current one and its solution is successful, then the solution can be copied, or there are slight differences in the problem descriptions and the solution has to be adapted. Adapting a solution can again be realized in two ways: either the previous solution strategy is used to generate a new solution, which is called derivational reuse (Aamodt & Plaza, 1994), or the solution itself is taken and transformed, what is meant by transformational reuse (Aamodt & Plaza, 1994), where the transformation is implemented by rules (Richter & Weber, 2013):

$$\Phi_1 \wedge \cdots \wedge \Phi_n \Rightarrow Action$$

where $\Phi_i, i = 1, \dots, n$ are preconditions referring to the attribute values that need to be fulfilled to perform an action. An action can be formalized as an operator

$$op\colon states \rightarrow states$$

where a *state* refers to a case description or parts of it. Operators may add, delete, or modify attribute values and be iterated. Particularly, several operators $op_i, i = 1, \dots, n$ may be concatenated in order to get the desired result:

$$op = op_n \circ \cdots \circ op_1$$

where the preconditions of each operator must not be violated by the results of the preceding operator.

If adapting a solution is difficult or not possible, query changes may pose another alternative particularly when they are insufficiently formulated (Richter & Weber, 2013). Here, rules may be applied to a problem description such as computing attribute values that are not specified or queries need to be corrected due to inconsistency, implausibility, or self-interest of the initiator of the CBR application. Furthermore, similarity and adaptation efforts may contrast to each other. That means a high similarity value does not implicate low adaptation costs. An idea is to account for the application costs of the necessary operator sequence in the final similarity value. Hence, the search for the most useful case would extend the search space by all possible adaptation operator sequences. The search may not terminate and hence should stop when the solution is sufficiently good. Heuristics may help to reduce the search space and realize an efficient adaptation (Richter & Weber, 2013). In general, measures to determine how well CBR works for a specific problem-solving topic can be appropriate (see Chapter 2.1.4).

Another form of adaptation is to reuse the solution process. For example in the field of planning, the path of decisions can be replayed by instantiating the specific variables in order to get a new plan. Thereby, decisions are reconstructed (Richter & Weber, 2013; M. M. Veloso & Carbonell, 1993). Particularly for plans, adaptation can be categorized to transformational and derivational adaptation. The latter corresponds to plan replay and transformational analogy refers to transformation operators converting existing plans into new ones (Hammond, 1986; Muñoz-Avila & Cox, 2008).

Adaptation does not only affect a single case but might regard several retrieved solutions as well. Sometimes a problem needs to be decomposed into several subproblems that are analyzed separately or several cases and their solutions are necessary to solve the current problem. Each solution may then be adapted and integrated into an overall solution afterwards. For this work, cases are decomposed (Chapter 3.1.1) and several solutions are reused as well (see Chapter 6).

Solutions can be adapted manually by the user or automatically by the system. For the latter, adaptation knowledge can be gained in advance or during the problem-solving process. Furthermore, learning techniques play an important role for acquiring adaptation knowledge as well, primarily by using domain knowledge and the case base (Craw, Wiratunga, & Rowe, 2006; Hanney & Keane, 1996; Jarmulak, Craw, & Rowe, 2001; Li, H., Li, X., Hu, D., Hao, T., Wenyin, L., & Chen, 2009; Wilke, Vollrath, Althoff, & Bergmann, 1997). For example leave-one-out retrieval experiments help generating adaptation examples by pair-by-pair case comparisons and by considering attribute value and solution differences, respectively, which are generalized by learning algorithms afterwards. Particularly, similarity values restrict the interesting candidates. Another learning technique refers to learning the number of neighboring cases to perform the weighted majority voting (Michie, Spiegelhalter, & Taylor, 1994) by applying leave-one-out tests as well (Wettschereck & Aha, 1995). However, besides choosing an appropriate algorithm and learning adaptation knowledge, the question how to integrate new adaptation knowledge into the available knowledge needs to be taken care of as well (Wilke et al., 1997). In addition, knowledge discovery techniques support semi-automatic adaptation knowledge acquisition (D'Aquin et al., 2007) or CBR can be applied to the adaptation process for learning and reapplying adaptation knowledge (Kinley, 2001; Leake, Kinley, & Wilson, 1995).

Different methods of adaptation can be classified according to domain knowledge requirement, type of adaptation knowledge, and if learning capabilities are included (Mitra & Basak, 2005). Figure 2.4 classifies adaptation knowledge distinguishing between static and dynamic adaptation, particularly between rule-based and model-based approaches and if the whole adaptation case or path towards adaptation is stored. Furthermore, weights being part of model-based approaches or ranking the retrieved cases may be inductively gained by the system.

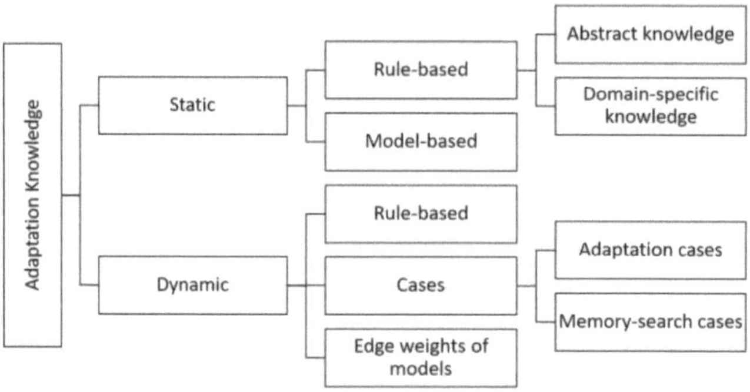

Figure 2.4: Types of adaptation knowledge (Mitra & Basak, 2005, Figure 4)

Figure 2.5 gives a brief overview of the different adaptation methods and their characteristics. The methods are depicted on a white background, the different classes are illustrated in grey rectangles. Adaptation methods found in the survey use genetic algorithms, Bayesian networks, are guided by constraint satisfaction, underlie a substitution-based model, apply derivational replay, use substitutions and transformations or calculate average values taking all relevant cases as input (ranking retrieved cases). Particularly the knowledge intensity distinguishes the different methods and if learning mechanisms are incorporated. Adaptive adaptation methods use machine learning techniques to learn adaptation knowledge whereas non-adaptive methods use static rules. Implementation dependent methods can be implemented in an adaptive and non-adaptive way, which is depicted by the dotted lines in Figure 2.5. The upper part illustrates classification based on domain knowledge requirement whereas the lower part indicates learning capabilities.

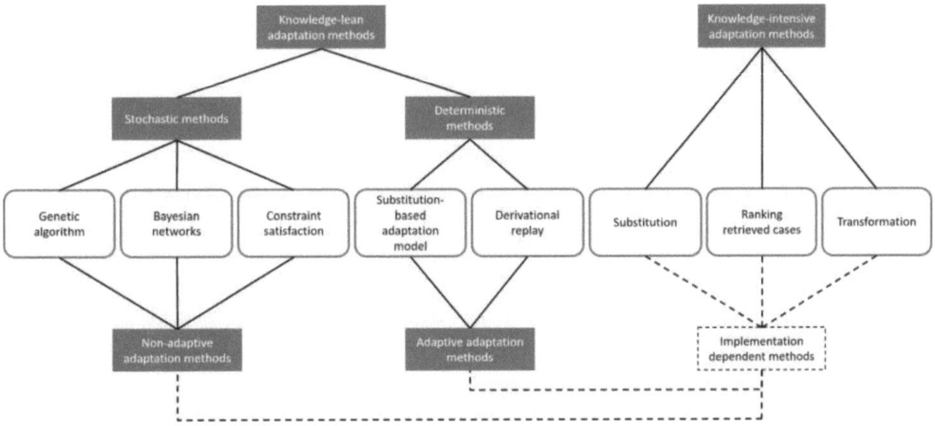

Figure 2.5: Classification of adaptation methods based on domain knowledge requirement and learning capabilities (Mitra & Basak, 2005, Figures 2 and 3)

2.1.4 Evaluation Measures

The core of the CBR approach is a case base that stores knowledge to be applied in the frame of a newly occurring problem. With regard to case acquisition, initial cases need to be provided, on which the system builds on further knowledge. The case base competence outlines the range of problems the CBR system can solve and may indicate if further cases are necessary to achieve a certain performance level or if other knowledge containers need to be enhanced (Leake & Wilson, 2011). Several empirical approaches estimate competence either by using the existing case base so far or uniformly sampling the problem space to test whether the sampled points are expected to be solvable and for which a criterion need to be defined. These approaches can particularly be used to predict marginal coverage benefit of next case addition as well as the number of cases required for maximal coverage (Leake & Wilson, 2011). Case base competence is particularly used during maintenance where knowledge is added, deleted, or modified (Smiti, 2011; Smyth & McKenna, 2001) where several approaches for modeling competence exist (Massie, Craw, & Wiratunga, 2005; Smiti & Elouedi, 2013; Smyth & McKenna, 1998, 1999).

Another method to evaluate a CBR system is to estimate the confidence in the solution by using information from the case base and values that are calculated as part of the CBR process (Cheetham, 2000; Cheetham & Price, 2004; García, Orozco, &

Arcos, 2007) or specifically to assess the confidence in adaptation rules (Jalali & Leake, 2013). 'Trustworthiness' is a synonymous concept supporting the user whether to use the suggested solution or not and whether the query falls within the realm of expertise of the case base (Chua & Tischer, 2004; Horsman, Laing, & Vickers, 2012; A. Yan & Wang, 2015). Another concept is the 'reliability' of a suggested solution that is the estimated probability that the solution is correct whereas the 'compatibility' reflects to what extent the case library supports the main assumption that similar cases have similar solutions (Xu, Wang, Ma, & Lin, 2010). This assumption may be challenged, for example, for classification tasks at class boundaries or if relevant factors affecting the solution are not integrated in the case representation.

In general, a variety of approaches to evaluate CBR systems exist ranging from measuring the quality of the generated solutions to, for example, computation time (Oehlmann, 1998). Furthermore, besides evaluating one CBR system and particularly to which degree an application problem has been solved, the notion of evaluation may also refer to comparing different systems as well as comparing system development methodologies (Althoff, 1995). In the frame of this work, evaluation and particularly the evaluation method are discussed in more detail in Chapter 7.

2.1.5 Uncertainty in Attribute Values

In real world problems, one may not assume that case descriptions are complete and each attribute value is available in a clear-cut manner but rather that the classical true-false paradigm often does not apply. Some description parts are missing, values are not known exactly or are vaguely described. Or, instead of exact values, the degree of a property or its probability is known (Richter & Weber, 2013).

Although cases are verified before entering the case base, it is not guaranteed that for each case the same amount of information is available. Hence, some attribute values might be missing or could not be described in the same precise manner as for other cases. The same goes with current problems being formulated incompletely, for example. Hence, uncertainties in the case base as well as query formulation have impacts on the similarity calculation, the reuse step, and obviously on the final result. To sum up, the crucial point here is the uncertainty that arises in the solutions which at least partly originates from uncertain initial descriptions.

When analyzing uncertainty in the context of decision-making, it is naturally connected to blocked or delayed action and depends on the decision-making model to be employed (Lipshitz & Strauss, 1997). A classification approach would be according to its issue and source. So, for decision-makers, the situation, the outcome, and the alternatives are uncertain caused by incomplete information, insufficient understanding, and undifferentiated alternatives (Lipshitz & Strauss, 1997). Three strategies are suggested to cope with uncertainty: (1) to reduce uncertainty by collecting additional information, deferring decisions or extrapolating with statistical methods, making assumptions or even predictions and scenario-building, respectively. Another approach is to react beforehand by controlling the source of variability; (2) to acknowledge uncertainty through consideration when evaluating options or completely avoid uncertainty by preferring clear outcomes; (3) to suppress uncertainty by denial or rationalization (Lipshitz & Strauss, 1997).

Hence, the notion of uncertainty is used differently. Within the scope of this thesis, the focus is particularly on *uncertainty in attribute values*, the representation possibilities and how to integrate them in the CBR cycle. One may distinguish between missing, vague, and probabilistic information. *Vague* information cannot be described in a clear-cut manner and may also refer to imprecisions resulting from measurement errors. For *probabilistic* information probability values reflect the correctness of a value. *Incomplete* information refers to missing values and is handled like information gaps. The objective is to extent modeling efforts and make uncertainty, at least in the retrieve and reuse step of CBR, transparent. To overcome other sources of uncertainty such as insufficient understanding and undifferentiated alternatives, may be alleviated by additional information and support in the problem-solving process or by integrating additional methods such as multi-criteria decision analyses (see Chapter 2.5).

The following chapter gives a brief overview on possibilities to represent uncertainty in attribute values and outlines consequences for retrieval. Other uncertainties that are linked with the method itself and the design of a CBR system, may be alleviated with the help of different evaluation measures (Chapter 2.1.4).

Vague information

Besides measurement errors, human usage of language is often prone to imprecise statements. Instead of exact temperatures, for instance, descriptions such as 'cold' or 'warm' are used. Different approaches may be used to handle such kind of information.

Multi-valued logic

The classical two-valued logic can be extended to finitely many or even infinitely many truth values (fuzzy logic), at first introduced by Jan Lukasiewicz (McCall, 1973; Woleński, 2004). The number of possible values may depend on the application domain, for example, suggesting no more than nine levels of distinction in ordinary human discourse (Schwartz, 1991). In case of a manageable amount of truth values, the similarities between them can be defined explicitly.

Interval arithmetic

Unprecise values may also be expressed with upper and lower bounds, which can be further processed by means of interval arithmetic (Moore, Kearfott, & Cloud, 2009). However, if a variable appears repeatedly in a formula, precision decreases. The interval width would be extended artificially. Another possibility to process intervals in the retrieve step is to examine interval intersections. One may note here, that intervals may intersect or one interval lies completely in another. The intersection width would be the same but possibly not the interpretation. If the query interval is subsumed of the case interval, the case may be more interesting than just intersecting query and case intervals. Similarities may also be determined between values and intervals and vice versa considering how symmetrical an interval encloses a value taking the interval width into account (Shi, Xin, & Dong, 2011).

Fuzzy Sets

Fuzzy sets (Zadeh, 1965) enhance ordinary sharp sets in which objects are either included or not. Given a set X as universe of discourse with elements x, a *fuzzy set* A of X is described by a *membership function* $\mu_A: X \rightarrow [0,1]$, where $\mu_A(x)$ represents the degree of membership of x in A. Basic definitions for sets such as union, intersection, and complementation as well as containment and emptiness are extended, always referring to membership functions (Zadeh, 1965). Integrating fuzzy sets into CBR and in particular into case representation and retrieval refers to membership functions as well (Bonissone & Cheetham, 1997; Dvir, Langholz, & Schneider, 1999). For retrieval, the integral method takes the intersection of the areas between the membership functions and the x-axis into account, assumed that the two fuzzy functions are not disjoint. The crisp method would regard the distance between the maxima of the membership functions (Richter, 2004). However, the shape of the curves would be irrelevant, hence making a combination of both approaches reasonable (Richter & Weber, 2013). Furthermore, similarities between crisp and fuzzy values may be assessed by corresponding degrees of membership. Different membership functions can be defined for different attribute-value pairs and hence making this approach case-specific.

Rough Sets

Another mathematical concept to handle imprecision is rough set theory (Pawlak, 1982). In contrast to fuzzy set theory, imprecision is expressed by a boundary region of a set instead of a partial membership. A famous example is the classification of cases given their attribute values. If a crisp classification is impossible, rough set theory allows lower- and upper-set approximations and cases belonging to a boundary between certain cases (Sankar K. Pal & Shiu, 2004). The lower approximation contains all objects that certainly belong to a specific set whereas the upper approximation contains all objects that possibly belong to that specific set. The boundary region that contains objects that neither can be assigned to that specific set nor cannot be assigned to it, poses the uncertainty area. If the boundary region is nonempty, the corresponding set is *rough*, otherwise the set is crisp. The role of that area is to give the user additional information and possibilities for precautionary actions (Richter & Weber, 2013).

Central for rough set theory is the indiscernibility relation, where attribute values of two objects are identical in relation to a considered subset of attributes (Rissino & Lambert-Torres, 2009) expressing the fact that some objects may not be discernable due to lack of knowledge. With respect to CBR, rough sets are typically used for feature weighting and selection and particularly memory size reduction (Fernández-Riverola, Díaz, & Corchado, 2007; Chun-che Huang & Tseng, 2004; Y.

Jiang, Chen, & Ruan, 2006; Z. Jiang et al., 2016; Salamó & López-Sánchez, 2011) or for developing a general similarity relation (Greco, Matarazzo, & Slowinski, 2006).

Probabilistic information

Probabilistic information deals with information whose correctness cannot be guaranteed, and that may underlie a certain probability distribution. The challenge here is to identify appropriate probability distributions to quantify uncertainty. Probability values for certain attribute values can, for example, enter the attribute weights to take into account their uncertainty in the similarity calculation. In order to handle probabilistic issues in CBR, other approaches such as Bayesian Networks (F. V. Jensen, 1996; Pearl, 1988) can be integrated. A Bayesian network models a set of variables and their conditional probabilities with a directed acyclic graph and provides its own inference mechanism. For instance, a hybrid system may handle common situations as well as outliers (Bruland, Aamodt, & Langseth, 2011) or Bayesian networks can be used for structuring the case base and calculate similarity (Gomes, 2004). Requiring a more in-depth domain knowledge, Bayesian networks contrast with the more heuristic philosophy of CBR. However, an appropriate integration in the CBR cycle or hybrid systems, respectively, may complement CBR in terms of probabilistic issues.

Incomplete information

One may think of several reasons, why problems can only be partially described, such as non-availability at a specific date, high procurement costs, effort, or expenditure of time. For countering incomplete information, initial descriptions can be refined or methods can be implemented to handle incrementally-built case descriptions, particularly for conversational CBR (Carrick, Yang, Abi-Zeid, & Lamontagne, 1999). In the following, several possibilities to handle unknown attribute values are presented to be applied to ordinal attribute types. The detailed overview can be found in (Bogaerts & Leake, 2004).

Default Difference

Here, a fixed default difference value is assigned whenever a feature is unknown. For a local similarity function, a value of 1 represents a very optimistic view whereas 0 assumes the worst case scenario. A local similarity function f_A is hence adapted to

$$\widetilde{f_A}(q_A, c_A) = \begin{cases} k, & c_A \text{ or } q_A \text{ unknown} \\ f_A(q_A, c_A), & \text{otherwise} \end{cases}$$

with $k \in [0,1]$, q_A the attribute value of the query for attribute A, and c_A the attribute value of the case for attribute A. If cases in the case base are completely described, a change in the default value does not affect the ranking of similar cases. However, decreasing k may favor stored cases for which more features are known, particularly if the query as well as descriptions of stored cases are only partially described. Furthermore, values of k need to be manually updated, especially to be aligned with the case base.

Full Mean

Here, missing values are replaced with the mean (or mode in case of symbolic attributes) of the corresponding attribute values. Denote CB the set of cases of the case base for which the attribute values are known. If the set is empty, a default value $k \in [0,1]$, is taken again:

$$k^* = \begin{cases} \frac{\sum_{c \in CB} c_A}{|CB|}, & CB \neq \emptyset \\ k, & \text{otherwise} \end{cases}$$

Where c_A is the value of the case for attribute A. Hence, a corresponding local similarity function is as follows:

$$\widetilde{f_A}(q_A, c_A) = \begin{cases} k, & c_A \text{ and } q_A \text{ unknown} \\ f_A(k^*, c_A), & q_A \text{ unknown} \\ f_A(q_A, k^*), & c_A \text{ unknown} \\ f_A(q_A, c_A), & \text{otherwise} \end{cases}$$

with $k \in [0,1]$, q_A the attribute value of the query for attribute A, and c_A the attribute value of the case for attribute A. If q_A and c_A are unknown, it might be better to choose a default value instead of replacing c_A and q_A with k^*, which would lead to maximal similarity.

Full mean ignores feature's distribution and dependencies between features. This should be partially tackled with the Nearest neighbor mean and Region mean, presented in the following. The computing effort for Full mean and Default difference is low, yet they both produce comparatively poor results (Bogaerts & Leake, 2004).

Nearest Neighbor Mean

In alignment with CBR, Nearest neighbor mean predicts attribute values based on values of the nearby cases. If values are missing, the approaches presented before may be applied. If attributes are interdependent, filtering the case base according to attributes correlated to the missing one enhance weighted nearest neighbor approaches (Jagannathan & Petrovic, 2009). Nearest neighbor mean is an expensive approach, since for each unknown attribute value, a retrieval before the actual CBR retrieval has to be conducted. However, the results are better than of Full mean or Default Difference (Bogaerts & Leake, 2004).

Region Mean

Region mean works with the positive aspects of Full mean and Nearest neighbor mean by clustering the case base to determine prototypes containing mean values of the corresponding classes. In the retrieve step of CBR, the missing value of an attribute is replaced by the value of the nearest prototype. Since the prototypes are calculated offline, the online computation is faster for Region Mean than for Nearest neighbor mean with similar error values (Bogaerts & Leake, 2004).

Further approaches

To handle unknown values, one may impute values that contribute to the similarity in an optimistic or pessimistic way that means maximizing or minimizing the final similarity values. Furthermore, values with the highest likelihood may pose an appropriate candidate (Richter & Weber, 2013). However, this approach may face a general problem in application domains of CBR, which is poor domain knowledge. If probability distributions are not taken into account and the domain of an attribute is known, one may estimate similarity by trying out all possible values for the specific attribute of which the value is unknown.

2.1.6 Advantages and Drawbacks of CBR

CBR offers many application possibilities and has been applied in various fields. One may distinguish two styles of CBR that are problem-solving and interpretive (Kolodner, 1992). The first style uses old solutions as a guide to solve new problems, which particularly depends on adaptation processes. Application examples are planning, diagnosis, or design tasks, or for explanation. With the interpretive style, new situations or solutions are evaluated, for example in situations, when computational methods are not available or cannot be run due to many unknowns. Old cases are used for classifying situations, argumenting classifications, justifying solutions, interpretations, or plans as well as predicting the effects of a decision or plan (Kolodner, 1992). Interpretation and problem-solving should not be considered separately but rather interpretive CBR as useful and crucial component of problem-solving (Kolodner, 1992).

Popular application areas of CBR are medical and technical diagnosis, call centers, electronic commerce, or law (Kolodner, 1992; M. Lenz, Bartsch-Spörl, Burkhard, & Wess, 2004). Furthermore, CBR is combined with other reasoning approaches such as rule-based reasoning, model-based reasoning, constraint satisfaction problem-solving, information retrieval or planning, amongst others for legal systems, planning nutritional menus, harmonizing melodies, speech synthesis, diagnosing heart failures or auditory diseases, for architectural design, decision support for managing patients with diabetes, or coloring industrial plastics (Marling, Rissland, & Aamodt, 2005). Further prominent research fields are route and project planning or tutoring systems (Greene, Freyne, Smyth, & Cunningham, 2010) as well as business process management, software process reuse, and trace-based reasoning (Montani & Jain, 2014). CBR for crisis and disaster management are particularly presented in section 2.3.

As outlined above, CBR is used for many different application areas. An advantage is that CBR allows for solving a problem quickly and solutions do not need to be generated from scratch (Kolodner, 1992; Leake, 1996a). This is especially advantageous when a problem being difficult to be solved once, is stored for later reuse avoiding a difficult reasoning the next time. Furthermore, CBR allows problem-solving in domains that are not fully understood (Kolodner, 1992). This is particularly useful in situations when certain combinations of problem characteristics have not happened before and a system that is based on a causal model would reach its limit. The proposed solutions may serve as starting point, even if they are not optimal or even wrong. Also, similar problems can also help to avoid mistakes (Kolodner, 1992). Furthermore, the solutions gained with CBR are based on prior cases and are hence explainable. User acceptance and transparency of the solutions derived are important factors for the later success in practice (Leake, 1996a).

Despite of the intuitive approach of CBR, the implementation meets several challenges. If a strong domain theory is not available or difficult to formalize, adapting existing high quality solutions may lead to good results (Cunningham, 2005). However, insufficient adaptation processes may weaken the quality of retrieved solutions and approaches such as rule-based or model-based approaches may be more appropriate (Cunningham, 2005). In general, adaptation is a crucial step in CBR that need to be carefully implemented. Otherwise the user may be unconsciously biased assuming solutions from previous cases are right without transferring them to the new problem situation (Kolodner, 1992).

2.2 Case-Based Planning

In planning, the task is to find a course of actions to achieve a specified set of goals given initial situations and constraints. These actions are described by operators changing the state of the world provided certain preconditions are met. In a classical generative planning process, the space of possible operators is traversed to solve a given problem where case-based approaches reuse plans often by making modifications (Bergmann, Muñoz-Avila, & Veloso, 1996). In case-based planning (CBP), the solution of case plays a major role for the reusability of that case and hence for the similarity assessment, particularly the preconditions that need to be satisfied for successfully applying the plan (Bergmann et al., 1995; Spalazzi, 2001). For reuse, as mentioned in section 2.1.3, either retrieved plans are modified with the help of, for example, domain dependent heuristics or the solution is used as a guide to construct a new plan. The revise and retain phase distinguish from case-based approaches for analytical tasks. The resulting plan is corrected with respect to the domain model and therefore needs to be validated in the real world. Furthermore, goals as well as the solution trace need to be identified and stored for future reuse (Bergmann et al., 1995).

Case-based planners are developed for various application domains, such as diagnosis and therapy or logistics. In an exhaustive survey, various CBP systems with diverse facets are presented (Spalazzi, 2001). They differ in terms of plan representation that can be purely featural or relational, such as abstractions, specializations or partonomic relations, or are logic-based. Furthermore, CBP systems either store plans or derivational traces or use an indexing scheme for retrieval referring to goals, initial situations and failures. The reuse step ranges from non-automatic to transformational, and derivational adaptation. As in other planning systems or general case-based reasoning approaches, plans need to be revised that includes evaluation and repair. Plan retention comprises decisions on what to store and how to eventually re-organize the plan memory for future retrieval.

Updated overviews regard systems as a whole (Borrajo, Roubíčková, & Serina, 2015) or focus on adaptation (Muñoz-Avila & Cox, 2008) as well as further developments of specific systems (Bonisoli, Gerevini, Saetti, & Serina, 2015; Borges, Dordal, Osmar, Ribeiro, Ávila, & Scalabrin, 2015; Garrido, Morales, & Serina, 2016).

CBP systems are specializations of CBR systems. This thesis goes beyond purely planning and aims at providing decision support in a more general manner. In particular, the type of decision support varies in the course of the event, which is explained more in detail in Chapter 3.

2.3 Application in Disaster Management

As presented before, CBR and CBP are applied in various fields. The following section particularly deals with applications in disaster management. 'Emergency management' and 'disaster management' are sometimes used synonymously (UNDRR, 2017) and is therefore taken into account in the literature review. The focus is on systems to be applied during response and recovery.

In general, a CBR system for disaster management supports information and knowledge sharing, minimizes stress by automating response processes and workflows, and prepares information such as lessons learned prior to a disaster (Otim, 2006). With varied specialized focus, CBR is utilized in various emergency response systems. For example, mobile technology is used to share information and to provide advice and assistance (Amailef & Lu, 2013). Here, short emergency messages are collected and analyzed automatically to be aggregated to a new problem description for CBR. Ontologies are used for case representation and similarity assessment. The system presented covers a range of disaster events such as bioterrorism, chemical agent, radiation, and terrorism and hence, in contrast to this thesis, the attributes have a more general character. Furthermore, the modeling of strategies in combination with their assessment differentiate this thesis from related work.

CBR is also embedded in a sequential group decision process combined with a Bayesian forecasting model to gain the prior distribution of absent features (Shen, Huang, Zhao, & Jin, 2008). Without explicitly modeling solutions, the setting is general, addressing uncertainty and dynamics in emergency situations. Also, fuzzy sets are popular to handle uncertainty during case retrieval and web crawlers can be used to gather information of solutions of previous disasters (Chao Huang, Huang, Zhong, & Chen, 2013). Relations between the attributes describing the event, and crawled texts explaining the solutions, can be displayed by associating rules that are translated into fuzzy sets aiming at adapting solutions with fuzzy reasoning (Chao Huang et al., 2013).

Spatial and temporal features such as geospatial data including maps, images with time stamps, and terrain information as well as critical infrastructure, and key resources are important for describing a disaster case (F. Wang & Huang, 2010). The focus here is exclusively on similarity functions handling geospatial data such as points or polygons.

Besides general decision support approaches, CBR can be found in the context of environmental emergencies including environmental pollution, biological security, and radioactive pollution (Z. Liao, Mao, Liu, Xu, & Hannam, 2011). The authors particularly concentrate on oil spills, integrate GIS technology, and provide an in-depth list of attributes to describe environmental emergencies. In contrast to this thesis, the course of the emergency is not regarded. Solutions are oil cleaning methods that need to be adapted according to the contaminated objects, such as water surface, retaining walls, rock slopes, water plants, and beaches. Similarity is calculated by aggregating local similarities for each attribute taking into account numerical as well as symbolic attributes, where unknown attribute values are excluded from calculation. Attribute weights are elicitated with the help of experts by determining their relative importance and adaptation is realized partly by rules as well as expert modifications. In contrast to this thesis, cleaning measures or their combination are not explicitly modeled (see Chapter 2.6).

Further environmental pollution accidents such as in river regions (L. Guo et al., 2009) are interesting application fields for CBR as well, utilizing the Analytical Hierarchy Process (Saaty, 1980) for determining weights for generally assessing similarity and without specifically modeling solutions. More sophisticated similarity measures are illustrated in a case study in the field of gas explosions (Fan et al., 2014) focusing on the retrieve step of CBR.

Another example is an interactive planning and scheduling assistant for hazardous material incidents where solution adaptation is partly carried out by the user (Gervasio, Iba, & Langley, 1998). Plans are represented by a tree where actions are equipped with time intervals and a set of resources providing capacity and quantity constraints. There are no causal links between actions. The assistant focus on determining initial candidate solutions retrieved from previous cases, adaptation mechanisms by expanding and deleting subtrees based on a set of rules, and providing a simulator for implementing and monitoring responses. The added value of a semi-automatic system in contrast to a fully automated approach is particularly emphasized (Iba & Gervasio, 2000). For similarity calculation, matching features are counted focusing rather on adaptation and planning assistance.

Furthermore, case-based support is provided in shipboard flooding emergencies where a set of prioritized counter-flooding tanks are searched for to handle flooding onboard ships and particularly to bring the ship into an upright position again (Ölçer & Majumder, 2006). The authors particularly combine CBR with multi-attribute decision-making, where research is particularly tailored to crises onboard ships.

Applications for the fire rescue service pose a vital research field for CBR as well (Avesani, Perini, & Ricci, 2000; Chakraborty, Ghosh, Maji, Garnaik, & Debnath, 2010; Krasuski & Kreński, 2009; Krupka, Kasparova, & Jirava, 2009; Lewis, 2004). For example, an advanced interactive planning system where CBR and constraint reasoning is combined is in use to fight forest fires (Avesani et al., 2000). Particularly, temporal issues are considered and interactive adaptation possibilities are provided. Plans are represented as a hierarchy of domain dependent information. The root represents the global plan that is composed of sub-plans for different fire front sectors and the leaves pose the actions. The temporal sequence can be described by an action graph where the user can insert or remove actions. The work of this thesis shares the division of an affected area into sub-areas but aims at compiling additional aspects that influence decisions on plans besides time and resources.

Other approaches that concern fire rescue services omit solution modeling or only adapt numerical values (Chakraborty et al., 2010), focus mainly on system architecture or ontologies (Krasuski, Maciak, & Kreński, 2009; Kreński, Krasuski, & Łazowy, 2011), or case representation and retrieval (Krupka et al., 2009). CBR and particularly the retrieval step are proposed in conjunction with developing a decision support system for fighting industrial fires (Auriol et al., 2004). CBP and especially the retrieval step is suggested for plan generation in conjunction with forest fire fighting where a plan tree structure for case representation is proposed (Rollón, Isern, Agostini, & Cortés, 2003).

CBR is proposed as decision support in flood crises focusing on retrieval (Luo, Xu, Shi, Jamont, & Zeng, 2007) and representing emergency plans as rules (Shen & Zhao, 2010) or as decision support in typhoon disaster management focusing on case specification and spatial awareness elements (X. Zhou & Wang, 2014).

The DIAL system is a case-based planner for disaster response plans, where research particularly focus on automated case or response plan adaptation (Kinley, 2001; Leake et al., 1995). Besides the disaster response plan that contains disaster characteristics, actions and performing individuals or groups (role fillers), memory search cases and adaptation cases are stored, containing search processes for finding relevant information for adaptation and traces of case adaptation. In order to retrieve plans of similar situations, features such as type of disaster, location or primary victims are regarded. When retrieving a plan, some role fillers may be directly mapped into the new situations whereby the user evaluates further role fillers afterwards. If possible, the system then uses prior knowledge to guide the solution process for the identified role filler problems. Hence, the adaptation is eventually case-based or realized rule-based or even manually. The DIAL system provides several learning methods including similarity assessment being guided by estimated adaptation costs. It is a pioneering work in the field of emergency response planning and case-based reasoning. Decoupling case learning and adaptation learning increases the effectiveness of a CBR system, since experience from adaptation may help to overcome current adaptation problems, although the corresponding response plan is not appropriate in the current context (Leake et al., 1995). The work of this thesis investigates the modeling of a disaster or nuclear accident, respectively, in more detail taking into account the changing appropriate measures, and explicitly models emergency strategies.

In summary, research on CBR and CBP in disaster management has special focus, either with regard to methodical issues or concerning the application domain or does not model strategies. CBR is particularly new in nuclear emergency management.

2.4 Enhancing the Case Base by Scenarios

Within the scope of this work, few past events exist that could enrich the case base and hence the core of the CBR system. Therefore, scenarios are generated to enhance the case base. The notion of *scenario*, generally describing possible future states and developments, is not consistent in the literature resulting in diverse typologies and scenario construction techniques (Börjeson et al., 2006). Without referring to actual construction techniques, scenarios can be characterized according to their goal, process design, and content (van Notten, Rotmans, van Asselt, & Rothman, 2003). The goals might be exploration or decision support where process design refers to formal or intuitive methods to construct scenarios, which could be of complex or simple nature. Scenario development techniques can be also categorized according to their historical roots referring to intuitive and hence non-quantitative or probabilistic approaches as well as a third prospective thinking approach for long-term strategic planning originated in France (Bradfield, Wright, Burt, Cairns, & Van Der Heijden, 2005). Furthermore, future states can be categorized as possible, probable, and/or preferable leading to further categories of scenario studies, namely 'predictive', 'explorative', and 'normative' (Börjeson et al., 2006). These classes are based on questions: "What will happen?", "What can happen?" and "How can a specific target be reached?" Each of these categories are further divided resulting in six types of scenarios (see Figure 2.6). Predictive scenarios comprise forecasts that are based on the most likely developments, and what-if scenarios regarding several forecasts on the condition of some specified events that are developed from the present situation on (Börjeson et al., 2006). Explorative scenarios are elaborated with a long-term horizon where a set of scenarios are worked out and profound and structural changes are explicitly regarded. They are either driven by external factors that are beyond the control of the relevant actors or are of strategic nature, describing consequences of a decision depending on which future development unfolds (Börjeson et al., 2006). The latter particularly takes internal and external factors into account. Instead of absolute goals, target variables are defined (Börjeson et al., 2006). Normative scenarios are distinguished by preserving or transforming system behavior being necessary to reach a certain target. Hence, for the latter, a marginal adjustment is not sufficient and rather back casting is necessary that means envisioning the desired target and work backwards since the actual structure is seen as a problem (Börjeson et al., 2006). Several scenario techniques exist, either, for example, on a general level (Börjeson et al., 2006) or more specific (Bishop, Hines, & Collins, 2007).

In the context of this thesis, scenarios are elaborated by considering varying accident characteristics, environmental conditions and locations, corresponding measures to prevent or reduce contamination or the likelihood of contamination of a target, and their effectiveness. They are of the same underlying structure as historical events. Hence, the scenarios in the frame of this thesis are of explorative character. In summary, following understanding applies:

Scenarios describe possible accidents and their developments as well as appropriate measures and their effectiveness, and are subject to the same structure as historical disasters. The term of 'cases' refers to historical disasters and scenarios equally. Hence, for case-based support, knowledge of historical events and scenarios is used, even though in different ways (see Chapter 3).

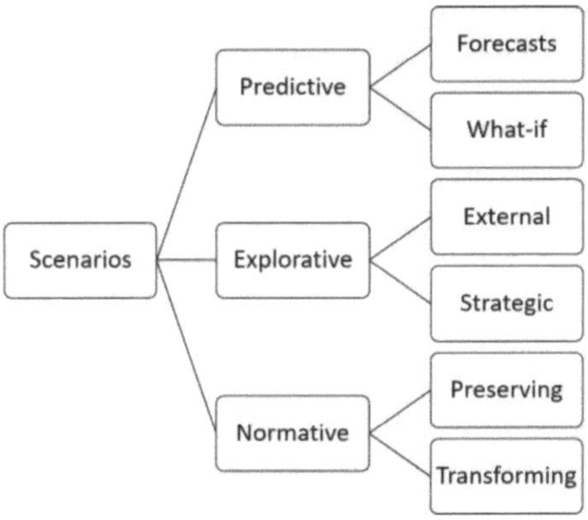

Figure 2.6: Scenario typology (Börjeson et al., 2006, Figure 1)

2.5 Multi-Criteria Decision Analysis for Additional Support

Similarity measures enable to rank retrieved cases automatically according to their closeness to the current problem. However, the solution of the most similar case or cases are not necessarily most appropriate in solving the current problem, since successful and less successful solutions may be stored in the case base. Further, the assumption that similar problems have similar solutions can be limited, amongst others, by the inability of a similarity measure to capture the usefulness of a case for a current problem or to identify the relevance of a feature in solving a problem as well as the absence of relevant features (Kar, Chakraborti, & Ravindran, 2012). In addition to approaches already presented in Chapter 2.1.5 to handle uncertainty in attribute values, another idea is to provide additional decisive criteria, particularly when several strategies are available, in the framework of a multi-criteria decision analysis (MCDA).

MCDA covers various methods supporting decision-making taking into account multiple objectives (decision criteria) in a transparent manner (Belton & Stewart, 2002; Triantaphyllou, 2000). MCDA comprises Multi-Objective Decision-Making (MODM) where several objectives are optimized simultaneously, and Multi-Attribute Decision-making (MADM), where the most preferable option is chosen from a discrete set of decision alternatives. The latter particularly covers several methods that differ in modeling of intra-criteria preferences (Bertsch, 2007), where performance scores of different alternatives with respect to one criterion are regarded. In the scope of this work, multi-attribute value theory (MAVT) belonging to MADM, is introduced only, since the values to be processed in decision analysis are deterministic and MAVT is successfully applied in the related research field as well as in combination with CBR as can be seen later in this chapter.

The key steps of MAVT, summarized in Figure 2.8, are as follows: First, the decision-problem is structured hierarchically comprising an overall goal, multiple criteria, attributes, and decision alternatives (Figure 2.7). Particularly, for the set of attributes, following properties are desirable (Keeney & Raiffa, 1976): The set should be *complete* and *operational* with meaningful attributes that support the understanding of the alternatives. A set of attributes is regarded as *complete*, if it clearly indicates to which degree the overall objective is met. Furthermore, the set should be *decomposable* and hence attributes can be analyzed independently from each other. Also, the *non-redundancy* to avoid double counting of impacts as well as *minimum size* of the set of attributes pose further properties important to be checked.

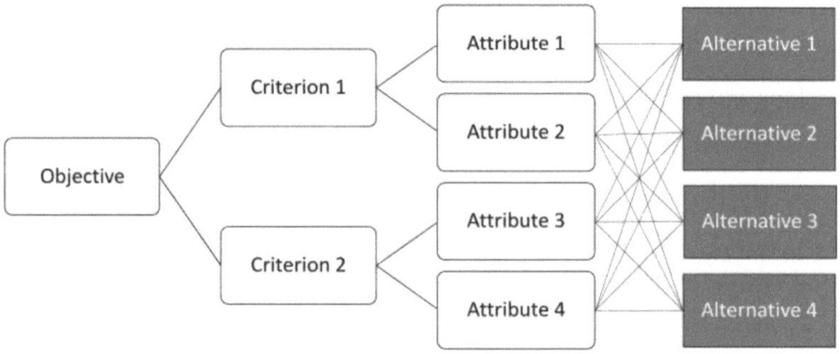

Figure 2.7: Hierarchical arrangement of objective, criteria, attributes, and decision alternatives

After problem structuring, the elicitation of the relative importance of the criteria follows. Thereafter, the elicitated information is aggregated resulting in a ranking of the decision alternatives. If desired, sensitivity analyses may be conducted. These steps are interactive and may be repeated, if necessary.

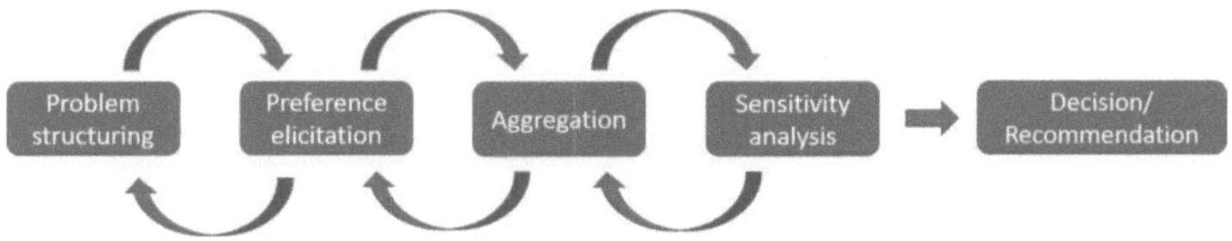

Figure 2.8: Key phases of MAVT (Bertsch, 2007, Figure 2.1)

In the following, a formal framework for MAVT is set up (Bertsch, 2007):

Definition 2.7 Score of decision alternatives

Let l denote the number of the decision alternatives, m the number of criteria, and n the number of attributes, $l, m, n \in \mathbb{N}^+$. For each decision alternative $da_i, i = 1, \dots l$ the *score* with respect to a specific attribute $at_j, j = 1, \dots, n$ is defined as

$$x(da_i, at_j) := x_{ij}.$$

These values can be summarized in a decision table (Table 2.2).

Table 2.2: Decision table of MAVT (Bertsch, 2007, Table 2.1)

Attributes [Units]/ Decision alternatives	at_1 [*unit* 1]	at_2 [*unit* 2]	...	at_n [*unit n*]
da_1	x_{11}	x_{12}	...	x_{1n}
da_2	x_{21}	x_{22}	...	x_{2n}
...	...	...	...	...
da_l	x_{l1}	x_{l2}	...	x_{ln}

In order to compare different alternatives with respect to several attributes underlying different units, the scores need to be mapped to a common scale by a value function:

Definition 2.8 Value function

A value function for an attribute at_j is defined as

$$v_j = \begin{cases} \mathbb{R} \to [0,1] \\ x_{ij} \mapsto v_j(x_{ij}) \end{cases}, j = 1, \dots, n$$

where x_{ij} denotes the score of an decision alternative $da_i, i = 1, \dots, l$ with respect to attribute $at_j, j = 1, \dots, n$.

The value functions represent the *intra-criteria preferences* that reflect how differences in the scores of the alternatives with respect to one criterion are judged enabling to compare different attributes on a common scale (Belton & Stewart, 2002; Bertsch, 2007). Here, the 'best' and 'worst' outcomes correspond to 1 and 0, respectively. Various possibilities exist to model value functions, such as applying linear or exponential functions (Bertsch, 2007). *Inter-criteria preferences* or the relative importance between different criteria, are modeled by weights on each level of the attribute tree, enabling to rank the different alternatives (Belton & Stewart, 2002; Bertsch, 2007). Hence, the final weight of each attribute is a product along the path from the objective to each attribute in the attribute tree (Bertsch, 2007). For the weight vector $w = (w_1, \dots, w_n)$ it holds

$$\sum_{j=1}^{n} w_j = 1$$

with $w_j \geq 0, j = 1, \dots, n$. There are different methods for weight elicitation (Belton & Stewart, 2002), where in context of this work a direct allocation of weights is assumed.

The overall scores of the alternatives are calculated taking into account the weights and value functions. For example, the overall value for alternative da_i can determined by means of an additive aggregation

$$v(da_i) = \sum_{j=1}^{n} w_j v_j(x_{ij}).$$

The aggregation by a weighted sum is commonly used and easy to understand by decision makers from different fields (Belton & Stewart, 2002) assuming that attributes are mutually preferentially independent (Keeney & Raiffa, 1976): An attribute at_1 is called *preferentially independent* of another attribute at_2 if preferences for certain outcomes and consequences, respectively, of at_1 do not depend on the level of outcome of at_2 (Clemen & Reilly, 2001). If the same applies vice versa, the two attributes are *mutually preferentially independent*. Several attributes $at_1, \dots, at_n$ are mutually preferentially independent if every subset of these attributes is preferentially independent of its complementary set (Keeney & Raiffa, 1976).

When proposing a solution, information on the achievement of defined objectives and on how they are derived is essential. In case of several available solutions, a ranking facilitates decision-making, in particular with the help of visualization, for example by stacked-bar charts that illustrate the contributions of the individual criteria and attributes to the performance scores, respectively. Furthermore, sensitivity analyses may help to investigate the influence of the preference parameters on the results and, amongst others, help to build consensus or understanding (French, 2003). One may investigate how sensitive the ranking is to changes in the criteria weights and to changing attribute values focusing on the best alternative or on changes in the ranking of any alternative, as well as determining smallest changes that cause actually a ranking change (Triantaphyllou, 2000).

As discussed before, applying MAVT intends to complement the case-based approach for problem-solving by evaluating each alternative solution in a quantitative manner. The aim is to provide a broader discussion basis and to support the understanding and trust in the determined solutions. A reasonable inclusion of MAVT is after adaptation and before revision within the CBR cycle.

Several approaches combine CBR and MCDA such as for stock analysis in the financial market (Sushmita & Chaudhury, 2007), for ranking alternatives (before adaptation) in the frame of tropical cyclone forecasting (San Pedro & Burstein, 2003), for decision support in case of supply chain interruptions (Merz, Hiete,

Bertsch, & Rentz, 2007) or to prioritize security measures against terrorist threats to public rail transport systems (L. Lin, Brauner, Münzberg, Meng, & Moehrle, 2013; Müller, Meng, Raskob, Wiens, & Schultmann, 2015) aiming at identifying the most preferred solution of some set of pre-selected cases. MCDA is also applied in the retrieval phase of CBR (Armaghan & Renaud, 2012), particularly for calculating weights (Alptekin & Büyüközkan, 2011), enhancing similarity assessment (Li & Sun, 2009), particularly by combining multiple similarity metrics (Lamontagne & Abi-zeid, 2006), or CBR is used for preference elicitation in MCDA (Chen, Kilgour, & Hipel, 2011).

Furthermore, explicitly for disaster and emergency management, MCDA methods are applied for flood risk management (de Brito & Evers, 2016; Hansson, Larsson, Danielson, & Ekenberg, 2011), nuclear remediation management (Geldermann et al., 2009), evacuation decisions (Kailiponi, 2010), emergency medical service assessment (Kou & Wu, 2014), as part of an incident information management framework (Peng, Zhang, Tang, & Li, 2011) or in the frame of helicopter mission planning during a disaster relief operation (Barbarosoğlu, Özdamar, & Cevik, 2002). MCDA is particularly beneficial for nuclear emergency management in general (Papamichail & French, 2013).

Several further approaches for assessing disaster management strategies can be found in humanitarian aid by means of a crisis performance measurement system with the dimensions relevance, efficiency, satisfaction, expectation, impact, and agility, that have to be aligned with the specific situation by corresponding indicators (Rongier, Lauras, Galasso, & Gourc, 2012). This specific application area is combined with performance measurements of commercial supply chains as well working with resource, output, and flexibility, as well as different metrics such as costs, response time, or types of supplies (Beamon & Balcik, 2008). Several approaches concentrate on one specific aspect to evaluate measures and support decision-making, such as the effectiveness of a strategy in the frame of earthquake mitigation measures using loss and response parameters (Gupta & Shah, 1998) or to evaluate emergency response operations in command and control taking into account human and property loss in conjunction with time after initializing response efforts (D. E. Brown & Robinson, 2005). Additional research investigates cost-optimal response actions (Hild, Fischer, Ott, & Glökler, 2010) or supports planning by calculating the duration and required resources of relief measures by means of key performance indicators (Moellmann, Engelmann, Braun, & Raskob, 2011). Another important concept is the robustness of decisions on strategies, since several options are possible on how the event will evolve or how environment will change. The objective is to select a strategy, which performs sufficiently well for many different scenarios (T. Comes, Hiete, Wijngaards, & Schultmann, 2010). All these solutions for assessing disaster management strategies are taken into account in the development of the multi-criteria assessment that is presented in Chapter 6.2.

As summarized above, plenty of successful MCDA and particularly MAVT applications, also in conjunction with CBR, exist in different research fields. The major advantages lie in the structured procedure for analyzing different information streams and thus preserving transparent decision-making as well as facilitating consensus finding in groups (Bertsch, 2007; Geldermann et al., 2009). In contrast to pure cost-benefit analysis, the strength of MCDA is the deliberate integration of subjectivity of decision-making by taking stakeholders preferences into account (Bertsch, 2007). In the frame of this work, parameters related to CBR as well as to future uncertainties are integrated in the multi-criteria decision support (see Chapter 6.2).

2.6 Modeling Disaster Management Strategies

A strategy consists of several measures which have a logical and temporal order of implementation. Furthermore, besides having a specific objective, a measure is directed towards a certain object. This means that for an object only certain measures can be applied to achieve the objective. Further factors that influence the choice of measures may also be taken into account. This information is especially important for the reuse step of CBR, not only to propose correct solutions but also to support understanding from the user side. Petri Nets (PNs) that are introduced in the following section, are a generic approach to model strategies. As presented later, adaptation and where appropriate, merging of several solutions should be possible, favoring the usage of PNs. Application areas and other approaches to model strategies are presented afterwards. Related work refers to general modeling as well as merging of PNs.

2.6.1 Petri Nets

Petri nets are a graphical and mathematical modeling tool useful for describing and analyzing information processing systems as well as for visual communication (Murata, 1989). They originate from the early work of Carl Adam Petri (Petri, 1962) and are defined as follows (Murata, 1989):

Definition 2.9 Petri Net

A Petri net is a tuple

$$PN = (P, T, F, W, M_0)$$

where:

- P and T are finite sets of places and transitions.
- $P \cap T = \emptyset$ and $P \cup T \neq \emptyset$.
- $F \subseteq (P \times T) \cup (T \times P)$ is a set of arcs (flow relation).
- $W: F \rightarrow \mathbb{N}^+$ is a weight function.
- $M_0: P \rightarrow \mathbb{N}$ is the initial marking.

Places are represented by circles, transitions by rectangles, and arcs are labeled by weights. The state of the system, which is called a marking $M: P \rightarrow \mathbb{N}$, is reflected by the distribution of tokens, represented by black dots, over places. The *input* and *output* places of transitions are defined as follows:

-$\bullet\, t = \{p | (p, t) \in F\}$ is called the set of input places of transition t,

-$t \bullet = \{p | (t, p) \in F\}$ is called the set of output places of transition t.

The dynamics of the system can be described by marking changes caused by firing a transition. A marking is changed according to following transition rule (Murata, 1989): A transition t is enabled if and only if each input place p of t contains at least $w(p, t)$ tokens where $w(p, t)$ denotes the weight of the arc from p to t. An enabled transition may fire. The firing of t removes $w(p, t)$ tokens from each input place p

and adds $w(t,p)$ tokens to each output place p of t where $w(t,p)$ is the weight of the arc from t to p.

There are different types of nets, which can be grouped into Low-and High-level PNs (LLPNs and HLPNs). In LLPNs tokens are indistinguishable. In HLPNs (K. Jensen & Rozenberg, 1991; Klink, Li, & Oberweis, 2008; K. Lenz & Oberweis, 2003), tokens have individual characteristics and can be therefore distinguished. Each place, transition, and arc is defined with respect to different token types. HLPNs allow for a more compact description than LLPNs. For practical applications, they are preferred to LLPNs (Oberweis & Sander, 1996). In the frame of this thesis, HLPNs are used to model strategies. Hence, following the standard documentation (International Organization for Standardization, 2000, 2004), the semantic model for HLPNs is introduced here in more detail. For this, the notions of multisets and their comparison are clarified in the first place:

A *multiset* B over a non-empty basis set A is a function

$$B: A \to \mathbb{N}$$

where $B(a), a \in A$ is called the multiplicity of a. A multiset B may be represented as a symbolic sum of basis elements scaled by their multiplicities

$$B = \sum_{a \in A} B(a)'a.$$

Multiset comparison is defined as follows: For two multisets $B_1, B_2 \in \mu A$ it holds

$$B_1 \leq B_2 :\Leftrightarrow \forall a \in A, \qquad B_1(a) \leq B_2(a)$$

where μA denotes the set of multisets over A.

A high-level Petri net is defined as follows (International Organization for Standardization, 2000):

Definition 2.10 High-level Petri Net

A *High-level Petri Net* is a tuple $HLPN = (P, T, D, Type, Pre, Post, M_0)$ where

- P and T are finite sets of places and transitions.
- $P \cap T = \emptyset$.
- D is a non-empty finite set of non-empty domains where each element of D is called a type.
- $Type: P \cup T \rightarrow D$ is a function used to assign types to places and to determine transition modes. A transition mode is a pair comprising the transition and a value from the transition`s type.
- $Pre, Post: TRANS \rightarrow \mu PLACE$ are the pre- and post-mappings with
  - $TRANS = \{(t, m) | t \in T, m \in Type(t)\}$
  - $PLACE = \{(p, g) | p \in P, g \in Type(p)\}$

  where $\mu PLACE$ is the set of multisets over the set $PLACE$.

- $M_0 \in \mu PLACE$ is a multiset called the initial marking of the net.

Hence a marking $M \in \mu PLACE$ is a multiset.

Enabling a single transition mode and concurrent enabling of transition modes are defined as follows (International Organization for Standardization, 2000):

Definition 2.11 Enabling of a single transition mode

A transition mode $tr \in TRANS$ is *enabled* at a marking $M :\Leftrightarrow Pre(tr) \leq M$.

Definition 2.12 Concurrent enabling of transition modes

A finite multiset of transition modes $T_\mu \in \mu TRANS$, is enabled at a marking $M :\Leftrightarrow Pre(T_\mu) \leq M$ where the linear extension of Pre is given by

$$Pre(T_\mu) = \sum_{tr \in TRANS} T_\mu(tr) Pre(tr).$$

All transition modes in T_μ are said to be *concurrently enabled* if T_μ is enabled.

A marking is changed according to following transition rule (International Organization for Standardization, 2000):

Definition 2.13 Transition rule

Given that a finite multiset of transition modes T_μ is enabled at a marking M, then a step may occur resulting in a new marking M' given by

$$M' = M - Pre(T_\mu) + Post(T_\mu)$$

where the linear extension of $Post$ is used. A step is denoted by $M[T_\mu\rangle M'$ or $M \overset{T_\mu}{\rightarrow} M'$.

2.6.2 Further Approaches for Strategy Modeling in Disaster Management

For analyzing existing approaches to model disaster and emergency management activities, papers in the areas of disaster recovery planning/strategies, disaster and accident rescue (processes), disaster/emergency response (activities), post-disaster rebuilding, disaster/emergency management, and emergency plans were studied with regard to modeling and the possibility of automatic processing.

The coordination of disaster response activities, for example, can be supported by an activity management system (Franke, Charoy, & Ulmer, 2010). Also, optimization approaches are applied in the frame of disaster management (L. Yan, Jinsong, Xiaofeng, & Ye, 2009) as well as performance analyses of post-disaster rebuild projects (Kim & Choi, 2012) without explicitly modeling strategies.

Modeling emergency management measures and plans by processes is a broad and important field using Event Driven Process Chains (La Rosa & Mendling, 2009), Workflow Management Systems (Jansen, Lijnse, & Plasmeijer, 2010; Rueppel & Wagenknecht, 2007; Sackmann & Betke, 2013; Sell & Braun, 2009) with an own approach for modeling workflows focusing on resources (J. Wang, Tepfenhart, & Rosca, 2009) or particularly Business Process Model and Notation (Betke & Seifert, 2017). Especially in the latter publication, the need for extensions to consider domain specific requirements such as different types of resources, their usage, states, spatial allocation as well as interdependencies are emphasized. A review on process-oriented approaches to disaster response management particularly reveals a lack of process modeling language fitting this specific domain (Hofmann, Betke, & Sackmann, 2015).

PNs are used for various emergency management applications: generalized stochastic PNs are used e.g. for modeling traffic accident rescue processes (Ju, Wang, & Che, 2007), and stochastic PNs are applied for performance analyses of coal mine emergency processes (Ma, Li, & Chen, 2011), emergency response decision-making processes (Shan, Wang, & Li, 2012), and urban response (Zhong, Shi, Fu, He, & Shi, 2010). Colored PNs, in particular, are used to model emergency plan business processes (W. Huang & Tong, 2011) and emergency response in the course of chemical accidents with continuous places and transitions (J. Zhou, 2013). They are used in combination with a queuing system for resource use (J. Zhou & Reniers, 2016) and in the framework of critical infrastructure protection (Cheminod, Bertolotti, Durante, & Valenzano, 2013) or for modeling the patients flow in an emergency medical department (Dilmaghani & Rao, 2009). Further examples of PNs are emergency management modeling in railway stations (Karmakar & Dasgupta, 2011), modeling of industrial fire management process (Bammidi & Moore, 1994), or accident modeling (Nývlt, Haugen, & Ferkl, 2015) whereat the difficulty is to transfer text into a formal model (Hill & Wright, 1997). Moreover, PNs have a huge potential in the field of risk analysis and accident modeling with the possibility of expressing common concepts into PN formalisms (Vernez, Buchs, & Pierrehumbert, 2003). PNs are particularly used in nuclear power plant emergency management, which aims at reducing the number of false evacuations (Tavana, 2008).

The PN applications presented so far focus on specific emergency response processes (i.e., in the framework of a specific accident scenario) for performance analysis or for execution support. In respect of strategy modeling, the research of this thesis has a different focus and which is discussed in more detail in Chapter 4.4.1. The papers by (W. Huang & Tong, 2011; J. Zhou, 2013; J. Zhou & Reniers, 2016) are thematically close to the approach of this thesis. They report on working with HLPNs and distinguishable tokens according to different resource types and the level of the fire state (J. Zhou, 2013). The application domain of nuclear emergencies can be found in (Tavana, 2008) who models a specific emergency management process addressing actions within a nuclear power plant with the help of LLPNs.

The combination of PNs and CBR is subject of research as well. PNs are used, for example, in the course of establishing a database and case retrieval is based on similarity calculations between markings (Lim et al., 2016). PNs also serve as mean to gain parameters that can be used in the case retrieval (Dharani & Geetha, 2013) or are used to model cases (Weber & Ontanón, 2010; Yang, Kwon Jeong, Oh, & Tan, 2004).

In summary, PNs are used in a variety of emergency management applications and are regarded as being suitable to model strategies in a structured and unambiguous manner. Furthermore, they enable an automated reuse in the framework of CBR and have analysis capabilities of structure and dynamic behavior and allow for analyses of resources. The latter is particularly interesting if several strategies are available for selection.

2.6.3 Merging Petri Nets

In this chapter, related work with regard to the reuse step of CBR is presented. As outlined before, the possibility of merging several solutions retrieved should be given. Since PNs are chosen for strategy modeling, the areas analyzed were process merging/PN merging and synthesis of processes.

Working with Event-driven Process Chains (EPCs), merging and uniting processes, respectively, can be realized with the help of maximum common connected subgraphs (La Rosa, Dumas, Uba, & Dijkman, 2010, 2013). Furthermore, EPCs can be reduced to their active behavior by considering and merging function graphs (Gottschalk, van der Aalst, & Jansen-Vullers, 2008). PNs are used for merging workflows on schema level, where the merged workflow net is the union of the original workflow nets being merged at specific merge points/places that are not specified further (S. Sun, Kumar, & Yen, 2006).

Processes may be also presented by a temporal formalism and merged at the language level (Bulanov, Lazovik, & Aiello, 2011). Another approach is to detect and resolve element and control flow differences between process models by decomposing a process model into fragments (Küster, Gerth, Förster, & Engels, 2008). In general, identifying correspondences is a key technique in process merging, such as by developing matchers that identify corresponding activities between two models (Weidlich, Dijkman, & Mendling, 2010). In particular, the classification of differences between processes needs to be discussed, since the purpose of process integration influences the determination of equivalence of activities and roles between two processes (Dijkman, 2007).

PN synthesis techniques can be divided into bottom-up, top-down, hybrid and knitting approaches. In the framework of bottom-up process synthesis (Jeng & DiCesare, 1993) systems are composed of incomplete sub-systems (modules) with the prominent application area of manufacturing systems (Cortadella, Kishinevsky, Lavagno, & Yakovlev, 1995). For synthesis, places are merged (Agerwala & Choed-Amphai, 1978; Narahari & Viswanadham, 1985) as well as common transitions, places, and paths (Ding, Wang, & Jiang, 2008). PNs are synthesized from modules that are modeled by strongly connected state machines (Jeng, 1995), colored PNs (Arjona, Bueno, & López-Mellado, 2010), generalized PNs (Koh & DiCesare, 1991), labeled partial orders/scenarios (Fahland & Woith, 2009; Mauser, 2010), or state-based models (Cortadella et al., 1995). Process synthesis is particularly embedded in the disaster response field by modeling adaptive disaster response processes, in which the behavior is synthesized by scenarios at run-time (Fahland, 2009; Fahland & Woith, 2009). Here, transitions (places) are merged if they are labeled equally and have equally labeled predecessors. In general, synthesis techniques may be susceptible to a possible loss of control in behavior of the composed system (Jeng & DiCesare, 1993). A further related research area is the composition of PNs (Guillen-Scholten, Arbab, de Boer, & Bonsangue, 2006; Hsieh & Chiang, 2011; Peres, Berthomieu, & Vernadat, 2011; Peťko & Hudák, 2012) either via common places, transitions, and arcs or specific nodes. The idea of merging at equally labeled nodes is particularly taken up in the framework of this thesis.

2.7 Discussion of the Methods Chosen

Addressing decision-making and decision support in (nuclear) emergency management opens up many possibilities for realization depending on the focus in mind, ranging from general system design issues to elaborated methods and algorithms. Research reported in this thesis pursues the development of a decision supporting method that can be applied when the possibility of an emergency situation is identified up to and including recovery. The results being presented in the following chapters cover a wide range of issues beginning with the general decision supporting paradigm to detailed solutions for specific problems. Prior to that, the choice of components building the solution is discussed.

Generally, three basic decision-making styles may be distinguished depending on uncertainty and time available. Firstly, when information is scarce and little time is available to decide, decisions of those who are experienced in managing crises result from recognition-primed decision-making (Klein, 2008; Paton & Flin, 1999) being more intuitive and based on heuristics without comparing several alternatives. Being assigned to naturalistic decision-making, field studies with decision-makers under difficult conditions such as limited time, uncertainty or high stakes, were conducted to find out how people in real world settings actually decide. Especially the usage of experience and pattern matching in combination with mental simulations to evaluate a course of action within the current context is highlighted. Simulations lead to initiating a certain action, adapting it or considering other actions. Recognition-primed decision-making challenges the idea to find the best possible option and combines intuition with analysis (Klein, 2008). In general, this type of decision-making style is feasible for experts, addresses highly complex problems in dynamic environments, and corresponds to the idea of CBR (Meso et al., 2002). Secondly, if more time and information are available, decision-makers may remember appropriate rules or procedures to apply. Thirdly, the analytical style as the most time consuming decision style, requires much information to select the best option out of several alternatives (Paton & Flin, 1999).

All three decision styles may be used during a disaster depending on the decision level or specific situation (Bouafia & Zahari Khairi, 2017; Paton & Flin, 1999; Sinclair, Doyle, Johnston, & Paton, 2012). The main difference between analytical and recognition-primed approaches is that for the latter the main effort and challenge lies in situation assessment whereas for the first approach the focus is on the choice of an option (Sinclair et al., 2012). However, all three styles are valuable for different purposes and are to be included in this thesis.

CBR as core method

Due to the nature of events regarded, CBR is chosen as the main decision supporting component, particularly to meet the uncertainty issue in respect of decision-making during the early stages of a nuclear emergency as well as promoting preparedness, in particular for recovery. For the latter, the aim is to handle issues of multiple measures and stakeholders but also little real world experience. According to the handbooks (for example, Nisbet et al., 2010) there are clear steps how to proceed when constructing a strategy (see Chapter 3.1.2) and constraints to take care of when choosing a measure. However, the exceptionality of each event, also with regard to users' preferences, requires decision supporting methods beyond fixed procedures. The multitude of measures and the need to decide in a societal consensus as well as negative experiences with implementation make advanced and automatization efforts highly valuable.

Contrasting to simulation-based systems, the case-based approach is particularly new in nuclear emergency management. Being aware of further development possibilities in various CBR-related directions, this research lays the foundation for applying experience-based decision-making in nuclear emergency management and particularly presents a prototype to show the applicability of the method.

Scenarios as extension of the case base

The shortage of documented historical events suggests to work with scenarios to prepare for possible future events and store existing expert knowledge in a structured manner. This approach particularly includes the usage of operational decision support systems such as JRodos that help constructing a strategy. Hence the work of this thesis motivates to develop strategies in advance to be better prepared in case of an accident.

Rules for complementing the similarity based approach

Although it might be somewhat contradictory to apply rules at times where almost nothing is known about the situation, the scheme integrated in this thesis is a European approach (HERCA & WENRA, 2014) and is based on four criteria that characterize the emergency situation in a very general manner. Hence, before any similarity calculation, the rules should help to roughly classify the situation and rapidly identify protective actions (see Chapter 5.1). This approach does not preclude the possibility to apply CBR. However, the similarity calculation favors a rough classification of the source term since the scenarios in the database result from JRodos simulations that are, amongst others, based on a source term. The rule-based approach does not integrate the source term or any classification of it.

Petri nets as modeling language for strategies

Petri nets provide means to describe a course of actions formally and unambiguously. Modeled as Petri net, a strategy can be further analyzed according to resources and also processed automatically in the reuse step of CBR. PNs are widely and successfully used and provide simulation capabilities useful for the purpose of this thesis.

MCDA for enhanced decision support

The multitude of decisive factors promotes the idea to combine CBR with MCDA to identify appropriate strategies. MCDA deliberately allows subjectivity, takes users' preferences into account, and supports participatory decision-making in a transparent manner. Analyses of nuclear events, discussions with experts as well as literature review strengthened the suitability of MCDA for additional decision support. As can be seen in chapter 6.2, applying MCDA in the frame of this work particularly refers to automatically determined values that are gained from the strategy modeling component, further promoting the automatization initiatives of this thesis.

The following chapter gives an overview of the whole method proposed, the assumptions on which it is based on, how the single components work together, the varying challenges of decision-making during an accident and how the presented solution provides support and complements existing systems.

3 Case-Based Decision Support

In order to answer the research question posed in section 1.2, a case-based decision support method enhanced by multi-criteria decision analysis is proposed. CBR is diversely applied in non-nuclear disaster management (section 2.3) which encourages to expand research to the nuclear field. In particular, experience gained in non-nuclear projects enters research on nuclear accidents and particularly the results of this work as outlined in the following.

First, CBR was applied in a general frame covering different kinds of disasters (Moehrle, 2012) particularly as part of the KRITIS project[1] supported by the Center for Disaster Management and Risk Reduction Technology (CEDIM). The objective was to support decisions on appropriate measures in case of a disaster, which was described by attributes that were inspired by the Tactical situation object (TSO) – a message structure for disaster and emergency management (CEN, 2009a, 2009b). The idea of TSO is to support the transfer of information between computer-based systems by encoding disaster/emergency relevant terms in an XML schema. TSO provides the relevant attributes to describe a disaster or emergency and defines a basic vocabulary for disaster management with unique expressions. The codes are arranged hierarchically providing a basic categorization of event features. So far, rail accidents involving hazardous and non-hazardous goods, fire disasters, chemical accidents, transport accidents, and power failure have been analyzed. The solutions were stored as temporarily ordered lists of measures. In case of an incident, the user could compose appropriate measures based on retrieved cases and particularly their solutions. This step included deleting inappropriate measures and supplementing necessary ones manually. This work constitutes the first steps in developing a generic decision support system for large-scale disasters. However, besides further necessary automatization developments, the employed attributes were too

[1] https://www.cedim.kit.edu/english/1959.php

general to describe an event in depth and the case base needed to be enhanced. Anyhow, since presenting potential solutions to handle a current disaster, the decision-making process as well as the implementation of measures were speeded up.

Research on security measures against terrorist threats to public rail transport systems combined CBR with scenarios and MCDA (L. Lin et al., 2013; L. Lin, Moehrle, Muenzberg, & Raskob, 2014) and was part of the RiKoV[2] project. The focus was on preventive measures to reduce the risk or mitigate the consequences of terrorist attacks. Due to the variety of possible scenarios, related measures, and diverse expectations of passengers, public authorities, and operators of the public railway transport systems, a prioritization approach for security measures was elaborated. For instance, levels of security may increase costs and public authorities and passengers may not tolerate the implementation of all kinds of security measures. Several historical attacks were analyzed and stored in a database. CBR had the pre-selection task of security measures where MCDA was used for prioritization among them afterwards. Again, TSO inspired the choice of attributes but was enhanced by event type dependent characteristics. For the evaluation of security measures, criteria such as physiological effectiveness, costs, and legal aspects were taken into account. In the frame of this work, all values needed for conducting MCDA were requested from the stakeholders. However, the whole approach supported a transparent and comprehensible decision-making process and particularly focused on strategic planning issues as well as developing an integrated framework. Research on evaluating the effectiveness of security measures was further deepened by integrating a process model describing the steps of an attack. The idea was to explore possible variations of a baseline scenario due to the implementation of security measures at several process steps and to evaluate the effectiveness of measures by means of efficacy, costs, and public acceptance and particularly MCDA. Both, the execution of the operation plan of the perpetrator and the effects of security measures were integrated in the process model. Here, experts' assessments on the probability of each variation would be necessary but enables to compare several strategies systematically taking into account plausible future developments.

[2] http://www.rikov.de

Research was then further conducted in the frame of CEDIMs Forensic Disaster Analysis (FDA)[3] that was concerned with near real-time analyses of disasters and their impacts such as in the frame of the central European flood in Germany (e.g. Khazai et al., 2013, 2014; Schröter et al., 2014). The objective was to quickly draw conclusions about a new and to a large extent unknown event, primarily by categorizing the event and assessing possible damages in the frame of natural disasters (Möhrle & Raskob, 2014). Especially storm events of the past, which were in the same category or which have similar frame conditions like imminent or just occurring storms, might give preliminary information (Möhrle & Mühr, 2015). For identifying useful historical events, particularly for estimating upper and lower limits for damaged buildings and direct loss, storm classes were defined taking the predicted affected area and wind speed into account. In particular, research on natural disasters was the starting point for developing the web interface, which was further enhanced when working in the nuclear field. As mentioned in the introduction, the central project in the nuclear field was PREPARE that aimed at closing gaps that have been identified in nuclear and radiological preparedness following the first evaluation of the Fukushima Daiichi nuclear power plant accident. In particular, existing operational procedures in dealing with long-lasting releases needed to be reviewed. Furthermore, monitoring and safety of goods transcending national borders, improved source term estimation, and dispersion modeling including hydrological pathways for European water bodies were subjects of research. Communication issues were addressed as well, aiming at investigating the conditions and means for relevant, reliable, and trustworthy information to be made available to the public at the appropriate time and according to its needs. In particular, the 'Analytical Platform' was developed exploring the scientific and operational means to improve information collection, information exchange, and the evaluation of such types of disasters. The case-based decision support method presented in this thesis, was partly integrated in the Analytical Platform (Raskob & Möhrle, 2014; Raskob, Möhrle, Bai, & Müller, 2016; Raskob, Müller, Möhrle, & Bai, 2016). In this context, scenarios were elaborated due to few events of the past (Raskob, Möhrle, & Bai, 2016).

[3] https://www.cedim.kit.edu/english/2863.php

In the following, the main assumptions and overall solution are presented before discussing the single components in a more detailed way in Chapters 4-6.

3.1 Assumptions and Chronology of a Nuclear Accident

The development of the decision support method is based on two **assumptions**: Firstly, it is assumed that the **whole problem can be divided into single sub-problems** that if solved, result in solving the whole problem.

> The *whole problem* in the course of a (potential) nuclear accident is the condition of not knowing which strategy is appropriate to protect public and environment from a possible radiation exposure.

Second, in order to solve these sub-problems, **experience** from former, particularly similar, problem situations **helps to determine appropriate solutions**. Experience does not relate to past accidents only but also to scenarios defined in advance of an accident which benefit from experience as well. This assumption particularly paves the way for applying CBR.

3.1.1 Dividing a Problem into Sub-Problems

The division of the whole problem occurring when an area that can be a region, city, or whole country, is threatened by a (potential) release of radioactive material from a nuclear power plant, is conducted according to temporal as well as area specific aspects. The German Commission on Radiological Protection suggests to break down an accident into phases (Figure 3.1) that reflect the varying status of release, type and urgency of measures, type and availability of resources, and relevance of exposure pathways (German Commission on Radiological Protection, 2014). The required and also implementable measures at a certain point in time are linked to these varying conditions and hence fit into a specific schedule.

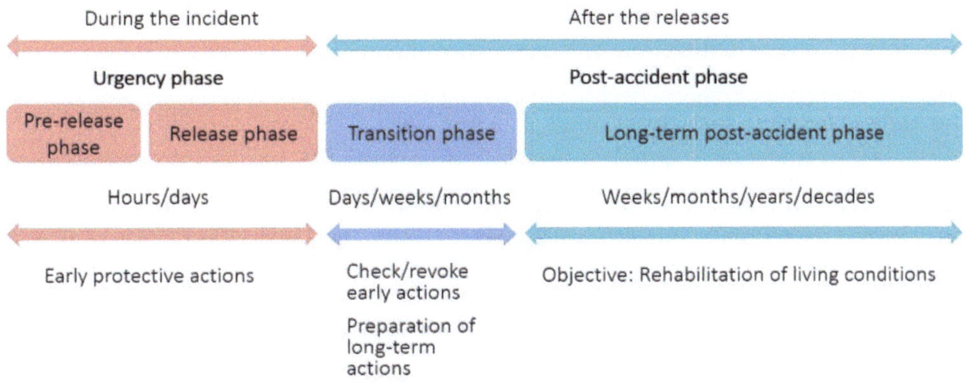

Figure 3.1: Phases of a nuclear accident (German Commission on Radiological Protection, 2014, p. 12)

Accident phases (German Commission on Radiological Protection, 2014, p. 11 ff.)

In the first instance, the urgency phase and post-accident phase are distinguished, which can be broken down into several sub-phases. The *urgency phase* consists of a *pre-release* and, if applicable, a *release phase.*

The *pre-release phase* starts if a possible major radionuclide release of radionuclides from a nuclear power plant is identified. The phase ends with the onset of such a release or the control of the incident. The pre-release phase may last for hours or days. During this phase, crisis management needs to be activated and the public has to be informed. If necessary and possible, precautionary measures, such as precautionary evacuation, should be initiated. If 'iodine thyroid blocking' is necessary, the pre-release phase should be used to distribute or collect iodine tablets. Decisions on precautionary measures are based on dose[4] criteria and depend on the forecast quality of the type, amount, and timing of radioactive material potentially to be released, the *source term,* and the dispersion and deposition mechanisms. The plant condition

[4] The *dose* refers to the quantity of ionizing radiation. In general, the *effective dose* is meant, which is the sum of weighted equivalent doses in all tissues and organs and hence *measuring the radiation exposure to human.* Hereby, the relative biological effectiveness of different radiation types as well as variation in the susceptibility of organs and tissues to radiation damage are taken into account (Nisbet & Watson, 2015b).

is important for the assessment of the source term. A small release that does not demand the implementation of measures, is not considered in this accident phase.

The *release phase* can last hours, days or a few weeks. If a precautionary evacuation was or could not (be) executed, measures considerably reducing the exposure on the propagation area are urgent, such as sheltering or the intake of iodine. More precautionary measures for civil protection, in particular evacuation, should be implemented in areas, where the radioactive cloud possibly approaches swiftly. Whether evacuation is possible during the passaging of the radioactive cloud has to be reviewed for each individual case. The release phase ends when dispersion and deposition of radioactive material have finished and the plant is under control again. This phase is characterized by the transition of the initial projection of the radiological situation to measuring the actual level of contamination by stationary or mobile monitoring facilities. Particular attention must be paid to the exposure pathways (which are explained later in this chapter) that are associated with the passing radioactive cloud and radiation protection of the action forces, which are primarily not occupationally exposed to radiation.

The *post-accident phase* consists of the *transition phase* and the *long-term post-accident phase.*

In the *transition phase* the radiation of the cloud including the direct inhalation of radioactive material and the deposition has ended or is not relevant any more. This phase can last days to several weeks or months. The beginning of the transition phase is characterized by a detailed analysis of the radiological situation. Particularly, the contamination values of food, drinking water, surfaces, soils, plants, and water bodies are determined with the help of a sufficient number of reliable measurements. At the end of the transition phase, the required data, resources, and time should be available to decide upon incident-based justification and optimization of measures for civil protection and of radiation exposure to emergency and support personnel and special groups among the population. At this late stage, changes in measures already implemented or additional measures, such as relocation, can just avert a part of the dose (averted dose) accrued without implementing the measures. Finally, the stepwise revocation of measures needs to be decided upon.

The *long-term post-accident phase* can last up to several years or decades after the accident and is characterized by a prolonged contamination of areas and the risk of a chronic low but constant human exposure. Organizing and shaping individual, social, and economic life in the affected areas as well as the implementation of radiation protection need to be discussed with the affected population and businesses. Decisions on strategies need to be realized in a societal consensus including aspects which are not radiologically significant. This particularly includes investigating people in more highly contaminated areas, conveying associated health risks, and a follow-up medical care to monitor the progress of their health. In general, multiple stakeholders such as politicians, experts, NGOs, or representatives of industry and consumers, are possibly involved in the decision process taking into account the many facets of a nuclear accident and aiming at deciding in a societal consensus.

The different accident phases may occur at various times for different places. This means that the categorization is area-specific and, for example, a country that is split up into different areas, may undergo different accident phases at the same time (International Atomic Energy Agency (IAEA), 2018).

As mentioned before, various *pathways* lead to human exposure where their importance vary in the course of a nuclear accident (German Commission on Radiological Protection, 2014, p. 13 f.). *External radiation* may be caused by the radiation from the passing radioactive cloud, due to contamination of the ground, skin, clothing, objects and solid or liquid waste as well as direct radiation from the plant. *Internal radiation* may be caused by inhaling airborne radioactive substances from the radioactive cloud, ingestion of contaminated foodstuffs, inhalation of resuspended radionuclides previously deposited on the ground, objects, and clothing, unintentional ingestion of contaminated earth as well as oral ingestion of contamination from the skin or clothing as well as contaminated drinking water. Contamination of foodstuffs result from direct contamination of leafy vegetables, root uptake by plants on contaminated ground, fodder crops containing radioactivity from contamination and root uptake, contaminated livestock and wild animals, and subsequent contamination of milk and meat. If no measures are taken, ingestion of contaminated food may be the most important pathway when observed over a prolonged period whereas inhalation of airborne radioactive material and radiation from contaminated ground pose the main pathways otherwise. In the case of wet deposition, radiation due to ground contamination have increased importance.

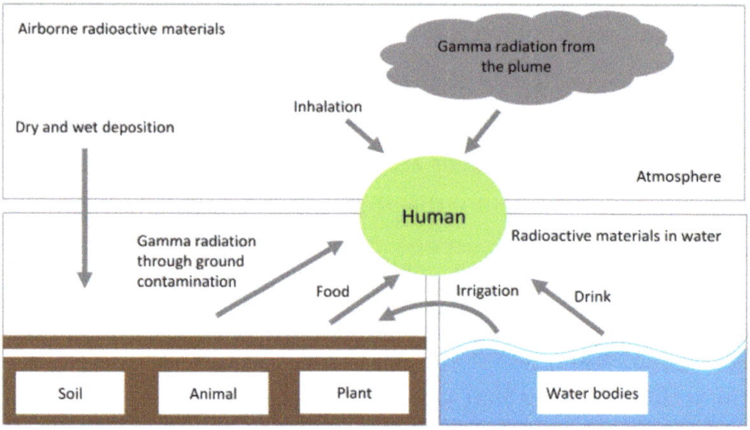

Figure 3.2: Exposure pathways that can lead to external and internal human radiation exposure (German Commission on Radiological Protection, 2014, p. 14)

Possible measures in the Urgency Phase (German Commission on Radiological Protection, 2014, p. 21 f.)

As introduced in the section before, a nuclear accident can be divided into phases during which specific measures may be implemented. The most important precautionary measures are introduced shortly in the following (German Commission on Radiological Protection, 2014):

Sheltering

This measure means that the public is told to stay indoors in protective rooms for a recommended period of time (that is typically limited to 1-2 days) to reduce inhalation of radionuclides and external radiation through shielding. The level of shielding heavily depends on the type of building, the construction materials, and surrounding buildings. During sheltering, windows and doors should be closed as well as ventilation systems shut off.

Evacuation

Evacuation is the swiftly organized relocation of the public to a safe location where accommodation, food, and drink is provided, with an undefined time of return. In case contamination remains high, evacuation might turn into a temporary or long-term relocation (see below). A well-organized evacuation provides the most effective protection against external and internal radiation exposure.

Iodine thyroid blocking

This measure helps to protect the thyroid gland against radioactive iodine entering the body and particularly concerns population groups that inhale radioactive iodine.

Interfering with the food supply

In the urgency phase, actions concerning food refer to issuing the public with a precautionary recommendation to avoid recently harvested foodstuffs and animal feed as well as fresh milk to avoid ingestion of contaminated foodstuffs.

Further actions refer to access restrictions and personal decontamination affecting external exposure and inhalation, particularly via skin, hair and clothing as well as radiation measurements for assessing the radiological situation and for medical screening purposes to affect external and internal exposure.

Possible measures in the Post-Accident Phase (German Commission on Radiological Protection, 2014, p. 21 ff.)

Relocation

This measure means to transfer residents of an area to a different area during the post-accident phase to prevent external irradiation from the ground and inhalation of resuspended material. The implementation and duration may be temporary or long-term. In case of temporary relocation, people are permitted to return to their homes at a later stage. Meanwhile, decontamination measures reduce the time period of relocation and affect the external exposure due to deposited radionuclides and incorporation. In contrast to long-term relocation, the social and economic impact is smaller. If contamination involves long-lived radionuclides, long-term relocation that means over an undefined period of time, might be necessary, implying organizational as well as social challenges.

Interfering with the food supply

In the later phases when radionuclide deposition has taken place, these actions refer to intervening in the supply of foodstuffs and animal feed as well as measures to reduce the presence of radionuclides in foodstuffs and animal feed and hence particularly affecting the exposure pathway 'ingestion'.

Decontamination

Decontamination is "the complete or partial removal of contamination by a deliberate physical, chemical or biological process [...]"(International Atomic Energy Agency (IAEA), 2007, p. 48) and is an umbrella term for various clean-up measures to reduce external doses and doses from resuspended material, possibly resulting in large volumes of waste (Nisbet et al., 2010).

Summary of time-dependent objectives

As already presented in the subsections before, each accident phase and strategy respectively, focus on specifics of the overarching objective to protect public and environment. Protecting the public is not always compatible with protecting the environment as some side effects of decontamination measures such as soil erosion risk or partial loss of soil fertility indicate (Nisbet et al., 2010). Figure 3.3 illustrates an objective hierarchy (German Commission on Radiological Protection, 2014; Nisbet & Watson, 2015b) where in the urgency phase the main focus lies on reducing the level of radiation exposure to human and in the post-accident phase, the objective is to return to normal living. Reducing the level of radiation exposure refers to two effects: (i) Deterministic effects, which are health effects for which a threshold level of dose exists above which the severity of the effect grows with the dose (International Atomic Energy Agency (IAEA), 2007); (ii) Stochastic effects, which are radiation-induced health effects (somatic or hereditary) where the probability of occurrence is greater for a higher dose but where the severity in case of occurrence is independent of dose (International Atomic Energy Agency (IAEA), 2007). For all objectives, commensurability of strategies needs to be taken into account that means balancing health risks against gravity of intervening in people's lives for the urgency phase and effectiveness against waste and societal aspects in the post-accident phase.

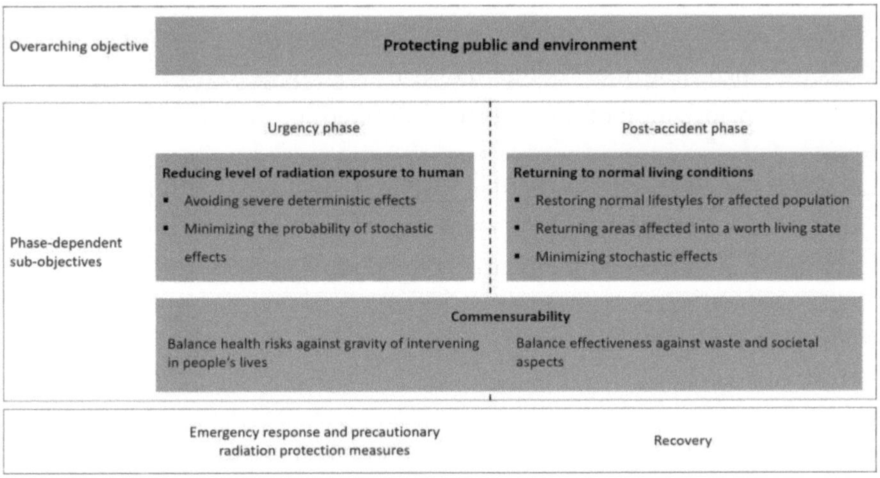

Figure 3.3: Objectives of strategies in the course of nuclear accidents

Definition of a sub-problem

Besides analyzing the problem concerning timely issues, the characteristics of the areas that are threatened by a nuclear accident are important for decision-making as well. Hence, an area-specific consideration is reasonable whereas areas can be regions or a whole country undergoing different accident phases. For example, a country can be divided into different affected areas that undergo different accident phases leading to different problems (due to different sub-objectives and area characteristics) and the need to decide upon different measures. This work particularly started with analyzing historical accidents such as the Chernobyl nuclear power plant accident resulting in a decomposition according to the location (cities, countries, etc.) and accident phase. Examples are Pripyat (Ukraine) which have been evacuated, several districts in the Ukraine as well as United Kingdom as whole, where dietary advices during the release phase where given and measures such as selective grazing regime or manipulation of slaughter times were ordered during the long-term post-accident phase. Consequently, a *sub-problem* in the course of a nuclear accident is the condition of not knowing which strategy is appropriate for a specific area and during a specific accident phase to protect public and environment from a possible radiation exposure.

As stated in the introductory chapter, a decision is a choice of a measure or of several measures including their combination to a strategy out of a set of possible measures, in consideration of the objectives defined for nuclear accidents.

Problem-solving in the course of a nuclear accident hence describes the transition from a condition of being faced with a problem to a condition where the objectives are achieved by means of the decision taken.

Figure 3.4 exemplarily illustrates the specification of an affected area undergoing different accident phases. If an area undergoes the pre-release or release phase, it is framed red. If an area undergoes the transition phase it is framed blue whereas for the long-term post-accident phase, the area is framed turquois. Assume a release of radioactive material is expected and hence, due to uncertain weather conditions, the whole area around the nuclear plant is potentially endangered. Here, the HERCA-WENRA approach (HERCA & WENRA, 2014) would be referred to and measures would be planned in a zone of 360 degrees around the installation and up to a specified distance. The accident proceeds, release has started and more information on the radiological situation becomes available. The weather forecast limits sectors concerned and hence the implementation areas for protective measures. First measurements can be evaluated to prepare for long-term actions. Step by step, the urgency phase for the defined areas ends and the post-accident phase starts.

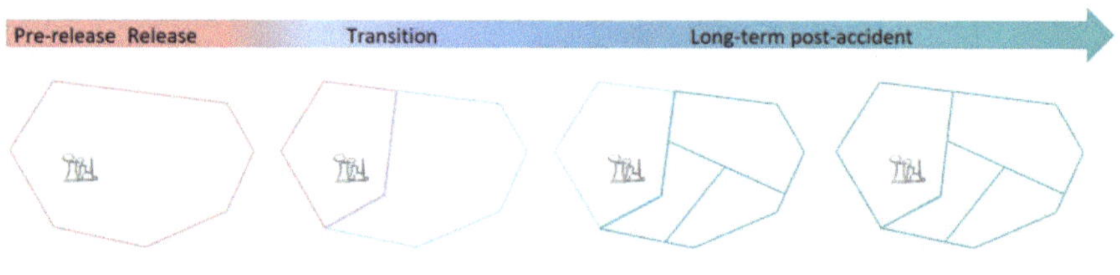

Figure 3.4: Several affected areas undergoing different accident phases

3.1.2 Constructing a Strategy

The objectives for nuclear emergency management introduced in the chapter before, can be specified by means of two dose levels: the *reference level for the residual dose*, which is the effective dose people receive during the first year via inhalation, external irradiation and ingestion, and the *intervention levels for individual measures* that are projected doses that could be reached or exceeded among the affected population if a certain measure is not implemented (German Commission on Radiological Protection, 2014). These levels particularly take into account the commensurability of measures within a social and economic frame.

In emergency exposure situations, the International Commission on Radiological Protection (ICRP)[5] recommends to set reference levels within a band of 20-100 mSv effective dose (acute or per year). A dose above 100 mSv poses no tolerable health risk and almost always justify protective measures (ICRP, 2007, 2009). In Germany, for example, a reference level for the residual dose of 100 mSv in the first year is used to plan and initiate measures. Especially for the protective measures, intervention levels that are compatible with the reference level for the residual dose, help in decision-making. They serve as radiological trigger levels for respective measures (German Commission on Radiological Protection, 2014) and are country-specific. In particular, the time span over which projected dose values are determined, may vary for different countries. For example, intervention levels in Germany for sheltering, iodine thyroid blocking, and evacuation refer to an early period of 7 days after release assuming that people are permanently staying outdoors. Table 3.1 sums up the intervention levels for the protective measures. If the specific intervention level is exceeded, the measure should be initiated. Especially decision support systems such as JRodos and dispersion, deposition, and dose models, respectively, help to determine areas for precautionary measures. Hereby, the source term, real-time and prognostic weather data, and environmental data are necessary to determine environmental contamination and projected dose values.

5 http://www.icrp.org/

Table 3.1: Intervention levels for selected measures(German Commission on Radiological Protection, 2014, p. 33)

Measure	Intervention level	Explanation
Sheltering	10 mSv	Effective dose due to external exposure + committed effective dose due to inhalation within a period of 7 days (permanently staying outdoors)
Iodine thyroid blocking	50 mSv for children and young people under the age of 18 and pregnant women 250 mSv for people aged 18 to 45	Thyroid dose (committed equivalent dose)[6] due to inhalation of radioactive iodine within a period of 7 days (permanently staying outdoors)
Evacuation	100 mSv	Effective dose due to external exposure + committed effective dose due to inhalation within a period of 7 days (permanently staying outdoors)

Evacuation may lead to temporary or long-term relocation where the reference level of the residual effective dose provides a decisive criterion.

In addition to dose criteria, further factors that are time- and location-dependent, influence decisions on an appropriate strategy (German Commission on Radiological Protection, 2014). These are the effectiveness and feasibility of measures, negative effects of measures, subjective influencing factors such as public acceptance, uncertainty parameters referring to inaccurate meteorological or radiological estimations as well as planning requirements where the challenge is to map areas determined by the dose model to the emergency response planning areas. In particular, expert advisors may provide information on these influencing factors and judge their relevance in the actual context (German Commission on

[6] The equivalent dose is the absorbed dose delivered by a specific radiation type averaged over a tissue or organ weighted with a specific radiation weight factor that considers the relative biological effectiveness of that radiation type (https://www.bfs.de, https://www.iaea.org). The committed dose particularly refers to the intake of radioactive material.

Radiological Protection, 2014) which supports the idea of this thesis to prepare and store information in a structured manner gained from experience and experts, respectively, in advance of an accident.

If little information is available, particularly in the pre-release phase, the HERCA-WENRA approach that was developed after the Fukushima Daiichi accident, may be used as first suggestion and which is integrated into this work. For the later phases, key steps in selecting and combining measures, as described in the European handbooks, are as follows (Nisbet et al., 2010, 2009):

(1) Identify the **targets** that are likely to be/have been contaminated

(2) Select the measures that are **applicable** to the specific targets

(3) Check the applicability of measures with regard to **radionuclides** being considered

(4) Check the **key constraints** for the measures with regard to the implementation

(5) Check the **effectiveness** of the measures to decide which of them to keep

(6) Check the type and quantities of **waste** produced by the measures as well as potential incremental dose[7] that may be received by individuals in connection with the implementation of the measures

(7) Check the relevant **constraints** of the remaining measures, particularly with regard to the site

(8) Select and **combine** measures left to a strategy

The handbooks provide recommendations or hints whether measures require further analysis. Particularly, site-specific customization with the help of relevant stakeholders is necessary. In this respect, the purpose of this work is to support the selection and construction process by reusing already defined scenarios that resemble the current problem situation to be solved and reuse already determined

[7] Additional dose received by a person due to the implementation of a measure (Nisbet et al., 2010).

measures. These measures can be used as a starting point for further discussions, save time, and indicate potential constraints for implementation. In particular, parts of the key steps referring to targets and radionuclides are integrated in the decision support method of this work in terms of attributes characterizing the problem (see Chapter 4). Furthermore, the constraints of implementing measures are implicitly taken into account when setting up the scenario. In particular, site-specific constraints are considered for specific location type categories. However, the categories are rough and when reusing a scenario and its measures, respectively, further discussions on the applicability of certain measures are possibly necessary. Furthermore, values on effectiveness and resources are adapted automatically (see Chapter 6).

3.2 Overview of the Case-Based Decision Support Method

The core of the decision support method is CBR. Here,

> the description of a (sub)-problem, corresponding strategies for problem-solving, their effectiveness, and further decision supporting information build a *case* in the case base. The description of a case is oriented towards a *case model*.

A case can be a historical accident as well as a scenario. Scenarios enhance the case base and result from simulations. Both are subject to a case model consisting of a problem and solution model (see Chapter 4.4). The solution model includes a strategy model that is based on HLPNs. The main idea is to allow the integration of triggering events of measures as well as their targets. The latter captures the effects of measures as well. The approach is generic and not solely developed for the nuclear field. Figure 3.5 depicts the development of the case model, compiled sources, the integration of experts that actually work in the field of application, and building the case base.

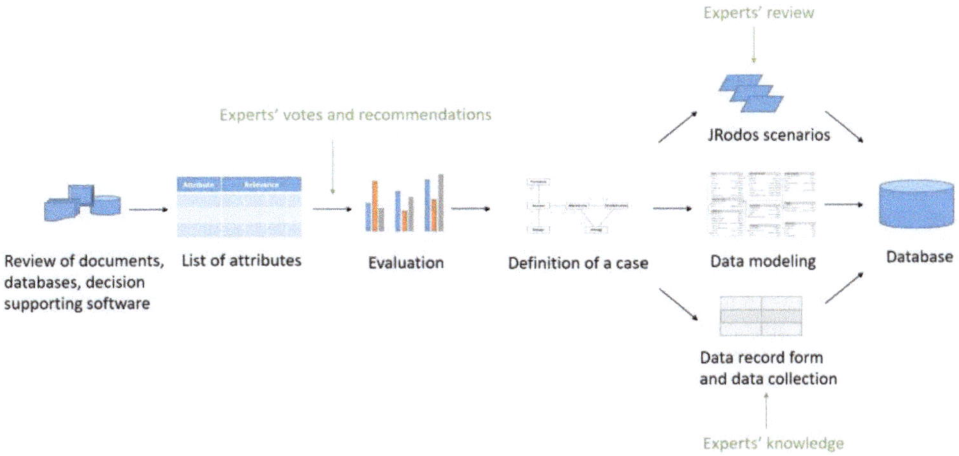

Figure 3.5: Process of case modeling and building the case base

The retrieve step is realized in two steps: First, candidates for the subsequent similarity calculation are selected whereas the filter attributes are the accident phase and further user-specified attributes. After delimiting the set of problem descriptions, similarities between the actual problem description and the problem descriptions of the remaining cases are calculated whereas the choice of attributes as well as weights are user-specified. The similarity function is defined according to the local-global principle. Finally, a fixed number of cases or cases whose similarities of their problem descriptions to the description of the actual problem exceed a certain threshold, are retrieved. The reuse step consists of merging and adaptation to transform solutions of most similar cases into a solution that fits into new circumstances. Merging aims at covering a wide range of actual targets whereas adaptation refers to area sizes, number of affected people, costs, and waste. Figure 3.6 briefly displays the realized retrieve and reuse steps of the CBR application, which is explained more in detail in Chapters 5 and 6.

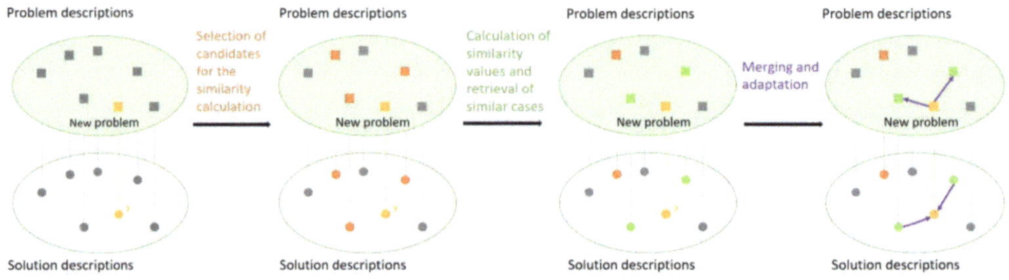

Figure 3.6: Two-level retrieval and reuse step of the CBR application. The illustration is inspired by Leake, 1996a, Figure 1

The reuse step comprises numerical adaptations, merging of several strategies, and a multi-criteria assessment. Merging is realized at equally labeled transitions aiming at covering a larger part of the current problem description than the single strategies retrieved do. If several strategies are available, a subsequent multi-criteria assessment helps to identify an appropriate strategy for the current problem situation. MCDA provides means to complement the case-based approach taking into account users' preferences as well as the exceptionality of nuclear accidents. The choice of suitable criteria is crucial. The approach pursued by this thesis (see Chapter 6.2) integrates different perspectives on the assessment of strategies: (i) The main idea is to reuse solutions of already experienced or at least considered problems and hence information on how the strategy works is integrated. (ii) Considerations with regard to future developments are integrated by evaluating the robustness of solutions. (iii) System-specific parameters, which depend on the underlying decision supporting method, are included indicating to which degree the user can trust the solutions identified. (iv) Current constraints such as concerning resources are regarded by running simulations of possibly suitable strategies.

Figure 3.7 sums up the components of the developed decision support method and illustrates the integration into the original CBR cycle (Aamodt & Plaza, 1994), which is marked in green. Particularly, several cases can be retrieved for further reuse. Note that cases comprise historical as well as fictitious accidents (scenarios) being simulated by JRodos. For decision support, the scenarios are of primary concern. The historical accidents provide additional information, especially experience gained with implementing measures.

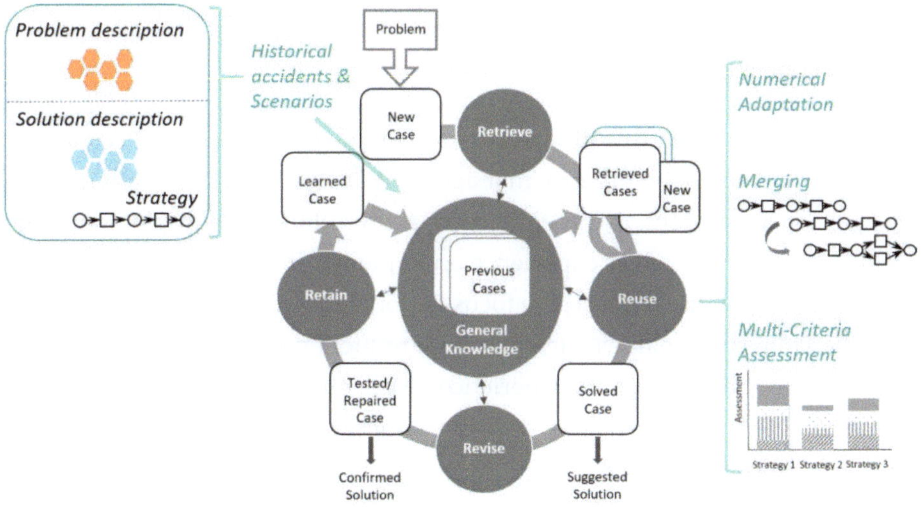

Figure 3.7: Overview of the case-based decision support method and integrations into the CBR cycle. The original CBR cycle is based on Aamodt & Plaza, 1994, Figure 1

3.3 Discussion of the Novel Approach

Decision-making in the course of a nuclear accident is complex due to the complicated but also varying frame conditions and requirements in each accident phase. This is also reflected in the changing objectives and corresponding possible measures. Systems currently in use support the decision-making process by ad hoc projections of the radiological situation and analyses in respect of measure combinations, for example with regard to their effectiveness – either computer-based or with the help of handbooks. In other words, they help in constructing a strategy by preparing or providing some decisive information. However, some issues are not sufficiently addressed: (i) Uncertainty, which is a crucial issue ranging from initial information on the accident to simulation results; (ii) Strategy building, which is very complex and would benefit from additional computerized support. Furthermore, non-radiological aspects need to be focused more. Also, there is lack of practical experience with regard to appropriate strategies and their implementation, especially with regard to long-term actions; (iii) Preparedness, which includes the preparation of scenarios in advance to save time, to avoid mistakes due to effects that have not been adequately thought through as well as to counter the complexity of decision-making due to various factors that need be considered. The structured integration of existing knowledge and experience from the past in the decision process would contribute to avoid pitfalls also.

The method presented in this thesis provides solutions for these issues and particularly supports nuclear emergency management during all accident phases: In the early stages of an accident, precautionary measures, the size of implementation areas, a shelter factor[8] as well as experience on implementing these measures are provided. In the post-accident phase, the focus lies on decontamination and hence strategies and effectiveness values such as a dose reduction factor[9] or waste produced, are presented to the user. Again, experience on the implementation of strategies are provided. In contrast to existing decision support, the **novelty** of the develop method is as follows:

- **Direct identification of strategies** instead of providing information to the user to build a strategy.
- **Strategies based on scenarios prepared in advance** of an accident are **reused** instead of developing strategies new in the course of an accident.
- Aggregation and **central storage of different knowledge sources** such as handbooks, experts' knowledge, and experience gained in former accidents as well as simulation results.
- Knowledge sources **are made available computerized and structured** to recognize potential pitfalls.
- **Modeling of strategies** with PNs allows to **capture orders of implementation and effects of measures.** Particularly with regard to the latter, the tokens in the nets are typed according to the target and the effect of a measure and degree of endangerment, respectively. This idea differs from

[8] The shelter factor is the ratio between the dose received with sheltering and the dose received without sheltering.

[9] The factor of dose reduction is the ratio between the dose received after implementing a specific strategy and the dose received without implementing this strategy.

existing approaches that mainly concentrate on process execution support or analysis according to performance parameters.

- **Multi-criteria assessment** of strategies by **adopting various perspectives** such as considerations on possible future developments, effectiveness, resources as well as confidence in the solutions retrieved. This approach particularly integrates different perspectives instead of pursuing a single one.

In summary, **computerized case-based decision support** is **new** in **nuclear emergency management.** Hence, this work pursues a completely new direction where each component of the solution is presented in the following chapters more in detail. The whole method is elaborated by means of nuclear accidents where some components such as the multi-criteria assessment and the strategy modeling are of generic nature. Furthermore, the case-based approach can be applied to other event types as well (Chapter 8). The reasons for focusing on nuclear accidents are the scientific relevance but were also the good frame conditions for modeling and data acquisition in close collaboration with experts. They provided knowledge on past accidents but also approved the developed scenarios and results of assessments. In contrast to other projects that focused on natural disasters, research on disaster management according to strategy building could be conducted. Furthermore, simulation results of a decision support system that is operationally used worldwide, helped to further extend the case base, which is the core of the whole approach.

4 The Case Base

The following chapter deals with the structure and content of the collection of cases and particularly addresses the questions what to store in a case, how to structure the case contents, and how the case base should be organized and indexed for retrieval and reuse. Especially with regard to the reuse step, the integration of general domain knowledge needs to be clarified (Aamodt & Plaza, 1994). Some parts of the case model have already been published (Moehrle & Raskob, 2015; Raskob & Möhrle, 2014).

In this work, the commonly used attribute-value-based case representation is central. Other representations such as pure texts or images are possible but were not pursued since decisive criteria could be directly discussed with experts. Furthermore, the attribute-value-based representation is flexible and hence suitable for the application domain and facilitates the later retrieve step. The choice of attributes results from gathering potentially relevant attributes from related documents, software, and databases and evaluating the obtained attribute catalogue by experts. This includes the evaluation of attribute domains as well. The attribute catalogue aims at covering all accident characteristics that are relevant for decision-making on strategies. The importance of the attributes are assessed according to each accident phase revealing changes during an accident.

This chapter outlines the sources that have been analyzed and the resulting attribute catalogue for evaluation. The catalogue covers radiological and non-radiological aspects which are, as stated in Chapter 3.1.2, important for decision-making as well.

Chapter 4.2 presents the results of the expert survey. Chapter 4.3 addresses the issue of uncertainty and makes suggestions with respect to the case base. Afterwards, the case model is introduced (Chapter 4.4) as well as the modeling of strategies using High-level Petri Nets (Chapter 4.4.1). The last part of Chapter 4 is dedicated to data collection.

4.1 The Attribute Catalogue

Various sources contribute to the list of attributes and in case of symbolic attributes, a set of allowed values. In the following, the notion of 'event' is used in a general sense and is not limited to nuclear accidents. As introduced in Chapter 1 an *event* is an occurrence of an incident that triggers the necessity of building and implementing a strategy. The term comprises historical and fictitious nuclear accidents as well as further disaster types.

In the following, a *hazard* is "a potentially damaging physical event, phenomenon and/or human activity, which may cause the loss of life or injury, property damage, social and economic disruption or environmental degradation [...] and "describes the probability of occurrence of a potentially destructive natural phenomenon in a defined area and within a defined time period." (Center for Disaster Management and Risk Reduction Technology, 2005, p. 13). The *vulnerability* describes the susceptibility of a system towards adverse impacts of hazards and can be expressed by the degree of loss (Center for Disaster Management and Risk Reduction Technology, 2005, p. 28). The term *risk* "[...] encompasses the probability and the amount of harmful consequences or expected losses [...]" being result of hazards and vulnerabilities (Center for Disaster Management and Risk Reduction Technology, 2005, p. 24). These notions are introduced for clarifying the next sections but are not further used in this thesis. Hence, an extensive discussion is omitted.

The first two sources are related to risk management and are primarily used for generally describing the affected area and covering different kinds of impact. Also, the approach for impact classification is used for the attribute catalogue. The third source provides means to describe an event in a general manner and particularly to be used in the event of a disaster. Especially, many symbolic attributes and their domains are made available. The last two sources are dedicated to the nuclear field and encompass results of current research.

Method of Risk Analysis for Civil Protection

The Federal Office of Civil Protection and Disaster Assistance (BBK)[1] in Germany, established in May 2004, acts as a federal service center for organizations and institutions working in civil protection and authorities at all levels of the administration. The BBK published a guideline 'Method of Risk Analysis for Civil Protection' (Federal Office of Civil Protection and Disaster Assistance, 2011) applicable to all administrative levels in Germany, with the aim to determine the extent of expected damage for different hazardous events, to compare a variety of risks related to different hazards, and consequently to implement measures to protect the population. In respect of expected damage assessment, attributes to describe the reference area and impact parameters are provided. The guideline lists information needed with regard to man, environment, economy, and supply as well as immaterial facts. Furthermore, parameters and central questions for describing a scenario are provided. The guideline resulted from research on methods of risk analysis as well as exchange with international and federal authorities and academia and respects international standards. Due to the generic approach, the attribute catalogue includes the descriptions of the reference area, a scenario, and impact parameters (Table A.1, Table A.2, and Table A.3) and the templates for impact classification (Appendix C).

Disaster Inventory System (DesInventar)[2]

DesInventar (Network of Social Studies in the Prevention of Disasters in Latin America, 2009) is a methodology and software tool to build databases containing loss, damages, or effects of disasters and emergencies. DesInventar originated from the Network of Social Studies in the Prevention of Disasters in Latin America (LA RED). The purpose is to provide a capacity for risk management to analyze hazards, vulnerabilities, and risks by supporting the acquisition, analysis, and visualization of disaster related information. In the methodological guide various events and causes are defined. Here, events are phenomenon of natural and anthropological

[1] https://www.bbk.bund.de/EN/Home/home_node.html

[2] https://www.desinventar.org/

origin having harmful effects on human lives, health, and economic or social infrastructure. Furthermore, adverse effects are provided, grouped into people, homes, infrastructure, and economic loss (Table A.4)

Tactical Situation Object (TSO)

TSO (CEN[3] Workshop Agreement Part 1 2009; CEN Workshop Agreement Part 2 2009) is a message structure for disaster and emergency management. The idea of TSO is to support the transfer of information between computer-based systems by encoding disaster/emergency relevant terms in an XML schema contributing to a shared situation awareness of various parties. TSO provides the relevant attributes to describe a disaster or emergency and defines a basic vocabulary for disaster management with unique expressions. The codes are arranged hierarchically providing a basic categorization of event features. TSO is used as an approach for a generic event description (Moehrle, 2012). Endangered objects, location type and environmental description, scale, type of area, and weather conditions are further used for the nuclear case (Table A.5).

Real-time On-line Decision Support System for Off-site Emergency Management in Europe (RODOS)

The decision support system RODOS (Ehrhardt & Weis, 2000) resulted from the RODOS project launched in 1989 and increased in size through the European Commission's 3rd, 4th and 5th Framework Programs. Up to 40 institutes from 20 countries were actively involved in the project. RODOS provides support for all stages of a nuclear accident and can be used at local, regional, or national level. The system can predict the dispersion and disposition of material released, models the transfer of radioactive material to feed- and foodstuff and to man, and supports decisions on countermeasures. RODOS covers nuclear power plant accidents, explosions of radiological dispersal service ('dirty bombs'), and radiological accidents with fire. The basis for calculations are the source term, real-time and prognostic weather data, and environmental data. The current version of RODOS is Java based and renamed into JRodos (Ievdin et al., 2010). The input parameters of JRodos (Table A.6)

[3] European Committee for Standardization

are added to the list of potential attributes, mainly to take the release phase into account.

Handbooks for assisting in the management of contaminated inhabited areas, food production systems, and drinking water in Europe following a radiological emergency

The handbooks for assisting emergency management in Europe (J. Brown et al., 2009; Nisbet et al., 2010, 2009) resulted from the 5-year project EURANOS: European approach to nuclear radiological emergency management and rehabilitation strategies[4] which started in 2004. The project was funded by the European Commission and 23 European Member States where 17 national emergency organizations and 33 research institutes participated. The generic handbooks serve as a guideline for planning, response, and training purposes. They include scientific, technical, and societal aspects which are important to the management of contaminated inhabited areas, food productions systems, and drinking water. The handbooks help in understanding the radiological aspects that are important for constructing a strategy, as already introduced in Chapter 3.1.2.

The first step in constructing a strategy is to identify the objects of concern (see Chapter 3.1.2), which are referred to as 'targets' in the attribute catalogue. Thereafter, appropriate measures can be determined depending on the radionuclides released. The period of exposure, the distance between people and contamination, and the presence of any shielding material are important for decision-making as well (Nisbet et al., 2010) and hence is integrated in the attribute catalogue. Furthermore, radionuclides differ in half-lives and type of radiation emitted (alpha, beta, or gamma radiation) penetrating human body in different ways. Consequently, these characteristics of radionuclides are integrated in the catalogue also. Furthermore, weather and particular the amount of precipitation at the time of deposition have a great influence on the radiation exposure and time people spend indoors and outdoors contributes to the doses in a different way (Nisbet et al., 2009) and hence need to be reflected in the catalogue of decisive criteria.

[4] https://euranos.iket.kit.edu/

Furthermore, the characteristics of the measures listed in the handbooks are integrated in the attribute catalogue. For example, the effectiveness and type and amount of waste restrict the set of possible measures.

Appendix B shows the attribute catalogue presented to the experts for evaluation. These attributes are grouped according to event, nuclear power plant, involved radionuclides, location, consequences, and measures. For symbolic attributes, a set of allowed values, often arranged in a taxonomy, are provided. Table B.7 exemplarily illustrates the TSO codes for the attribute 'location type'.

4.2 Evaluation of the Attribute Catalogue

The attribute catalogue was evaluated independently by nine experts according to its relevance for decision-making. The experts participated in the PREPARE project and work in research institutions as well as nuclear safety authorities. In particular, the importance of each attribute for an accident phase was assessed. The objective was to identify the smallest set of attributes that covers all important aspects of decision-making. The advantages of a small set are as follows:

- Time pressure may not allow to specify unnecessary accident characteristics that are possibly already covered by other attributes.
- The retrieval results may not be clearly distinguishable if too many attributes are involved in the similarity calculation. The more attributes are involved, the more possibilities exist to cancel out major differences between attribute values. The similar cases might not be differentiated properly from each other.
- In the later data acquisition step, values need to be provided for the attributes. If too many attribute values are missing, the retrieval step might be impaired also.

For evaluation, a scale from zero to four was offered to the experts to give their votes (Table 4.1). The intention was to strike a balance between rough relevant/not relevant assessments and fine granular scales that would overreach the objective to identify relevant attributes for each accident phase. Hence, 'medium relevance' serving as judgement between two extremes as well as intermediate values between two adjacent judgements were given. However, a less granular scale would have been preferred by the experts (see 4.2.1).

Table 4.1: Scales to assess the relevance of an attribute for an accident phase

Scale	Explanation
0	No relevance
1	Little relevance
2	Medium relevance
3	Great relevance
4	Strictly necessary

In total, 151 attributes were offered in the survey. Table 4.2 illustrates the number of possible values for the symbolic attributes 'targets', 'location types', 'environmental hazards', 'area types', and 'weather categories'. These domains were adopted from TSO. More symbolic attributes are included in the catalogue, such as 'time of release' where only 'day', 'night' or 'day and night' are available, for example.

Table 4.2: Number of possible values for symbolic attributes with large domains.

Attribute	Domain cardinality
Targets	234
Location types	53
Environmental hazards	17
Area types	79
Weather categories	48

The experts were asked to provide value ranges for specific impact categories such as the number of fatalities and injured in case of a disastrous event (see Appendix C).

4.2.1 Experts' Feedback

As part of the project, nine experts were addressed to rank the attributes and complete the impact classification form where all of them provided feedback and shared their experience when fulfilling this task:

- The attribute catalogue has been regarded as well-chosen and comprehensive but mainly as too large.
- The scores might have been reduced to three or even two scores: no relevance/some relevance/great relevance or relevant/not relevant.
- The domains for some symbolic attributes have been regarded as too detailed. The domain for the targets have been shortened and re-organized as a hierarchy (see Appendix E).
- In general, changes in some attribute names have been suggested in alignment with the radiological terminology, particularly those gained from TSO. Particularly, the INES scale has been added to the attribute catalogue.
- The meaning of the accident phases was not clear for everyone due to differing country-specific terms.
- It was not clear who in the end should provide values for the attributes defined.
- The question arose how to integrate different operational guidelines and approaches in different European countries as well as the quantification of loss since monetary values may have different meanings in different European countries.
- The impact classification form has generally been regarded as very difficult to fill. Only two experts provided numbers for some categories. This is owed to country-specific regulations but also to the range of interpretation possibilities and hence subjectivity. One expert commented that an incident that causes no immediate fatalities or injuries might be still categorized as disastrous if it has serious impact on the area, environment, or economy or result

in other issues such as stigmatization or economic recession. Furthermore, the expert questioned the classification of an event concerning environment and particularly on the basis of impairment of protected area, water bodies, ground water, and agricultural land since i) the implications of impairment would probably depend more on available alternative resources than on the actual contaminated area and ii) isolated treatment might not be useful since even small contaminated land could lead to stigmatization and large economical loss for the entire region. To summarize, the complexity of the topic does not easily allow a categorization in such simple terms when it comes to economy, supply, and immaterial impacts. In the following, the two examples for impact classification are presented based on Belgian and Ukrainian regulations.

Impact classifications

The approach of the experts was to translate their country-specific emergency classifications into the classification form provided.

Belgium

For the Belgian emergency levels, there is usually no sharp division between fatalities or injuries. The main levels of emergency are divided into A, B, and C levels where C is the highest (Table 4.3).

Table 4.3: Belgian emergency levels

Number of casualties (death & injuries)	Emergency level declaration
5 heavily injured 10 moderately injured 20 of an unknown situation	Trigger level A emergency plan
21-40 wounded	Trigger level B emergency plan
40+	Trigger level C emergency plan

These levels were translated into the classification form. Here, a disastrous event starts with 40+ casualties where the lowest level of emergency is declared when 5 people are heavily injured which is reflected by classifying an event as 'moderate' (Table 4.4).

Table 4.4: Belgian impact classification with regard to man based on the country-specific emergency levels

MAN

Classification	Casualties (Fatalities & Injured)		
Disastrous		>	40
Significant	10	-	20
Moderate	5	-	9
Minor	2	-	4
Insignificant		≤	2

In respect of impact classifications with regard to environment and supply, the specification approach is questioned again since impairments and disruptions cannot be regarded isolated. With regard to water bodies not only the area contaminated but also the speed of stream and dilution of contamination respectively is important. Furthermore, with regard to drinking water, the number of people affected, alternative sources as well as the industry dependence on water plays an important role. Also, with regard to energy and gas supply, the season influences how damaging a disruption is. In general, disruptions may be measured not only with regard to time or affected area but in the dimension of how many persons may be affected.

Ukraine

In Ukrainian legislation there are no classes of emergencies as 'disastrous', 'significant', 'moderate', 'minor', 'insignificant'. Ukrainian classification of emergencies is based on the administrative status of territories involved, number of casualties and scope of economic losses, and emergencies are divided into emergencies of 'national level', 'regional level' and 'local level'. Based on this logic, an event is classified as disastrous if more than 10 fatalities and more than 300 injured are involved. In case of less than one fatality and less than 20 injured, the event would be classified as insignificant (Table 4.5).

Table 4.5: Ukrainian impact classification with regard to man

MAN

Classification	Fatalities			Injured		
Disastrous		>	10		>	300
Significant	5	-	10	100	-	300
Moderate	3	-	5	50	-	100
Minor	1	-	2	20	-	50
Insignificant		≤	1		≤	20

Environmental classification could not be conducted since the territories involved are characterized as administrative units such as region, populated locality etc. and not expressed in ha or km. With regard to economy, the general term 'losses' is in use in Ukrainian legislation. Figures are provided for the cases when no casualties are involved and were calculated based on the minimum official salary valid for September 2013 and currency exchange rate at that time. Here, losses exceeding 16 million Euro would refer to a disastrous event (Table 4.6)

Table 4.6: Ukrainian impact classification with regard to economy

ECONOMY

Classification	Losses		
Disastrous		>	16 million Euro
Significant	1.6 million Euro	-	16 million Euro
Moderate	0.02 million Euro	-	1.6 million Euro
Minor		-	
Insignificant		≤	0.02 million Euro

In Ukrainian legislation there is no classification on the type of living conditions (as 'disruption of water supply', 'disruption of energy supply', 'disruption of gas supply', and 'disruption of telecommunication'). Ukrainian legislation provides general definition – 'disruption of living conditions'. Here, as disastrous event means that the living conditions of 50000 persons are disrupted for more than 3 days (Table 4.7). The immaterial classification was not clearly understood.

Table 4.7: Ukrainian classification of disruption of living conditions

SUPPLY

Classification	Disruption of living conditions				
Disastrous			>	50000	persons
		for	>	72/3	hours/days
Significant		10000	-	50000	persons
	for		>	72/3	hours/days
Moderate		1000	-	10000	persons
	for		>	72/3	hours/days
Minor		100	-	1000	persons
	for		>	72/3	hours/days
Insignificant			≤	100	persons
		for	≤	72/3	hours/days

Interim conclusion

The forms for the impact classifications were only partly filled of two experts. Due to the different country-dependent legislations, the classification of an event and its impacts is very individual. For example, classifying an event as disastrous by means of the number of fatalities and injured differs between the two countries regarded. This may be partly owed to the differing country and population size as well as population density. Exemplarily, the numbers are listed in Table 4.8.

Table 4.8: Country size, population size, and population density for Ukraine and Belgium. Date of information July 2017

Country	Country size	Population size	Population density
Ukraine	603.550 km^2	44.033.874	73/km^2
Belgium	30.528 km^2	11.491.346	376/km^2

Another conclusion is that impacts on man, supply, economy, as well as immaterial implications cannot be regarded separately for categorization and a specific size for an affected area cannot be automatically assigned to the category 'disastrous'. The categorization depends on, for example, how many people are affected and if strategies can be developed to overcome the impairment. Consequently, the impacts need to be considered together with country-specific characteristics in order to classify the severity of an accident. Due to the reserved response to the impact classification form, further attempts of clarification have not been undertaken. The experts rather recommended to work with the number of affected people and the international nuclear and radiological event scale (INES) to classify nuclear power plant accidents (International Atomic Energy Agency (IAEA), 2008). The scale has seven levels and events are considered according to their impact on people and environment, on radiological barriers and controls at facilities, and on defense in depth. The latter particularly takes into account events with no but potential consequences. Actually, the INES scale is applied after an accident. During an accident, the notion of 'iodine equivalent' is used and reflects the amount of radioactive material released from a nuclear power plant accident. There are specific conversion factors for radiological equivalence to Iodine 131 (International Atomic Energy Agency (IAEA), 2008, Table 2). However, only regarding an accident from a radiological point of view is insufficient and further attributes were taken into account as can be seen in the following.

Importance of the attributes for decision-making during each accident phase

The results of evaluating the attributes and particularly the median values for each accident phase can be found in Appendix D. If it is not mentioned that an attribute is deleted, the attribute is integrated in the final set. Attributes that are marked with the note 'add' are provided additionally by the experts. For being integrated in the final set, an attribute needs to be voted at least by a 3 (great relevance) for at least one accident phase. Attributes for describing a measure have all been regarded as decisive. In summary,

- Most of the domains of symbolic attributes needed to be reduced since many values TSO offers have been regarded as not necessary.
- Several attributes were adapted to the nuclear domain.

- Depending on the expertise of the evaluator, some very specific attributes were suggested to add to the catalogue.
- The taxonomy of targets subsumed many attributes.
- Several attributes could be merged.
- Except of the attributes describing consequences, the degree of importance of attributes varied depending on the release status. Many attributes assigned high relevance during the pre-release and release phase were less important during the transition and long-term post-accident phase.
- Consequences are not important for the pre-release phase. However, most of the offered attributes were regarded as having great relevance or were strictly necessary for decision-making during the other accident phases.

After the evaluation, the original aggregation in 'event', 'nuclear power plant', 'location', 'radionuclide', 'consequences', and 'measures' was almost completely revised. The structure was particularly aligned with the problem division into affected areas and accident phases (see Chapter 3.1.1). The evaluation particularly revealed, which attributes are relevant to describe an affected area, which are phase-specific, and which belong to a general description of the event. Figure 4.1 illustrates the basic structure of an accident, which is linked to a release or potential release (indicated by 'pre-release'), to several affected areas, where each area can be assigned to one or several accident phases. A strategy is specified for an affected area during a specific phase. 'Release' and 'pre-release' indicate general characteristics whereas 'accident phase' includes phase-specific information. Hence, a case in the case base contains *general information on the accident*, such as the nuclear power plant involved, information on the *affected area*, such as the population distribution, information on *release* such as the release duration, and *phase-specific information*. The latter refers to targets, for example, which change in the course of an accident. Roofs, for example, are objects of interest in the later phases in terms of decontamination whereas specific food needs to be regarded earlier. Furthermore, each case includes a strategy and further decisive information such as the effectiveness of this strategy. The latter can be specified by the dose reduction, for example.

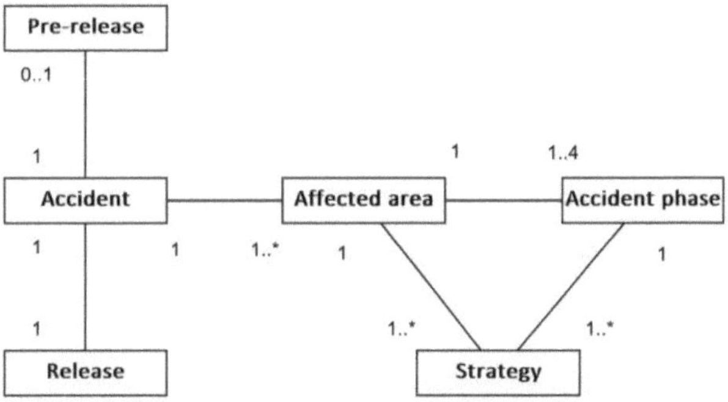

Figure 4.1: Basic structure of an accident

4.3 Uncertainty Handling

Thinking of a nuclear accident or potential accident scenario, there is likely to be uncertainty, for example in the source terms, weather conditions, observation errors in the monitoring data, in processing models like e.g. atmospheric dispersion, the public compliance with any measure, the demography of the population affected and so on (French, 1997). From the earliest moments of an accident when a release threatens, through the release phase, to the long-term consequences arising from the resulting contamination, there are many uncertainties to be weighted in selecting strategies. Many of these uncertainties can be reduced through careful collection and analysis of a variety of data.

In Chapter 2.1.5, several solutions are presented on how to handle uncertainty in the problem description. Within the scope of this thesis, the first step in handling uncertainty is to offer categories for description instead of demanding exact values for a specific attribute. As could be already seen in the attribute catalogue, several symbolic attributes can be used for problem description. The accident scenario type, for example, indicates a possible event development, such as a large leak in the containment which may lead to a steam blast. Furthermore, attributes such as weather which could have a very detailed description, can be categorized as well. For instance, a first distinction into 'no rain' or 'rain' indicates the extent of contamination where precipitation may lead to a higher contamination of an area. Refinements are necessary as can be seen in Chapter 4.5 when the simulation results are analyzed.

Working with pre-defined domains of symbolic attributes and categorization of certain characteristics are the first steps to limit additional uncertainty generated in the model by uncertain input data. Furthermore, the assignment of important attributes for decision-making to accident phases, help to reduce uncertainty by focusing on relevant characteristics as well. Table 4.9 shows some examples of symbolic attributes and corresponding domains.

Table 4.9: Examples of symbolic attributes with corresponding domains

Attribute	Categories
Accident type	explosion of radiological dispersal service nuclear power plant accident radiological accident with fire spread of contamination following radiological poisoning
Iodine equivalent	1-7 Comment: There is a significant difference in the measures between the top level 7 of the iodine equivalent and the other lower level no less than 5. For the cases of less than level 5, no recommended strategies could be offered.
Population distribution	rural urban metropolitan
Weather	rain no rain no rain low wind no rain medium wind no rain stable wind Comment: When the iodine equivalent achieves the top level 7, the weather significantly changes the sizes of evacuation/sheltering area or the distribution area of iodine tablets for adults/children from the data analysis of the scenarios calculated by JRodos (see also Chapter 4.5).

4.4 The Case Model

In the following, the structure of a case is introduced formally (Moehrle & Raskob, 2015). Basically, a case consists of a problem and solution description which in turn encompasses a strategy, its effectiveness, and further decisive information. For description, attributes are used (based on Stahl, 2003, Definition 2.1):

Definition 4.1 Attribute

> An attribute A is a pair $(A_{name}, dom(A))$ where A_{name} is a unique label and $dom(A)$ is the domain. The value of an attribute A is denoted by $a_{name} \in dom(A)$.

Note that the domain of an attribute particularly contains *NULL* in case the attribute value is not known. One part of a case is the problem description being subject to a problem model (based on Stahl, 2003, Definition 2.2):

Definition 4.2 Problem model

> A problem model D consists of finitely many attributes $D = (A_1, A_2, \dots, A_n), n > 0$. Denote $\widehat{D}$ as the set of all problem models.

The problem model comprises descriptions of the affected area, the accident phase and the related event that in turn refers to the description of release (if happened) and involved nuclear power plant. As mentioned before, the solution part of a case consists of a strategy:

Definition 4.3 Strategy model

> A strategy model $S = (M, E)$ where $M = \{(M_1, \dots, M_v) | v \geq 0\}$ is a set of tuples of attributes where $E \subseteq M \times M$ indicates the implementation order of the measures. Denote $\hat{S}$ as the set of strategy models. A strategy is a pair $s = (m, e)$ with $m = \{(m_{i1}, \dots, m_{iv}) | m_{ir} \in dom(M_r), r = 1, \dots v, i \in \mathbb{N}^+\}$ and $e \subseteq m \times m$. Denote $\overline{S}$ the set of all strategies that are subject to a strategy model S.

Note that each tuple of M represent the measure, the target of the measure, and further information on the measure. A case further consists of effectiveness values of a strategy:

Definition 4.4 Solution model

> A solution model L is a pair $L = ((L_1, .., L_k), S)$ consisting of finitely many attributes $(L_1, \dots, L_k), k \geq 0$ and a strategy model S. Denote $\hat{L}$ the set of all solution models.

The attributes $L_1, \dots, L_k$ particularly specify the effectivenss of a strategy. Finally, the parts introduced so far can be joined to a case model (based on Stahl, 2003, Definition 2.4):

Definition 4.5 Case Model

> A case model C is a pair $C = (D, L) \in \hat{D} \times \hat{L}$. Denote $\hat{C}$ the set of all case models.

A case is then defined as follows:

Definition 4.6 Case

> A case according to a case model C is a pair $c = (d^c, l^c) = ((a_1^c, .., a_n^c), ((l_1^c, \dots, l_k^c, s^c))$ with $a_i^c \in dom(A_i), i = 1, \dots, n, l_j^c \in dom(L_j), j = 1, \dots, k$ and $s^c \in \overline{S}$. Further, d^c is called the problem description and l^c the solution description of the case c.

The core of a CBR system is the case base which is defined as follows:

Definition 4.7 Case base

> The case base $CB = \{c_1, \dots, c_K\}$ is a finite set of valid cases according to a given case model $C \in \hat{C}$.

Note that the solution description part may be empty in contrast to the problem description part (based on Stahl, 2003, Definition 2.7):

Definition 4.8 Query

> Given a case model C, a query is a case $q = (d^q, l^q)$ with an empty solution description that means for $l^q = (l_1^q, \dots, l_k^q, s^q)$ it holds $l_i^q = NULL, i = 1, \dots, k$ and $s^q = (\emptyset, \emptyset)$.

The strategy model introduced so far provides means to present measures and their characteristics as well as their implementation order by pairwise considerations. For example, for a strategy $s = (m, e)$ with $e \subseteq m \times m$, $e_1 = (\tilde{m}_1, \tilde{m}_2) \in e$ indicates that the measure specified in $\tilde{m}_1$ is implemented before the measure specified in $\tilde{m}_2$. This is a first approach to capture the order of implementation. The next chapter introduces a more sophisticated modeling of strategies.

4.4.1 Modeling of Strategies Using High-Level Petri Nets

In the following, the strategy model (Moehrle, 2013b, 2013a; Moehrle & Raskob, 2019) is presented. The **requirements for strategy modeling** resulted from analyses of related work, flood reports (Arbeitsgruppe Hochwasser (Sachsen-Anhalt), 2003; Unabhängige Kommision der Sächsischen Staatsregierung, 2002), and fire department regulations (Feuerwehr-Dienstvorschriften FwDV) dealing with leadership and command in emergency operations command and control systems as well as research within the PREPARE project. The fire department regulations particularly guide situation assessment which is based on locality, time, weather, damage, damaged objects, the extent of damage as well as resources determining the planning process and the resulting measures. In this work, location, context of event, or the initial situation are primarily covered by the retrieve step of CBR.

- *Independence of the type of event*. This requirement originated from research in the field of natural disasters and analyses of different types of events allowing now to transfer the model to nuclear emergencies as well.
- *Capturing the implementation order of measures*. In general, measures cannot be executed in an arbitrary order, such as decontamination measures that may have timely or logical constraints with regard to the implementation order (Nisbet et al., 2010).

- *Comprising short- and long-term decisions as well as possible event developments*. Being part of the preparedness phase of disaster management, this work aims at providing support for response and recovery and hence short- and long-term decisions.

- *Capturing the effects of measures.* This requirement is important for the comparability of strategies.

- *Capturing crucial factors influencing decisions on measures.* This requirement particularly refers to the learning capability of CBR. The crucial factors are important for identifying similar cases from the case base. Some of them are important for the reuse step as well.

- *Allowing performance analysis,* which is important for the assessment of strategies. Hence, simulation possibilities are of great value.

- *Supporting a graphical representation of strategies* facilitating user understanding. A structured storage and possibilities for automatic processing are of first priority. A graphical presentation would mainly be useful for communication and manual adaptation of strategies, if desired.

- *Facilitating automatic processing* which is important for the reuse step of CBR.

- *Allowing easy extensibility*. The modeling capabilities should not be limited. This work does not claim to have integrated all decisive factors but rather focuses on a general model for strategies.

The strategy model is based on ISO/IEC 15909 (International Organization for Standardization, 2000, 2004). Moreover, the labeling of transitions (Murata, 1989) is integrated. The strategies in the case base are instances of the strategy model. In consideration of the requirements listed before, the following **assumptions** are made:

(i) The model contains two active components with different behaviors: measures and events.

(ii) Events cause the endangerment of targets, which may also be surfaces that have been contaminated. Here, 'endangerment' needs to be understood in a wider sense.

(iii) Measures are decided upon and implemented because of an event and its resulting targets.

(iv) Measures reduce the endangerment of the targets and do not create endangerment.

(v) Measures consume resources.

Definition 4.9 HLPN-based strategy model

The strategy model S is a tuple

$$S = (P, T, Dom, Type, Pre, Post, M_0),$$

where:

- P is a finite set of places.
- $T = T_m \cup T_e$ is a finite set of transitions where T_m denotes the set of measures and T_e denotes the set of events. It holds that $P \cap T = \emptyset$. Moreover, there are finite sets of labels for measures Σ_m and events Σ_e and labeling functions

$$L_k: T_k \to \Sigma_k, k \in \{m, e\},$$

  which assign labels to the transitions from a predefined domain.
- $Dom = \{B, B \times [0,1], R, B \times [0,1] \times R, \{\cdot\}\}$ is a set of domains where each element of *Dom* is called a type. The type B is a predefined set of targets. The interval $[0,1]$ indicates the degree of endangerment expressed as real number between 0 and 1. With reference to a contam-

inated surface, 1 indicates 100 % contamination and 0 indicates a successful decontamination[5]. The type R is a predefined set of resources. The type $\{\cdot\}$ does not have any characteristics.

- $Type: P \cup T \rightarrow Dom$ is a function used to assign types to places and to determine transition modes. A transition mode is a pair comprising the transition and a value taken from the transition's type.

- $Pre, Post: TRANS \rightarrow \mu PLACE$ are pre- and post-mappings with

$$TRANS = \{(t, m) | t \in T, m \in Type(t)\},$$

$$PLACE = \{(p, g) | p \in P, g \in Type(p)\},$$

  $\mu PLACE$ is the set of multisets over the set $PLACE$.

- $M_0 \in \mu PLACE$ is the initial marking of the net.

For $(t, m) \in TRANS$ the pre-and post-mappings of the transition t and its mode (t, m) can be written as symbolic sums of elements of $PLACE$ scaled by their multiplicities:

$$Pre(t, m) = P_\mu = \sum_{x \in PLACE} P_\mu(x)'x, P_\mu \in \mu PLACE$$

and $Post(t, m)$, respectively, where $P_\mu(x)$ is the multiplicity of $x \in PLACE$ in P_μ.

Let

$$TRANS|T_m = \{(t, m) | t \in T_m, m \in Type(t)\}$$

$$TRANS|T_e = \{(t, m) | t \in T_e, m \in Type(t)\}$$

Assumptions (ii) and (iv) can be formalized as follows:

Let $(t, m) \in TRANS$ with $m = (b, y) \in B \times [0,1]$.

[5] A successful decontamination does not necessarily correspond to a pre-release status but rather to the achievement of specific effectiveness values and the restoration of a worth-living environment.

For $(p_1,(b,y_{pre}))\in Pre(t,m),(p_2,(b,y_{post}))\in Post(t,m)$ it holds

$$y_{pre}\leq y_{post}\ if\ (t,m)\in TRANS|T_e \tag{4.1}$$

$$y_{pre}\geq y_{post}\ if\ (t,m)\in TRANS|T_m \tag{4.2}$$

Note that $\{\cdot\}$ is equivalent to $(p,(b,0))$ for any $p\in P$ and $b\in B$. Inequality (4.1) formalizes assumption (ii): events may create endangerment. Inequality (4.2) refers to assumption (iv): measures may reduce endangerment.

Assumption (iii) can be formalizes as follows:

$$Type(t_m)=B\times[0,1]\times R \text{ for all } t_m\in T_m \tag{4.3}$$

Assumption (v), which refers to the consumption of resources, can be formalized as follows:

Let $(t,m)\in TRANS|T_m, P_\mu = Pre(t,m)$ and $P_{\tilde{\mu}} = Post(t,m)$. There exists at least one $x = (p,r)\in P_\mu$[6] with $r\in R$ for which it holds that

$$x\in P_{\tilde{\mu}} \text{ and } P_\mu(x)\geq P_{\tilde{\mu}}(x) \text{ or } x\notin P_{\tilde{\mu}} \tag{4.4}$$

where $x\notin P_{\tilde{\mu}}$ indicates a complete consumption of resources.

The tokens contain information on targets and their endangerment as well as on resources. A strategy is an instance of the strategy model. The implementation of this strategy corresponds to a run of this instance.

4.4.2 Example

For illustration purposes, CPN Tools[7], a modeling and simulation tool for Colored Petri Nets (CPNs), is used. CPNs belong to the class of HLPNs and are characterized by the combination of PNs and programming languages (Jensen & Kristensen,

[6] x is a member of the multiset P_μ denoted by $x\in P_\mu$ if $P_\mu(x)>0$

[7] http://cpntools.org/ CPN Tools particularly denotes multisets as $l`A++m`B, l,m\in\mathbb{N}$, for example.

2009). The CPN modeling language particularly conforms to the ISO/IEC standard the definition of the strategy model is based on.

The following example shows different implementation possibilities of measures excluding the consumption of resources. Figure 4.2 illustrates an event *E1* triggering an endangerment on targets *B*1, *B*2, and *B*3. Measures directed towards *B*1 and *B*3 as well as *B*2 are implemented concurrently. The endangerment of target *B*3 is reduced stepwise by the measures *M*1 and *M*3. An intermediate event *E*2 increases the endangerment of target *B*3 again. Measures *M*1 and *M*3 as well as *M*4 are particularly illustrating sequentially implemented measures directed towards different targets. Measures *M5* and *M6* are both directed towards target *B*2. They are implemented concurrently. Measures *M*2 and *M5* and *M6*, respectively, illustrate sequentially implemented measures directed towards the same target. With regard to target *B*2, *M*2 as well as *M7* and corresponding subsequent measures can be applied particularly anticipating the merging of several strategies that is discussed in Chapter 6.

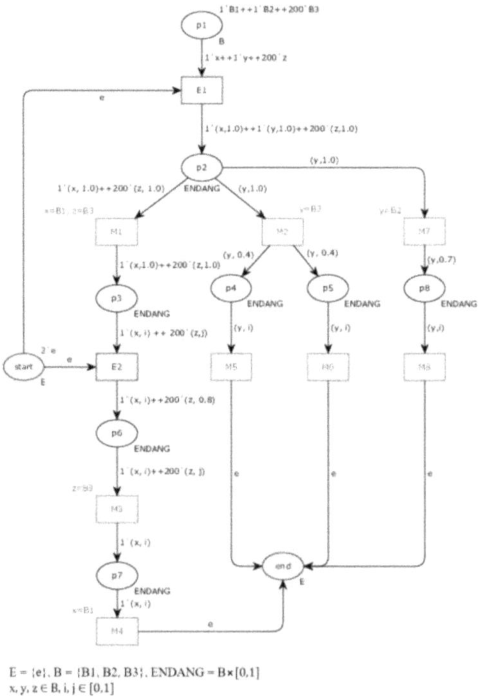

Figure 4.2: Example strategy illustrating different orders of implementation

4.4.3 Discussion of the Model

The strategy model developed in this thesis represents a solution to capture the order of implementation, event developments, the targets involved as well as their endangerment and effects of measures on the endangerment. Strategies that are stored according to the strategy model can be further used in the reuse step of CBR. First, to merge several strategies if necessary, and second to further analyze possibly alternative strategies in the course of a multi-criteria assessment. The strategy model supports a structured storage, automatization of the reuse step, and analyses. However, the model serves as an integral part of the decision support method and does not intend to be utilized by the user directly. In respect of implementing the decision support method, a suitable interface is necessary. In the examples so far, tokens represent different targets. The degree of endangerment may be specified by the achievement of objectives. Furthermore, the HLPN-based strategy model enables to take performance indicators, such as the implementation duration of a strategy, into account.

This thesis particularly considers following implementation possibilities of measures:

- Sequential implementation of measures directed towards a target.
- Concurrent implementation of measures directed towards different targets.
- Concurrent implementation of measures directed towards the same target.
- Several strategy possibilities depending on the targets involved.
- Sequential implementation of measures directed towards different targets.
- Event happening during the implementation of a strategy.
- Combinations of these.

More possible constellations are conceivable, such as measures that are implemented several times, but which are not investigated in this thesis.

As can be seen in the examples, it is implicitly assumed that

(i) The net has exactly one initial and one final node of the type $\{\cdot\}$ (or E in the Figures).
(ii) Endangerment generated is completely reduced in each net.

These assumptions are particularly important for the merging of several strategies which is presented in Chapter 6.

4.5 Data Collection

For building the case base, the experts that voted on the attribute catalogue, were asked to provide knowledge on historical events, simulations were run by JRodos for the release and long-term post-accident phase, and the HERCA-WENRA approach was translated into 8 cases for the pre-release phase. In general, the problem descriptions of the historical events are more comprehensive than of the JRodos scenarios. In contrast to strategies that are received from the simulations, experts provided additional knowledge on the experience with implementation and their effectiveness. For a structured data collection, a data record form based on the structure illustrated in Figure 4.1 was built for the experts to fill in their knowledge. Four historical events have been analyzed to populate the case base: the Chernobyl nuclear power plant accident, the Fukushima Daiichi nuclear power plant accident, the Windscale fire, and the poisoning of Alexander Litvinenko. Each event is subdivided into accident phases and affected areas. Finally, 16 cases result from four historical events. For each affected area, a strategy is provided that are directed towards specific targets and exposure pathways. Furthermore, the experts shared their expertise in respect of implementation. Table 4.10 shows to which phases the cases belong to and which affected areas are regarded.

Table 4.10: Number of cases gained of historical events for the different accident phases

Phase/event	Chernobyl nuclear power plant accident	Fukushima Daiichi nuclear power plant accident	Windscale fire	Poisoning of Alexander Litvinenko
Release	3	1	1	1
Transition	1	-	1	1
Long-term post-accident	4	1	1	1
Affected areas	Pripyat Narodichskiy district of Zhitomirskaya oblast Bryansk region Novo Bobovichi United Kingdom	Fukushima Prefecture	Milk ban area	Population who were given urine tests (includes both United Kingdom and overseas testing)

The simulations for the release phase are based on variations in the values of four symbolic attributes (Table 4.11). Since the approach to countering uncertainty is to work with rough classifications, symbolic attributes are regarded only. Although the INES scale range from 1-7, only INES 5-7 are regarded since INES 4 would result in 'do nothing'. The four weather categories are a first approach to roughly classify different weather situations (Table 4.12) assuming three wind speed categories: low, medium, and stable. The categories define the wind speed at a grid point and the direction of the wind. 'Low' refers to a wind speed of 1 m/s and a changing wind direction with time, 'medium' to a wind speed from 1 to 3 m/s and a changing wind direction with time, and 'stable' to a wind speed of 4 m/s with a more specific wind direction and less direction changes with time. 96 scenarios result from this approach. The results of the simulations are (i) The size of evacuation area and the number of affected people; (ii) The size of the sheltering area and the number of affected people; (iii) The size of the distribution area of iodine tablets for adults and the number of affected people; (iv) The size of the distribution area of iodine tablets for children and the number of affected people; (v) Costs; (vi) Average shelter factor.

Table 4.11: Attributes and domains for constructing scenarios

Attribute	Values
INES	5 (FKI)[8] 6 (FKF) 7 (FKA)
Season	Spring Summer Autumn Winter
Weather	No rain low wind No rain medium wind No rain stable wind Rain
Population distribution	Urban (high population area) Rural (low population area)

Table 4.12: Explanation of the weather categories

Weather category	Explanation
No rain low wind	Low wind speed and changing wind direction
No rain medium wind	Medium wind speed and changing wind direction
No rain stable wind	High wind speed and a specific wind direction
Rain	Rain, medium wind speed and changing wind direction

Table 4.13 shows exemplarily calculated areas for evacuation, sheltering, and the distribution of iodine tablets for adults and children for the different INES values in an urban area averaged over all seasons. The values show that the largest areas result from INES 7 events. INES 6 events, for example, include less contaminants and with changing wind directions contaminants are dispersed. Hence, the areas resulting from the weather category 'no rain stable wind' are often larger since most contaminants are blown into one direction. Furthermore, the different weather conditions result in variations in the area sizes. Rain leads to the largest areas for evacuation and sheltering. Since inhalation is the main exposure pathway for radioactive iodine, rain may lead to smaller areas in contrast to other weather conditions.

[8] The FKI, FKF, and FKA denote different release scenarios (Walter et al., 2016).

In summary, the variations in the results show that a refinement of weather categories is reasonable to get more precise results.

Table 4.13: Area sizes for measures resulting from simulations

Weather category / INES	No rain low wind	No rain medium wind	No rain stable wind	Rain
Evacuation areas in km^2				
5	0	0	0	0
6	0	0.2	0.65	1.1
7	81.88	33.88	22.8	195.7
Sheltering areas in km^2				
5	0	0	0.4	0.3
6	1.38	11.1	12.32	54.42
7	1327	516.4	730.4	4127.0
Areas for the distribution of stable iodine to adults in km^2				
5	0	0	0	0
6	0	3.9	5.4	3.1
7	555	251.4	202.7	254.8
Areas for the distribution of stable iodine to children in km^2				
5	0	0	2.3	0
6	78.2	99.9	99.7	96.2
7	12516.4	6394.5	2641.4	2465.4

The cases for the long-term post-accident phase are either gained from historical events or determined by JRodos. Again, values for symbolic attributes are varied (Table 4.14).

Table 4.14: Attribute values for constructing long-term scenarios

Attribute	Values
INES	6
Season	Summer
Weather	Rain
	No rain
Population distribution	Urban
	Rural

Figure 4.3 depicts exemplarily a combination of measures and their order determined by JRodos for the long-term post-accident phase in an urban area under rainy weather conditions during release. This result includes the duration of each measure and needs to be developed by hand. JRodos calculates the costs, amount of waste, and factor of dose reduction. However, the composition of measures needs to be reviewed by an expert to identify possible pitfalls and side effects. An expert of the project, for example, stated that grass cutting would generally not be an option for wet deposition scenarios as most of the contamination would from the beginning be in the soil rather than on the grass.

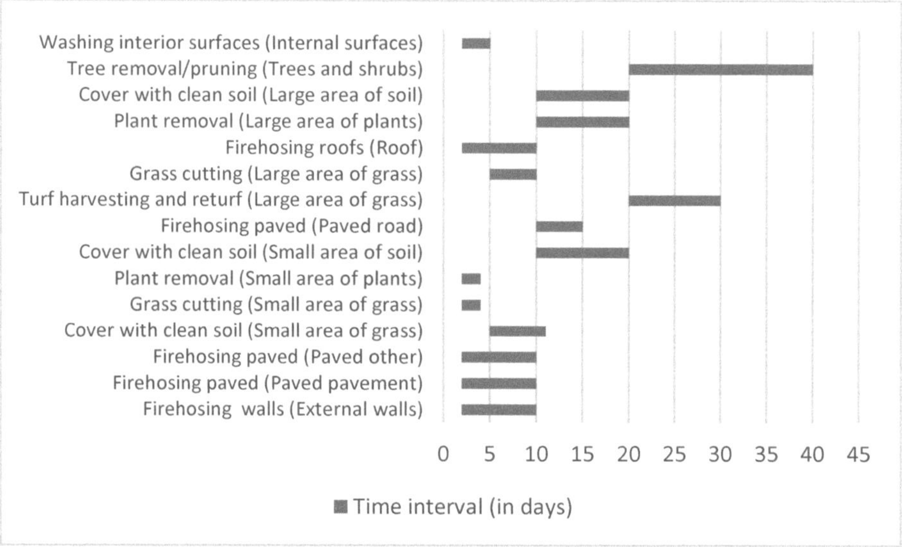

Figure 4.3: Combination of measures for an urban area and rain during release

As mentioned before, the cases for the pre-release phase are derived from the HERCA-WENRA approach. Table 4.15 exemplarily shows a value assignment of the four attributes regarded and the corresponding recommendation.

Table 4.15: Example result of the HERCA-WENRA approach

Attribute	Value
Risk of core melt?	Yes or unknown
Maintaining of containment integrity?	Yes or unknown
Wind direction	Variable or unknown
Estimated release time	Unknown
Recommended strategy	
Evacuation and iodine thyroid blocking up to 5 km in a zone of 360 degrees Sheltering and iodine thyroid blocking from 5 to 20 km in a zone of 360 degrees	

Figure 4.4 depicts an excerpt of the scheme developed for the storage of the cases in a database. The excerpt reflects the structure of an accident and shows some of the attributes describing, for example, a release or an affected area. 77 attributes are available for problem description and 34 for describing a strategy and its effectiveness. However, some attribute values remained (predominantly) empty which was taken into account when determining the retrieval criteria (see Chapter 5.1). For reasons of clarity, mainly those attribute that are used in the retrieve and reuse step of CBR are illustrated in Figure 4.4. The database is structured in 43 tables including domains for symbolic attributes. For example, the table 'release_characteristics' has a many-to-one relationship to the table 'weather_at_release', which includes different weather categories. Again, for reasons of clarity, tables that include the domains of symbolic attributes are not illustrated in Figure 4.4.

Figure 4.5 illustrates the distribution of cases in the database according to historical events, scenarios, and rules as well as accident phases. The database so far mainly builds upon scenarios that are simulated by JRodos and are assigned to the release phase. As part of future work, the database needs to be enhanced in order to cover a wide range of different scenario types. An approach would be a finer granularity of specific symbolic attribute domains such as weather categories (see Chapter 8).

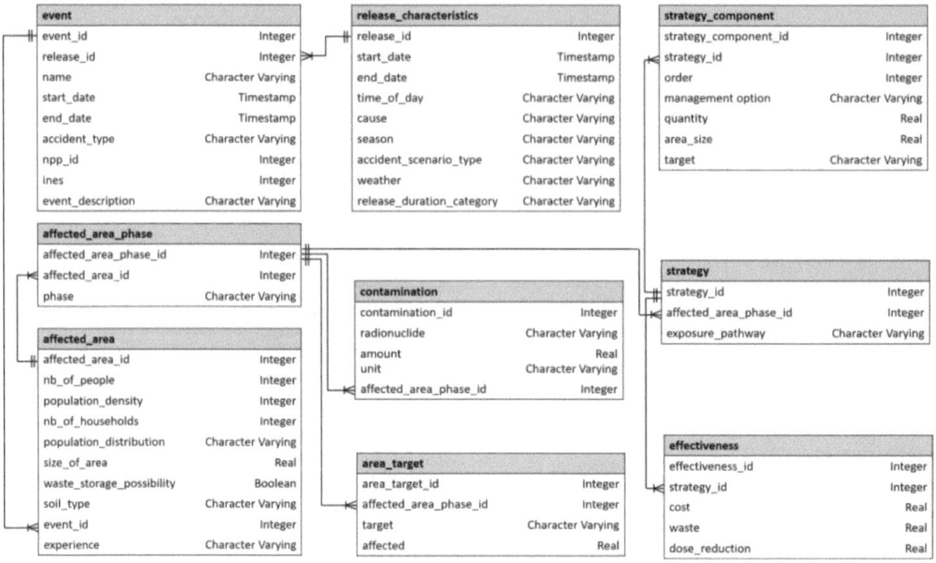

Figure 4.4: Excerpt of the database scheme for the storage of nuclear events (Moehrle & Raskob, 2015, Figure 4)

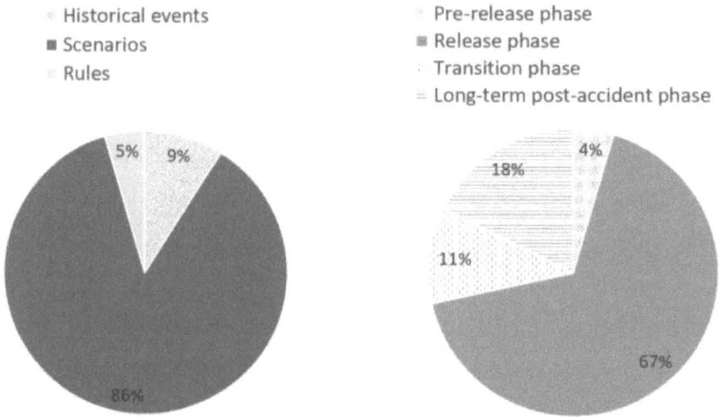

Figure 4.5: Overview of cases in the database categorized in historical events, scenarios, rules, and accident phases

4.6 Summary and Discussion

The first step of developing the case base was to elicitate relevant problem- and solution characteristics for decision-making. The approach was to collect possibly relevant attributes from the nuclear as well as general disaster management field to be evaluated by experts to identify the set of decisive criteria. Many symbolic attributes with predefined domains were integrated to be particularly used in times when little information is available to describe a problem in a detailed way. The evaluation reduced the set of attributes partly being adapted to the nuclear domain. The current set of attributes does not claim to be complete. Since the whole approach is new in nuclear emergency management, adaptations and extensions are expected in the course of time. This refers also to the domains for symbolic attributes. The domains that already existed were evaluated by the experts resulting in reduction, rearrangement, or completely revision. For example, the weather categories that are mainly oriented towards precipitation, wind speed, and wind direction, are regarded as sufficient in the first instance. However, refinements in this regard are necessary. The evaluation also showed that the problem description characteristics relevant for decision-making vary in the course of an accident. Hence, the timely development of an accident plays an important role when defining cases. The attempt of an (European-wide) impact classification (as discussed in Chapter 4.2.1) was less successful due to country specific regulations and the complexity of the topic that does not easily allow a categorization in such simple terms when it comes to economy, supply, and immaterial impacts.

The topic of uncertainty needs to be taken into account throughout the CBR cycle. With regard to the case base the focus is on vague descriptions and the use of symbolic attributes and predefined domains as a first approach to handle this issue. The idea is to allow categorical descriptions under the assumption that these may be specified more easily and possibly faster than numerical values, especially in times when little information is available. Also with regard to the later phases the idea is to start with some rough categorizations to cover a wide range of different scenario types to be refined stepwise. The whole approach particularly contributes and promotes to prepare for possible accident scenarios in advance.

Data collection revealed the complexity of building a case base since not for all attributes values could be assigned and hence information content varied from case to case. Hence, the actual set of attributes used for retrieval is a subset of the initial attributes describing problem and solution. Moreover, some attributes are for information only, such as date or name. A more detailed discussion can be found in

Chapter 5.1. Retrieval is divided into two steps: First the set of problem descriptions is filtered, first according to the accident phase, and second according to further filter attributes selected by the user. Second, the actual similarity calculation is performed. The general approach is to maintain flexibility that means to allow variations in the set of retrieval attributes. The actual choice of attributes is left to the user. Table 4.16 sums up the number of case describing attributes and the number of attributes that are used for retrieval.

Table 4.16: Number of attributes for case description and retrieval

# Attributes available	Usage
77	Problem description
34	Solution description
9	Filtering
26	Retrieval criteria

Due to the also flexible implementation of the whole method (see Chapter 7) and the freedom of the user to configure the retrieve step, additional characteristics that might be relevant for decision-making can be included easily.

In respect of scenario construction, only a small set of primarily symbolic attributes were chosen to set up the simulations. The first approach was to work with categories of release scenarios, weather situations, and affected areas with rather rough granularity. The resulting area sizes and number of affected people as well as effectiveness values and experiences made during historical events support decision-making in the early stage of an accident. The attributes chosen are particularly input parameters of the JRodos system. The next steps would be to specify further attributes and refine the strategies with the help of experts or refine the categories worked with for the simulations to improve the results.

The case model is composed of a problem model and solution model which, in turn consists of a strategy model and attributes for, amongst others, specifying the effectiveness. In particular, in respect of the HLPN-based strategy model, the regarded implementation orders are limited, at first. The generic model that integrates event developments, measures, and increasing and decreasing endangerment of targets, allow enhancements according to time, for example. In general, this chapter presents the basic ideas for a case model being generic and expandable.

5 Similarity Assessment of Nuclear Accidents

This chapter introduces the retrieve step of the case-based decision support method. Retrieval aims at identifying those cases from the case base whose solutions are useful for solving the current problem. Their usefulness is indicated by a similarity value and depends on how similar the problem descriptions are. In other words, the similarity value indicates to which degree the problem descriptions correspond to each other. The main assumption of CBR is that similar problems have similar solutions. Hence, the objective of the retrieval step is to identify problem descriptions in the case base which are close to the current problem description and the query, respectively, in order to solve the current problem.

Within the frame of this thesis, similarity is reflected by a similarity function which operates on problem descriptions. Another way is to express similarity via relations, which is independent of the case representation. However, stating quantitatively how similar two cases are, is preferred. A higher similarity value is understood as 'more useful' and hence this approach is regarded as more expressive. Based on the notation introduced by (Stahl, 2003, Definition 2.6), D_D denotes the set of all problem descriptions according to a problem model $D \in \widehat{D}$. A problem model D (Definition 4.2) is a tuple of attributes $D = (A_1, A_2, \dots, A_n), n > 0$.

A *similarity function* (Definition 2.3) for D is a function

$$f: D_D \times D_D \rightarrow [0,1].$$

Here, a value of 1 reflects a useful case for solving the current problem whereas a value of 0 indicates a useless case. For cases that contain negative experiences, the solely comparison of problem descriptions could lead to a similarity value of 1 as well. Hence, the similarity value needs to be enriched by additional information on the effectiveness of the solution. A similarity value smaller than 1 indicates that the case does not capture the current problem description completely and consequently the solution stored needs to be adapted. The similarity values enable to rank the retrieved cases (Chapter 5.1). The higher the similarity value the more useful the case is.

Case and query are compared to attribute-wise posing a flexible way for similarity assessment when cases are represented by attributes. With regard to the application domain, the individual view on the problem of each expert, missing information that might be excluded in the comparison as well as varying information available for different events and during different accident phases, favor the attribute-wise comparison of case and query. Hence, each attribute needs its own similarity function:

A *local similarity function* (Definition 2.4) for attribute A is a function

$$f_A: dom(A) \times dom(A) \rightarrow [0,1].$$

Each attribute may have different relevance in the similarity assessment which can be reflected by weights assigned to the attributes:

For attributes $A_1, \dots, A_n$ characterizing the cases,

$$\vec{w} = (w_{A_1}, \dots, w_{A_n}) \text{ with } w_{A_i} \in [0,1] \text{ and } \sum_{i=1}^{n} w_{A_i} = 1$$

denotes the *attribute weight vector* (Definition 2.5), where each w_{A_i} is called the *attribute weight* for A_i.

The overall similarity between a query and a case is determined by a *global similarity function* (Definition 2.6) $f: D_D \times D_D \rightarrow [0,1]$ with

$$f(d^q, d^c) = \sigma(f_{A_1}(d^q_{A_1}, d^c_{A_1}), \dots, f_{A_n}(d^q_{A_n}, d^c_{A_n}), \vec{w}),$$

where $\sigma: [0,1]^{2n} \rightarrow [0,1]$ is called *aggregation function* and $d^q_{A_i}$ denotes the value of the query d^q for attribute A_i, f_{A_i} the local similarity function for A_i, and $\vec{w}$ the attribute weight vector. d^c is defined accordingly.

The local similarity function for an attribute takes its type as well as domain properties into account. The global similarity function controls the influences of the attributes on the overall similarity. Local and global similarity functions together need to reflect the meaning of a useful solution in the application domain and for the user, respectively

The retrieve step consists of two steps: First, candidates for solving the current problem are selected. This step is realized by filtering the set of problem descriptions. Second, the similarities between these candidates and the query are assessed (Figure 5.1). Chapter 5.1 introduces retrieval as a whole. In Chapter 5.2, local similarity functions for attributes possibly being part of the similarity assessment are proposed. Table 5.1 lists (possible) retrieval attributes. Some of them are suitable for candidate selection (see Chapter 5.1). The configuration possibilities of retrieval are flexible and particularly left to the user (see Chapter 5.1). Note that in the course of specifying retrieval, attributes used for adaptation only are specified as well (Table 5.1).

Table 5.1: Overview of retrieval attributes and attributes for adaptation

Attributes for retrieval and similarity assessment	
Risk of core melt	Maintaining of containment integrity
Wind direction	Estimated release time
Accident type	Event description
Iodine equivalent	Environmental hazard
Nuclear power plant type	Average thermal power
Area size	Number of people
Population density	Population distribution
Waste storage possibility	Contamination
Target	Time of release
Season	Weather at release
Category of release duration	Cause
Accident scenario type	Number of events
Similarity threshold[1]	Accident phase
Attributes for adaptation only	
Soil type	Exposure pathway
Attributes used for retrieval and adaptation	
Target	Number of people
Area size	Accident phase

1 A similarity threshold is a value $x \in [0,1]$, which the similarity values of the cases retrieved should exceed.

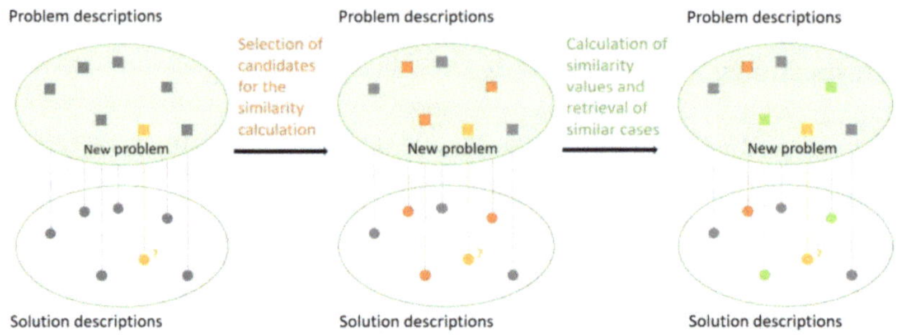

Figure 5.1: Illustration of the retrieve step

5.1 Two-Level Retrieval of Similar Cases

The retrieval step aims at identifying cases from the case base that are useful for solving the current problem. Similarity functions help to judge the usefulness whereas similarity values are used for ranking several retrieved cases. Based on the notation of Stahl, 2003, Definition 3.4, the *retrieval task* is defined as follows:

Let $C = (D, L)$ be the case model, $CB = \{c_1, \dots, c_K\}$ the case base, f a similarity function, and $q = (d^q, l^q)$ a query. The retrieval task is to determine an ordered list of cases $R = (c_1, \dots, c_\kappa)$ with

$$f(d^q, d^{c_i}) \geq f(d^q, d^{c_j}), 0 \leq i \leq j \leq \kappa$$

where one of the following conditions, which can be specified by the user, holds:

1. $|R| = x$ meaning that a fixed number $0 < x \leq K$ of cases to be retrieved is demanded[2].

2. $f(d^q, d^{c_i}) \geq \theta, i = 1, \dots, \kappa$ meaning that the similarity values need to exceed a threshold $0 < \theta \leq 1$.

---

2 $|R|$ denotes the length of the list R.

3. $|R| \leq x$ and $f(d^q, d^{c_i}) \geq \theta > 0, i = 1, \dots, \kappa$ meaning that the number of retrieved cases should not exceed a specific number $0 < x \leq K$ and within those cases, the similarity values should exceed a threshold $0 < \theta \leq 1$.

Retrieval may be realized in different ways (Lopez De Mantaras et al., 2006) and often depends on the specific application domain. Within the framework of this thesis, only a few of the problem describing attributes are used for retrieval. This is owed to the different number of attribute values that could be determined for historical events and specified for generating the scenarios. In respect of historical events, experts provided many values for attributes. For generating the scenarios, only few attribute values have been specified. For specifying comprehensive scenarios with detailed problem descriptions, an extended expert involvement is necessary. However, these detailed descriptions are not necessary in respect of the objectives defined (Chapter 1.2), since some attributes (i) Refer to disruption of critical infrastructure, which is important with regard to the feasibility of a strategy. However, the focus of this thesis is identifying an appropriate strategy in the first instance. Feasibility studies are to be conducted afterwards; (ii) Are implicitly taken into account such as the dose, which is integrated in the simulation results; (iii) Have an informative and less decisive character, such as the name or date.

Denote $\widetilde{D} = (A_i | i \in J), J \subseteq \{1, \dots, n\}$ the possible retrieval attributes. The specification of the accident phase is mandatory and is particularly used as filter attribute. For the release, transition, and long-term post-accident phase, retrieval is realized as follows:

(i) The user selects the retrieval attributes $\widetilde{D}_R = (A_i | i \in J_R), J_R \subseteq J$.

(ii) The user specifies the query by assigning values to each $A_i, i \in J_R$.

(iii) The user selects the filter attributes $F = (A_i | i \in J_F), J_F \subseteq J_R$.

(iv) The user assigns weights to each $A_i, i \in \tilde{J} := J_R \backslash J_F$. Denote $= \left(w_{A_i}\right)_{i \in \tilde{J}}$ the weight vector.

(v) The case base is filtered according to the accident phase and the filter attributes specified by the user. Denote CB_F the filtered case base $CB_F = \{c = (d^c, l^c) | d^c_{A_i} = d^q_{A_i}, i \in J_F\}$.

(vi) The retrieval task is applied to CB_F, with $q = ((d^q_i | i \in \tilde{J}), l^q)$ and

$$f(d^q, d^c) = \sigma\left(f_{A_i}\left(d^q_{A_i}, d^c_{A_i}\right), \vec{w} | i \in \tilde{J}\right), c \in CB_F$$

and $\vec{w} = (w_{A_i})_{i \in \tilde{J}}$.

For the aggregation function σ, which aggregates the local similarities, the weighted sum can be applied

$$\sigma\left(f_{A_i}\left(d^q_{A_i}, d^c_{A_i}\right), \vec{w} | i \in \tilde{J}\right) = \sum\nolimits_{i \in \tilde{J}} w_{A_i} \cdot f_{A_i}(d^q_{A_i}, d^c_{A_i})$$

In the framework of this thesis, the weighted sum particularly is preferred due to its widespread use and common understanding.

As introduced above, a two-level retrieval is realized: First, candidates for the similarity assessment are selected by means of filter attributes. Second, similar cases are determined within the filtered set of cases. The choice of filter attributes and attributes for similarity assessment are made by the user providing the flexibility to state mandatory equality for certain attribute values as well as to configure the similarity assessment individually. The attributes appropriate for filtering have the following names: 'accident type', 'iodine equivalent', 'population distribution', 'time of release', 'season', 'weather at release', 'category of release duration', 'cause', and 'accident scenario type'. Filtering according to the 'accident phase' is mandatory. This approach takes into account the exceptionality and temporary uncertainty of these events as well as users' individual view on the problem. In respect of uncertainty, attributes might be excluded in the retrieval for which values are not available yet. In addition, users may assign weights to the attributes to control their influence on the overall similarity. The majority of retrieval attributes are symbolic. The aim is to offer categories instead of demanding numeric values, particularly in times information is sparse and may be rather stated qualitatively than quantitatively.

For the pre-release phase, retrieval corresponds to a rule-based approach that is based on the attributes (*risk of core melt*, {yes or unknown, no}), (*maintaining of containment integrity*, {yes or unknown, no}), (*wind direction*, {variable or unknown, stable}), and (*estimated release time*, {unknown, before evacuation within 5 (or 20) km distance, after evacuation within 5 (or 20) km distance}). Table 5.2 shows the corresponding measures.

Table 5.2: HERCA-WENRA approach (HERCA & WENRA, 2014)

Risk of core melt	Maintaining of containment integrity	Wind direction	Estimated release time	Measures
Yes or unknown	Yes or unknown	Variable or unknown	Before evacuation within 5 km distance	Sheltering + Iodine Thyroid Blocking up to 20 km in a zone of 360 degrees
Yes or unknown	Yes or unknown	Variable or unknown	After evacuation within 5 km distance/ Unknown	Evacuation + Iodine Thyroid Blocking up to 5 km in a zone of 360 degrees Sheltering + Iodine Thyroid Blocking from 5 to 20 km a zone of 360 degrees
Yes or unknown	Yes or unknown	Steady	Before evacuation within 5 km distance	Sheltering + Iodine Thyroid Blocking up to 20 km in selected 30 degrees sectors
Yes or unknown	Yes or unknown	Steady	After evacuation within 5 km distance/ Unknown	Evacuation + Iodine Thyroid Blocking up to 5 km in selected 30 degrees sectors Sheltering + Iodine Thyroid Blocking from 5 to 20 km in selected 30 degrees sectors
Yes or unknown	No	Steady	Before evacuation within 20 km distance	Sheltering + Iodine Thyroid Blocking up to 100 km in selected 30 degrees sectors Additional Iodine Thyroid Blocking actions specific to children
Yes or unknown	No	Steady	After evacuation within 20 km distance/ Unknown	Evacuation + Iodine Thyroid Blocking up to 20 km in selected 30 degrees sectors Sheltering + Iodine Thyroid Blocking from 20 to 100 km in selected 30 degrees sectors

Risk of core melt	Maintaining of containment integrity	Wind direction	Estimated release time	Measures
				Additional Iodine Thyroid Blocking actions specific to children
Yes or unknown	No	Variable or unknown	After evacuation within 20 km distance/ Unknown	Evacuation + Iodine Thyroid Blocking up to 20 km in a zone of 360 degrees Sheltering + Iodine Thyroid Blocking from 20 to 100 km in a zone of 360 degrees Additional Iodine Thyroid Blocking actions specific to children
Yes or unknown	No	Variable or unknown	Before evacuation within 20 km distance	Sheltering + Iodine Thyroid Blocking up to 100 km in a zone of 360 degrees Additional Iodine Thyroid Blocking actions specific to children

5.2 Assessing Local Similarities

Let $q_A := d_A^q$ the attribute value of attribute A of the query description d^q and $c_A := d_A^c$ the attribute value of attribute A of the case description d^c. The local similarity functions are sorted according to attribute types.

Symbolic attributes

Accident type, Population distribution, Nuclear power plant type, Cause, Accident scenario type, Release duration category

The *accident type* roughly categorizes the type of emergency. Let B_1 = {explosion of radiological dispersal service, nuclear power plant accident, radiological accident with fire, spread of contamination following radiological poisoning}.

The *population distribution* describes the population density of the affected area quantitatively and hence reflects the number of people affected. Let B_2 = {metropolitan, urban, rural}.

The *nuclear power plant type* may state something about the controllability of an event. Let B_3 = {advanced boiling water reactor, boiling water reactor, fast breeder reactor, gas cooled reactor, graphite reactor, heavy water moderated reactor, high temperature gas cooled reactor, light water cooled reactor, light water graphite reactor, pressurized heavy water reactor, pressurized water reactor}.

The specification of the *cause* of the accident may have psychological implications. Let B_4 = {accidental, deliberate, natural}

The *accident scenario type* provide means to implicitly describe the accident, what is potentially released, and hence the source term. Let B_5 = {burst pipe, large leak in containment, loss-of-coolant accident, medium leak in containment, overpressure failure, small leak in containment, station blackout with core melt, steam blast}.

Before the Fukushima Daiichi nuclear power plant accident, there was no experience with long-lasting releases and the operational procedures in dealing with long-lasting releases needed to be reviewed. As an example, decisions on early measures need to take the *release duration* into account. Let B_6 = {short, long}.

Let

- A_1 = (accident type, B_1)
- A_2 = (nuclear power plant type, B_2)
- A_3 = (population distribution, B_3)
- A_4 = (cause, B_4)
- A_5 = (accident scenario type, B_5)
- A_6 = (release duration category, B_6)

For these attributes the overlap measure (e.g. Boriah et al., 2008)

$$f_{A_i}(q_{A_i}, c_{A_i}) = \begin{cases} 1, & q_{A_i} = c_{A_i} \\ 0, & otherwise \end{cases}$$

with $i \in \{1,2,3,4,5,6\}$ is chosen as local similarity function. This function only checks for an exact match. For example, with regard to the accident type, the number of radionuclides involved varies for the different categories. Also the nuclear power plant types differ and, as stated before, the population distribution reflects the number of affected people. The different causes for an accident can be also clearly distinguished and the different accident scenario types lead to different source terms (Löffler, Mildenberger, Sogalla, & Stahl, 2012). Furthermore, the release duration category only distinguishes two different durations. As a first approach, the overlap measure is regarded as sufficient for these attributes.

Time of day of release

For A = (*time of day of release,* (day, night, day and night)) a similarity table (Stahl, 2003, Definition 3.14) is proposed as local similarity function:

Given a symbolic attribute A with $dom(A) = (\mu_1, \dots, \mu_n)$, the matrix $(s_{ij})_{i=1;\dots,n;j=1\dots,n}$ with $s_{ij} \in [0,1]$ and

$$f_A(q_A, c_A) = f_A(\mu_i, \mu_j) = s_{ij}$$

is called a *similarity table* for $dom(A)$.

A similarity explicitly states the interrelations between attribute values (Table 5.3).

Table 5.3: Similarity values of different release times

q_A/c_A	Day	Night	Day and night
Day	1	0	0.5
Night	0	1	0.5
Day and night	0.5	0.5	1

During night, there is less mixture in the lower atmosphere which leads to a higher concentration of contaminants. Hence, release during day or night needs to be treated differently. If release lasts longer and for day and night, depending on the release time of the query, the local similarity is reduced by 50 %. Note that this attribute does not refer to the release duration but the concentration of the contaminants. It may be discussed further if the symmetrical reduction of 50 % is reasonable. However, the similarity table serves as first idea to compare between different release times.

Iodine equivalent

The *iodine equivalent* corresponds to the International Nuclear and Radiological Event Scale (INES) that ranges from 0 to 7 for particularly classifying nuclear accidents. In the frame of this work, only INES 5 to INES 7 events are regarded since events below INES 5 would result in the strategy 'do nothing'. The local similarity function for A = (*iodine equivalent*, (5, 6, 7)) is

$$f_A(q_A, c_A) = \begin{cases} 1, & q_A = c_A = 7 \\ 0, & q_A < 7, c_A = 7 \\ 1 - 0.5|q_A - c_A|, & q_A < 7, c_A < 7 \end{cases}$$

This function resulted from analyses of the JRodos results of the evacuation and sheltering areas as well as areas for the distribution of iodine tablets (Table 4.13). The calculations provide a representative spectrum of possible simulation results without being complete. The differences of the areas between INES 7 events and events of a smaller scale are considerable. Hence, if the query corresponds to an INES 7 event only cases from the same scale are useful. If the query is of smaller scale, a possibly useful case does not have to be of the same scale. Since INES 7 events reflect a large amount of released material, the scale of event plays an important role for the long-term phases as well.

Season of release

For A = (*season*, (spring, summer, autumn, winter)) a similarity table is proposed as well (Table 5.4).

Table 5.4: Similarity values of different seasons

q_A/c_A	Spring	Summer	Autumn	Winter
Spring	1	0.75	0.5	0
Summer	0.75	1	0.5	0
Autumn	0.5	0.5	1	0.75
Winter	0	0	0.75	1

The *season of release* not only affects deposition mechanisms but may also have influence on strategy implementation due to climatic conditions. However, depending on the position on earth, season does not necessarily imply the same climatic conditions. In the course of the JRodos scenarios, German climatic conditions are used. In future, seasons in different countries need to be translated accordingly. The values that can be found in Table 5.4 serve as a first approach to define similarity values between seasons but may be refined if necessary. Especially with regard to the long-term phase, season is an important criteria for decisions in respect of agricultural production areas.

Weather

Weather at release is a decisive factor strongly influencing, for example, the area sizes for the early measures (Table 4.13) and in general the deposition mechanisms. For A = (*weather*, (rain, no rain, no rain low wind, no rain medium wind, no rain stable wind)) a similarity table as local similarity function is proposed (Table 5.5).

Table 5.5: Similarity values of different weather categories

q_A/c_A	Rain	No rain	No rain low wind	No rain medium wind	No rain stable wind
Rain	1	0	0.5	0.5	0.5
No rain	0	1	0.5	0.5	0.5
No rain low wind	0	0.5	1	0.5	0.5
No rain medium wind	0	0.5	0.5	1	0.5
No rain stable wind	0	0.5	0.5	0.5	1

Since the wind conditions have a great influence, the additional information on wind reduce the similarity value by 50%, if on the other hand, only the condition 'no rain' is available. The area sizes vary for the weather categories depending on the scale of event and the corresponding measure. Here, the refinement of the weather categories and hence adaption of the similarity values poses another research direction for the future.

Target

Let B = {adults, airplane, cars buses motorbikes, cereals, children, crop growing, dairy cows milk, detached external surfaces, detached external surfaces gutters and downpipes, detached external surfaces roofs, detached external surfaces walls, detached internal surfaces, detached precious objects, football stadium, fruit, game, horticulture, hospital patients, hospitals, hotel, hotel bar, inhabited areas, kindergarten, large area of grass, large area of plants, large area of soil, mobile homes and tents, mobile homes and tents external surfaces, mobile homes and tents internal surfaces, mobile homes and tents precious objects, multi-storey external surfaces, multi-storey external surfaces gutters and downpipes, multi-storey external surfaces roofs, multi-storey external surfaces walls, multi-storey internal surfaces, multi-storey precious objects, offices, paved pavement, paved other, paved road, people, recreational, residential, restaurant, roads, schools, semi-detached external surfaces, semi-detached external surfaces gutters and downpipes, semi-detached external surfaces roofs, semi-detached external surfaces walls, semi-detached internal surfaces, semi-detached precious objects, sewage and water treatment, sheep meat, sheep milk, small area of grass, small area of plants, small area of soil, soil grass and plants, trees and shrubs, vegetables, water environment, woods and forest} and $A = (target, B)$. The local similarity function for A is defined as follows:

$$f_A(q_A, c_A) = \begin{cases} 1, & q_A \subseteq c_A \\ 0, & otherwise \end{cases}$$

Here, A is a multi-valued attribute and hence q_A and c_A are sets. The idea of the similarity function is that the contribution to the overall similarity is highest, when the targets stated in the query are completely included in the set of targets considered by the case. In the reuse step, the targets play an important role as well since measures are directed specific targets.

Contamination

Let B = {Ba140, Ce141, Ce144, Cm242, Cs134, Cs136, Cs137, I131, I132, I133, Kr85, La140, Mo99, Nb95, noble gases, Np239, Po210, Pu238, Pu239, Pu240, Pu241, Pu242, Ru103, Ru106, Sr89, Sr90, Te129, Te132, U, Xe133, Xe33, Y90, Zr95} and A = (*contamination, B*). For this attribute, a local similarity function for many-valued attributes (Richter & Weber, 2013, p.159) is applied:

$$f_A(q_A, c_A) = \frac{1}{|q_A|} \sum_{x \in q_A} \max\{sim(x, y) | y \in c_A\}$$

with $|q_A| > 0$ and

$$sim(x, y) = \begin{cases} 1, & x = y \\ 0, & otherwise \end{cases}$$

Basically, the function determines if the radionuclides specified in the query appear in the regarded case as well. A possible enhancement of the function would be to include the similarities between the radionuclides. Furthermore, since measures are applicable to specific radionuclides, a more sophisticated approach for calculating local similarities is conceivable (Möhrle, Schoknecht, Raskob, & Oberweis, 2015). Also, the amount of contamination is excluded so far.

Textual attributes

Event description

This attribute is a textual attribute and intends to capture general information on the case that may not be provided by a predefined set of allowed values. Hence, the domain is the set of all sequences of characters. The Jaccard coefficient (Jaccard, 1901) is proposed to handle comparisons between texts. The texts are split, stop words are removed, and words are stemmed. Afterwards, the remaining sets of words are compared to each other: For A = (*event description, dom(A)*) let J_q the set of resulting words after splitting and processing q_A and J_c the corresponding set for c_A. The Jaccard coefficient for A is defined as[3]

[3] $|X|$ denotes the cardinality of the set X.

$$f_A(q_A, c_A) = \frac{|J_q \cap J_c|}{|J_q \cup J_c|}.$$

The Jaccard coefficient is useful for identifying duplicates of text and does not take into account synonyms and the semantic of event descriptions. An underlying ontology would contribute to a more in-depth similarity assessment. However, this work prefers to structure nuclear accidents and hence textual descriptions play a minor role. The attribute 'event description' allows the user to add further information. Important aspects are assumed to be covered by the other attributes.

Numeric attributes

Number of people, Population density, Average thermal power, Release height

Let A_1 = (*average thermal power*, $\mathbb{R}^+$), A_2 = (*number of people*, $\mathbb{N}$), A_3 = (*population density*, $\mathbb{R}^+$) and A_4 = (*release height*, $\mathbb{R}^+$). For these attributes following local similarity function is proposed:

$$f_{A_i}(q_{A_i}, c_{A_i}) = \frac{\min\{q_{A_i}, c_{A_i}\}}{\max\{q_{A_i}, c_{A_i}\}}$$

with $i \in \{1,2,3,4\}$.

The *average thermal power* indicates the amount of radioactive material that can potentially be released. Besides the iodine equivalent, the *number of people* is another important criterion for classifying the scale of an event. This information is particularly important to judge the feasibility of a strategy. The *population density* can be specified if more information is available. Otherwise, the attribute 'population distribution' is used. Hence, 'population distribution' and 'population density' are not used simultaneously. The release height indicates the possible transport distances of the radioactive particles. The release height in the Chernobyl accident (2000m) was much larger than in the Fukushima accident (mostly 0-300 m, but some up to 1000 m) contributing to a much larger affected area. The local similarity functions for these attributes are ratios between the values of the query and the case. With regard to the number of affected people, a difference-based similarity function was applied first. However, it is difficult to judge, from which size difference on the local similarity in- or decreases the global similarity. In general, difference-based approaches require a subsequent mapping to the interval [0,1]. A general approach for defining local similarity functions for numeric attributes is (Stahl, 2003)

$$f_A(q_A, c_A) = \begin{cases} f_1(\delta(q_A, c_A)), & c_A < q_A \\ 1, & c_A = q_A \\ f_2(\delta(q_A, c_A)), & c_A > q_A \end{cases}$$

where δ is a difference function $\delta: dom(A) \times dom(A) \to \mathbb{R}$. Working with difference-based similarity functions assumes that a decreasing distance results in an increasing similarity value. Usually, f_1 is monotonic increasing and f_2 monotonic decreasing (Stahl, 2003).

Examples for f_1 and f_2 are threshold, linear, exponential, and sigmoid functions:

$$f_i(\delta(q_A, c_A)) = \begin{cases} 1, & \delta(q_A, c_A) < \theta \\ 0, & \delta(q_A, c_A) \geq \theta \end{cases}$$

$$f_i(\delta(q_A, c_A)) = \begin{cases} 1, & \delta(q_A, c_A) < min \\ \dfrac{max - \delta(q_A, c_A)}{max - min}, & \min \geq \delta(q_A, c_A) \geq max \\ 0, & \delta(q_A, c_A) > max \end{cases}$$

$$f_i\big(\delta(q_A, c_A)\big) = e^{\delta(q_A, c_A) \cdot \alpha}$$

$$f_i\big(\delta(q_A, c_A)\big) = \frac{1}{e^{\frac{\delta(q_A, c_A) - \theta}{\alpha}} + 1}$$

With $i \in \{1,2\}$. The challenge is to define the difference function, base functions and corresponding parameters.

Area size

The area size is an important criterion for classifying the event as well. Furthermore, when discussing decontamination strategies, an expert of the PREPARE project particularly emphasized the dependency on the possibility to store waste. Hence, when comparing two areas concerning size, their similarity would decrease if one area has possibilities to store waste and the other area not. For the early phases, waste storage is not relevant. The exact area sizes are important in the reuse phase of CBR.

Hence, for A_1 = (*area size*, $\mathbb{R}^+$) the attribute A_2 = (*waste storage possibility*, {TRUE, FALSE, NULL}) is introduced. The local similarity function for A_1 is as follows:

$$f_{A_1}(q_A, c_A) = \begin{cases} \dfrac{\min\{q_{A_1}, c_{A_1}\}}{\max\{q_{A_1}, c_{A_1}\}}, & q_{A_2} = NULL \vee c_{A_2} = NULL \\ 0, & q_{A_2} = FALSE \wedge c_{A_2} = TRUE \\ 1, & q_{A_2} = FALSE \wedge c_{A_2} = FALSE \\ \dfrac{\min\{q_{A_1}, c_{A_1}\}}{\max\{q_{A_1}, c_{A_1}\}}, & otherwise \end{cases}$$

If the user does not make any specifications in respect of waste storage, the ratio between the area sizes is regarded. If in a current event, waste storage is not possible, the area size of a case that has taken waste storage into account, does not contribute to the overall similarity. Inversely, a case that has not included any waste storage possibilities is regarded as highly valuable for the current problem situation. Hence, a situation in which it is known that waste cannot be stored in the affected area is regarded as more crucial for decision-making than the other way round.

5.3 Summary and Discussion

The retrieve step and similarity assessment of nuclear accidents are implemented in a flexible manner. The user may choose criteria to be included in the similarity assessment. Two events are compared attribute-wise and the user determines for which attribute values equality is required. Furthermore, the influence of each attribute can be controlled by assigning weights to each non-filtering attribute. Finally, the similarity threshold or number of cases envisaged to be retrieved is set individually.

The local similarity functions proposed so far depend on the attribute type as well as its domain properties. The functions result from discussions on the role of the attributes in decision-making as well as analyses of their domains. The latter refers to the influence of specific attribute values on the results. For example, as stated before, INES 7 events result in larger area sizes for measures than other events, which is reflected in the similarity function defined. Furthermore, similarity tables provide good opportunities to state similarity values between specific attribute values. As with all local similarity functions and attribute domains, further refinements are possible and envisaged. The local similarity function for the attribute 'affected area' for example, is rather general since only the ratio between area sizes is regarded. A possible improvement is to work with difference-based similarity functions where the shape of the function reflects how the area sizes of query and case associate.

Especially in the early phases of an accident, uncertainty complicates decision-making. Symbolic attributes allow to describe a problem qualitatively and indirectly such as the accident scenario type indicating potentially released material. The local similarity functions proposed reflect the demanded differentiation between attribute values. For example, weather categories might be closer to each other than different accident types. Furthermore, in terms of attribute selection, filtering, and weights, retrieval can be defined individually for each new query. Unavailable information, for example, may be implemented by omitting the corresponding attribute. Furthermore, uncertainty on attribute values may be reflected in low attribute weights. Hence not only users' preferences but also uncertainty are taken into account in the retrieve step. To improve this approach, stating value ranges for numeric attributes as well as estimating missing values from the case base or other sources are conceivable. The flexibility of the retrieval step proposed open up improvements in various directions. Furthermore, more attributes that are part of the problem description, can be included in the retrieval as well. Once uncertainty decreases and strategies for the long-term post-accident phase are of interest, the characterization of release and the affected area is particularly important for deciding on agricultural and decontamination strategies. Here, new challenges appear such as the problem description of a case only covers parts of the query description in respect of targets as well as users' individual preferences concerning effectiveness parameters that now increasingly reveal. Chapter 6 particularly deals with these issues.

6 Reusing and Merging Strategies

This chapter presents the reuse step of the case-based decision support method comprising numerical adaptation, merging of strategies, and strategy assessment. Numerical adaptation concerns the number of affected people, the area size, the amount of waste, and costs. Merging aims at combining several strategies where each of them covers a subset of the set of targets currently specified. Strategy assessment deals, inter alia, with several effectiveness parameters to compare strategies. The reuse step considers the identification of suitable strategies in diverse ways by (i) adapting numerical quantities to current circumstances, (ii) by taking into account several solutions to cover the entire problem, and (iii) by offering the user a wide decision basis. The numerical adaptation for the number of affected people and the area size is realized by computing the proportion of query and case values for the corresponding attributes. For decontamination strategies, the amount of waste, and costs are adapted according to the area size. For the release phase, costs are oriented towards the number of affected people. Merging (Moehrle, 2013b, 2013a; Moehrle & Raskob, 2019) and strategy assessment (Moehrle, 2014) are presented in the following.

6.1 Merging Strategies of Similar Cases

A strategy corresponds to an instance of the strategy model introduced in Chapter 4.4.1. The strategy model takes into account the targets a measure is directed towards. If a strategy of a retrieved case does not cover all targets currently endangered, another strategy directed towards the missing targets possibly provides additional decision support. The question is how to combine these strategies to cover all targets?

Assume that k similar cases are retrieved from the case base to solve a current problem. Hence, k strategies are available to be reused.

For the sake of clarity, the following **assumptions** are made:

(i) Each net has exactly one initial node and one final node. The initial and final nodes are places of type $\{\cdot\}$.

(ii) Endangerment is produced and reduced completely in each net.

(iii) Resources are completely consumed in each net.

In the course of merging, the focus is on following situations starting with two strategies to be merged. The strategies have a joint event resulting in targets.

(i) Both strategies cover disjoint subsets of targets.

   a. They do not have any measures in common resulting in concurrently implemented measures.

   b. They share the same measure, which enhances the set of transition modes and essentially refers to the situation when a measure is directed towards different targets. The demanded resources rise accordingly.

(ii) Both strategies are directed towards the same targets. The strategies do not have any measure in common resulting in a choice of measures for specific targets.

These situations may be combined and generalized arbitrarily. The purpose of merging is to identify possible strategies if a single strategy only covers part of the problem. The latter primarily refers to the targets currently endangered. Furthermore, if the addressed targets are the same but different strategies are available, the choice of measures should be identified. Hence,

> *merging* of two strategies and hence two Petri nets is conducted at their common equally labeled transitions including corresponding pre- and post-mappings and may result in an extension of place types and transition modes.

Merging focuses on (i) combining several strategies that cover subsets of targets currently endangered; (ii) providing runs taking into account newly combined targets (iii) preserving the original runs of the nets.

Let S_1 and S_2 be two strategies

$$S_i = (P_i, T_i, Dom_i, Type_i, Pre_i, Post_i, M_{0,i})$$

with

$$Pre_i, Post_i: TRANS_i \rightarrow \mu PLACE_i$$

and $L_{m,i}$, $L_{e,i}$ the labeling functions of $S_i, i \in \{1,2\}$. In the following, transitions are referred to by their labels

$$T_i := \{L_{k,i}(t) | t \in T_i, k \in \{m, e\}\}, i \in \{1,2\}.$$

Denote $start \in P_i$ and $end \in P_i, i \in \{1,2\}$ the start and end nodes of the nets.

The merging of the two nets is based on merging the transitions with the same labels, the nodes *start* and *end,* and places that are involved in the pre-and post-mappings of the merged transitions. In the following, the merging of two transitions is investigated further, especially the merged places involved.

Let $t_1 \in T_1$ and $t_2 \in T_2$ with $t_1 = t_2$. Denote

$$TRANS|t_i = \{(t_i, m) | m \in Type(t_i)\}, i \in \{1,2\}$$

$$\tilde{P}_i^{pre} = \{p \in P_i | (p, Type(p)) \in Pre(TRANS|t_i)\}$$

and

$$\tilde{P}_i^{post} = \{p \in P_i | (p, Type(p)) \in Post(TRANS|t_i)\}, i \in \{1,2\}$$

the places involved in the pre- and post-mappings of t_1 and t_2. Two places $p_1 \in \tilde{P}_1^{pre}$ and $p_2 \in \tilde{P}_2^{pre}$ are merged if $Type(p_1)$ and $Type(p_2)$ both belong either to the targets and their endangerment, resources or do not have any characteristics. The merging generates a new place $p \in P^M$ which denotes the set of all new places originating from merging a place of P_1 with a place of P_2. The same applies to places that belong to $\tilde{P}_i^{post}, i \in \{1,2\}$. *Start* and *end* nodes are always merged.

Let

$$I: P_1 \times P_2 \rightarrow P^M$$

a bijective function assigning places $p_1 \in P_1$ and $p_2 \in P_2$ to a place $p \in P^M$. Denote

$$\pi_i: P_1 \times P_2 \to P_i$$

the i-th projection mapping, $i \in \{1,2\}$, and

$$\tilde{P}_i = \{p \in P_i \mid \exists \bar{p} \in P^M: \pi_i(I^{-1}(\bar{p})) = p\}, i \in \{1,2\}$$

the places of S_1 and S_2 that are merged.

Definition 6.1 Merged nets

Let S_1 and S_2 be two strategies with

$$S_i = (P_i, T_i, Dom_i, Type_i, Pre_i, Post_i, M_{0,i}), i \in \{1,2\}$$

The merged nets result in

$$S = (P, T, Dom, Type, Pre, Post, M_0)$$

where

(i) $P = (P_1 \cup P_2 \cup P^M) \backslash (\tilde{P}_1 \cup \tilde{P}_2)$

(ii) $T = T_1 \cup T_2$

(iii) $Dom = Dom_1 \cup Dom_2$

(iv) $Type(p) = \begin{cases} Type_i(p), p \in P_i \backslash \tilde{P}_i, i \in \{1,2\} \\ Type_1(\pi_1(I^{-1}(p))) \cup Type_2(\pi_2(I^{-1}(p))), p \in P^M \end{cases}$

(v) $Type(t) = \begin{cases} Type_i(t), t \in T_i, t \notin T_1 \cap T_2, i \in \{1,2\} \\ Type_1(t) \cup Type_2(t), t \in T_1 \cap T_2 \end{cases}$

(vi) $TRANS = TRANS_1 \cup TRANS_2$

(vii) $Pre, Post: TRANS \to \mu PLACE$ with

$$PLACE = \{(p, g) \mid p \in P, g \in Type(p)\}$$

and for $(t, m) \in TRANS \backslash TRANS_j$

$$Pre(t,m) = \widetilde{Pre}_i(t,m) \tag{6.1}$$

$i \neq j, i, j \in \{1,2\}$ with

$$\widetilde{Pre}_i(t,m) = \sum_{\substack{(p,g)\in PLACE \\ p\notin P^M}} P_\mu^i(p,g)'(p,g) + \sum_{\substack{(p,g)\in PLACE \\ p\in P^M}} P_\mu^i(\pi_i(I^{-1}(p)),g)'(p,g)$$

with $P_\mu^i = Pre_i(t,m)$

and for $(t,m) \in TRANS_1 \cap TRANS_2$

$$Pre(t,m) = \widetilde{Pre}_1(t,m) \text{ or } \widetilde{Pre}_2(t,m) \tag{6.2}$$

The same applies to *Post*, respectively.

(viii) $\mathrm{M}_0 = \mathrm{M}_{0,1} + \mathrm{M}_{0,2}$

6.1.1 Example

Assume three similar cases retrieved from the case base and hence three strategies available for solving the current problem situation. The first strategy (Figure 6.1) is targeted towards 'playground' and 'dairy cow', suggesting 'topsoil removal' and 'cover with clean soil' as well as 'clean feeding'. The first two measures can be implemented concurrently to the last measure.

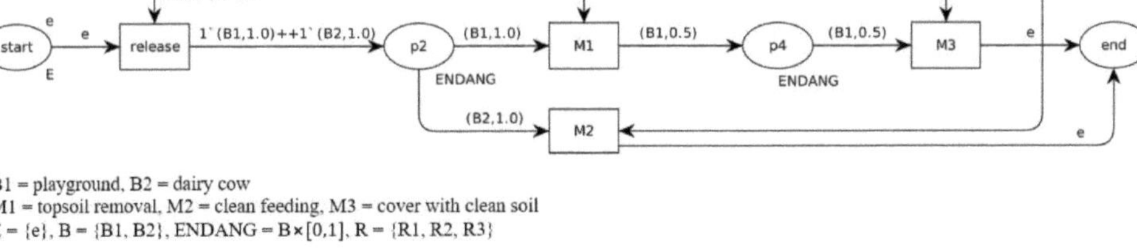

B1 = playground, B2 = dairy cow
M1 = topsoil removal, M2 = clean feeding, M3 = cover with clean soil
E = {e}, B = {B1, B2}, ENDANG = B×[0,1], R = {R1, R2, R3}

Figure 6.1: Strategy directed towards 'playground' and 'dairy cow'

The second strategy (Figure 6.2) suggests 'topsoil removal' and 'plant and shrub removal' to decontaminate the playground. Both measures are implemented sequentially.

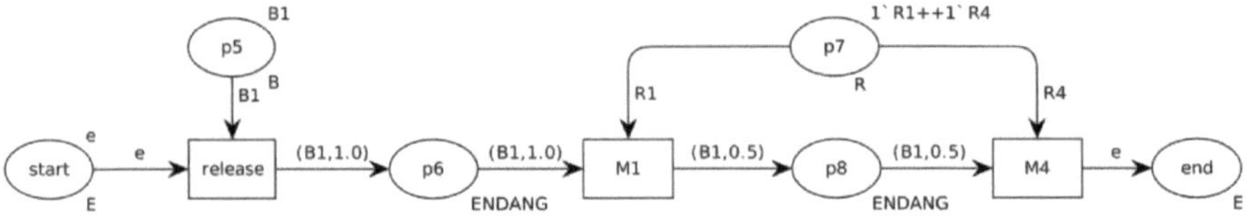

B1 = playground
M1 = topsoil removal, M4 = plant and shrub removal
E = {e}, B = {B1}, ENDANG = B×[0,1], R = {R1, R4}

Figure 6.2: Strategy directed towards 'playground'

The third strategy (Figure 6.3) is directed towards 'park' and suggests 'ploughing' and 'cover with clean soil', both implemented sequentially.

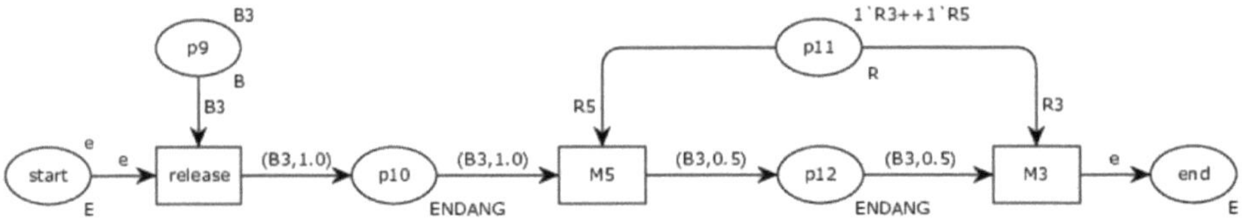

B3 = park
M3 = cover with clean soil, M5 = ploughing
E = {e}, B = {B3}, ENDANG = B×[0,1], R = {R3, R5}

Figure 6.3: Strategy directed towards 'park'

To begin with, the first two strategies are merged (Figure 6.4). The common transitions are 'release' and M1 = topsoil removal. Hence the places involved in the pre- and post-mapping are merged accordingly. The resulting strategy offers a choice of measures with regard to the target 'playground'. After topsoil removal (M1), either 'cover with clean soil' or 'plant and shrub removal' can be implemented. The set of targets is not extended in the course of merging and hence there is no new combination of targets. The functions g and f with B1 = playground and B2 = dairy cow reflect the possible runs:

$$g(i) = \begin{cases} 1`B1 + 1`B2, & i = 1 \\ 1`B1, & i = 2 \end{cases}$$

$$f(i) = \begin{cases} 1`(B1,1.0) + 1`(B2,1.0), & i = 1 \\ 1`(B1,1.0), & i = 2 \end{cases}$$

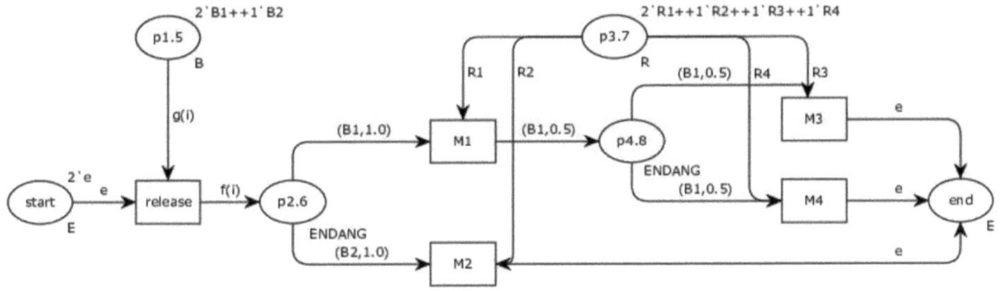

B1 = playground, B2 = dairy cow
M1 = topsoil removal, M2 = clean feeding, M3 = cover with clean soil, M4 = plant and shrub removal
E = {e}, B = {B1, B2}, ENDANG = B×[0,1], R = {R1, R2, R3, R4}

Figure 6.4: Petri net resulting from merging Petri nets of Figure 6.1 and Figure 6.2

Figure 6.5 illustrates the final merged net and merging the net of Figure 6.4 and Figure 6.3, respectively. The merging is based on the common transitions 'release', M1 and M3. The set of targets is enhanced by B3 = park where new combinations of targets are possible now:

$$g(i) = \begin{cases} 1`B1 + 1`B2, & i = 1 \\ 1`B1, & i = 2 \\ 1`B3, & i = 3 \\ 1`B1 + 1`B2 + 1`B3, & i = 4 \\ 1`B1 + 1`B3, & i = 5 \end{cases}$$

$$f(i) = \begin{cases} 1`(B1,1.0) + 1`(B2,1.0), & i = 1 \\ 1`(B1,1.0), & i = 2 \\ 1`(B3,1.0), & i = 3 \\ 1`(B1,1.0) + 1`(B2,1.0) + 1`(B3,1.0), & i = 4 \\ 1`(B1,1.0) + 1`(B3,1.0), & i = 5 \end{cases}$$

The measure M3 is directed towards 'playground' and 'park' and hence the user may choose between M3 and M4 with regard to 'playground': $h(x, 0.5) = 1`(x, 0.5), x \in \{B1, B3\}$.

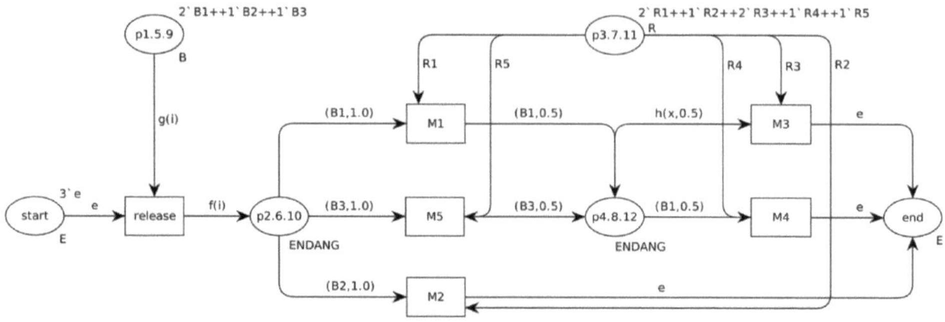

B1 = playground, B2 = dairy cow, B3 = park
M1 = topsoil removal, M2 = clean feeding, M3 = cover with clean soil, M4 = plant and shrub removal, M5 = ploughing
E = {e}, B = {B1, B2, B3}, ENDANG = B×[0,1], R = {R1, R2, R3, R4, R5}

Figure 6.5: Petri net resulting from merging Petri nets of Figure 6.3 and Figure 6.4

6.1.2 Discussion of the Merging Approach

Several strategies are merged in case each strategy retrieved only covers a part of the problem description of the query and a subset of the current targets, respectively. Merging aims at identifying strategies that cover all targets specified in the query. The basic ideas are to merge the common transitions and their pre- and post-mappings where a predefined set of transition labels is assumed. The pre- and post-mappings for common transition modes can be chosen from the pre-and post-mappings of the respective Petri nets that are merged. The pre- and post-mappings of transitions that are not merged remain unchanged. The merging preserves the original runs of the Petri nets and identifies possible new runs for newly combined targets.

The merging approach is generic and neither linked to a specific event nor measure type. So far, the strategy model integrates two decisive factors for measure selection i.e., the targets and the resources needed for implementation. With reference to the key steps in constructing a strategy (see Chapter 3.1.2), a missing factor would be the radionuclides involved. However, the model can be extended according to more decisive factors by including more types. The key steps in selecting and combining measures (see Chapter 3.1.2) include the consideration of the effectiveness and the reduction of contamination as well, which is covered by the strategy model by the degree of endangerment. The notion of effectiveness is discussed in Chapter 6.2.

The consequences of implementing measures e.g., the waste produced or the resulting costs, which are important for the strategy assessment (Chapter 6.2), could be modeled through the post-mappings of the transitions. A subsequent strategy assessment is necessary if several strategies are available for selection. In general, Petri nets offer various possibilities for enhancement such as the duration of implementing a measure or the probability of the occurrence of an event. The duration of implementing a measure might be uncertain and be endowed with a probability distribution as well. Performance analyses related to the duration of a strategy and resource utilization may be used in the assessment providing the user a wide decision basis.

The assumptions stated at the beginning of this chapter reflect to which strategies the decision support method refers to, namely strategies that are endorsed by experts. Constructing scenarios means identifying possible accidents and useful strategies to counter them. The latter refers to, inter alia, eliminating the endangerment. The assumption that a strategy has a fixed start and end node is for reasons of clarity. The start node is a place of type $\{\cdot\}$ that is part of the pre-mapping of the event that triggers the endangerment of certain targets and hence serves as modeling element to enable the initial event transition. The end node is a place of type $\{\cdot\}$ as well, determining the achievement of eliminating the endangerment. Resource modeling can be extended e.g., by modeling alternative resources or resources that are set free after implementing a measure. However, a Petri net in the case base models a strategy with defined type and amount of resources. Hence, within the scope of this work, modeling a complete consumption of resources is sufficient but does not entail any restrictions.

The chapter primarily focuses on strategies underlying a joint event that cause the endangerment of objects, e.g. in the example of Chapter 6.1.1, the release of radioactive material. However, a specialization of the event is possible, resulting in different events that cause the endangerment of targets but which does not limit the merging approach. It is also possible to model an event between two measures, which has effects on the endangerment of the targets. If two strategies have the same intermediate event, the pre- and post-mappings of the merged Petri net is determined according to Equations (6.1) and (6.2) and hence the mappings of the transition modes originally defined.

A transition mode comprises the transition, the target, its degree of endangerment, and possibly resources. The pre- and post-mappings define how transitions change the endangerment of a target. Hence, more special strategies including, for example, a repeated implementation of the same measure until the endangerment is eliminated, is covered by the strategy model as well. Furthermore, assume a strategy that suggests a reversed implementation order of measures than another strategy. The merging of these two strategies would result in a Petri net that reflects the arbitrary implementation order. The merging particularly does not interpret this situation as a contradiction.

As mentioned above, the merging may result in several strategies available for selection. In this case, a subsequent strategy assessment helps the user to decide. The method proposed in the next chapter, mainly integrates different perspectives on assessing a strategy, namely the experience with implementation, robustness towards future uncertainties, quantifiable ratios which can be deduced from simulations, and system-specific parameters, which depend on the underlying decision supporting method. The following chapter discusses an integrative approach bringing different perspectives on a sub-problem together, however, without in-depth investigation but indicating possible research directions.

6.2 Multi-Criteria Assessment of Strategies

For assessing strategies, multi-attribute value theory (MAVT) is proposed supporting participatory decision-making taking into account multiple objectives (decision criteria) in a transparent and structured manner and facilitating consensus finding in groups (Bertsch, 2007; Geldermann et al., 2009). The decision problem is structured hierarchically comprising an overall objective, multiple criteria, attributes, and decision alternatives. Here, attributes make the criteria measurable. After problem structuring, a preference model is constructed that includes elicitating the relative importance of the criteria and hence attribute weights and defining value functions that map the scores of the alternatives with respect to a specific attribute to a common scale. The latter particularly makes the alternatives comparable. Thereafter, the scores of a specific alternative are aggregated in consideration of the value functions and weights, resulting in a ranking of the decision alternatives. If desired, sensitivity analyses may be conducted. These steps are interactive and may be repeated, if necessary (Bertsch, 2007). The focus is on MAVT, since (i) the attribute values are assumed to be deterministic, (ii) the set of alternatives (strategies) is discrete, and (iii) MAVT is successfully applied in related research field (Papamichail & French, 2005) as well as in combination with CBR (see Chapter 2.5).

The strategy assessment aims at (i) ranking different strategies in a transparent manner, (ii) providing a broad discussion basis, and (iii) preserving flexibility to account for the variability of disasters and users' preferences. In particular, the contributions of the different criteria to the overall assessment should be revealed. This can be supported visually, e.g. by stacked-bar charts.

As discussed in Chapter 2.5, various approaches exist to evaluate measures, mainly in terms of performance, through costs, response time, loss, required resources etc. as well as public acceptance. Another approach is to evaluate the robustness and especially to select a strategy that performs sufficiently well for many different scenarios and hence event developments and a changing environment (T. Comes et al., 2010). In addition, strategies that are determined by a decision support system are based on certain methods. Therefore, quantities that help to judge the usefulness of the solution identified, provide decision support as well. In respect of CBR, a confidence value, for example, reflects the accuracy of a solution and besides the similarity values of the retrieved cases, the number of similar cases, the deviation in the solutions of the retrieved cases, the percentage of cases retrieved suggesting a specific solution or the span of the solutions could be taken into account (Cheetham, 2000). Evaluation measures are particularly introduced in Chapter 2.1.4.

The contribution of this chapter is to integrate different perspectives on strategy assessment. Existing assessment approaches either focus on system-specific parameters solely, or the robustness of strategies by elaborating scenarios, or focus on costs, efficacy, or public acceptance and hence current conditions. MAVT enables to integrate these different approaches taking into account users' preferences. The strategy assessment proposed in this chapter is independent of the event but depends on CBR and related parameters such as the similarity value. A previous publication (Moehrle, 2014) discusses this topic independently of the event and assumes a case base of historical events. In the framework of nuclear emergencies, the majority of cases are scenarios where the strategies are based on reference levels for the residual dose and are judged according to costs, the amount of waste produced, public acceptance, or feasibility in general. Hence, one branch of the proposed attribute tree (Moehrle, 2014) is adapted to nuclear emergencies and particularly quantities that are actually computable. The paper treats strategy assessment from a more general point of view by regarding fatalities, injured, damage to economy, and environment. Furthermore, the terminology is adapted and the former notion 'old assessments' that reflects historical values on damages is changed into 'effectiveness'. The effectiveness of a strategy measures how well the strategy achieves the objectives (Rongier et al., 2012) and i.e., reducing the level of radiation exposure to human and returning to normal living conditions. Depending on the type of measure, there are concrete definitions of effectiveness (J. Brown, Watson, Nisbet, 2015; Nisbet & Watson, 2015b, 2015a) that mainly express the reduction of contamination in or on the target after implementing a measure[1]. In particular, the effectiveness refers to radiological aspects solely. In the frame of this thesis, societal aspects as well as produced waste are subsumed under the branch 'effectiveness' since they contribute to the objective of returning to normal living conditions as well. Their importance may vary during an accident such as the amount of waste, which is relevant in respect of decontamination. Hence the notion of effectiveness actually changes in the course of an accident but which can be taken into account in MAVT. The effectiveness of a strategy is one branch of the hierarchy for assessment and reflects a current status in contrast to discussions on robustness by investigating possible future developments. The other branches of the hierarchy utilize that strategies are derived by JRodos and are based on a Petri net model and that the core method, CBR, has its own ranking induced by the retrieval task as defined in Chapter 5.1. The strategy assessment is mainly formulated for the long-term accident phase when more time is available and particularly the merging of several strategies is applied and the set of targets is more diverse. This chapter intends to round off the identification of a suitable strategy for decision support, mainly by integrating the approaches elaborated so far as well as in consideration of the application field. The following hierarchy of criteria (Figure 6.6) proposes how the

[1] Owed to the type of measure, the effectiveness of fixing measures is defined differently and refers to the reduction of the inhalation dose after implementing a measure (Nisbet & Watson, 2015b).

integration could be realized. Especially, the choice of attributes may be refined but which goes beyond the scope of this thesis.

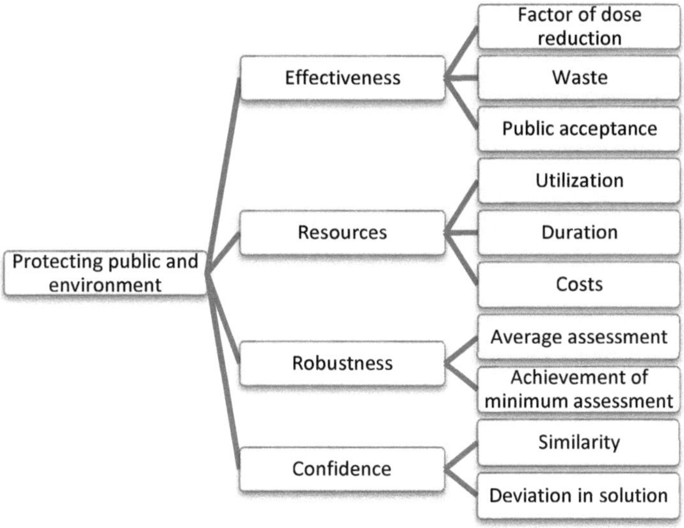

Figure 6.6: Hierarchy of criteria and attributes for strategy assessment

The overall objective is to protect public and environment (Figure 3.3) being decomposed into 'effectiveness', 'resources, 'robustness', and 'confidence'. The effectiveness can be measured according to (i) the factor of dose reduction, which is the ratio between the dose received after implementing a specific strategy and the dose received without implementing this strategy (see chapter 3.3), (ii) the amount of waste, and (iii) public acceptance. Introducing the factor of dose reduction intends to generalize the definitions of effectiveness mentioned above. Public acceptance may be measured qualitatively, such as in the categories 'high' and 'low' (L. Lin et al., 2014).

The criterion 'resources' states through which means the objectives are achieved and e.g., which resources and to what extent they are utilized. Resources are particularly covered in the strategy model, as introduced in chapter 4.4.1., which allows the refinement according to time for implementing a measure or the entire strategy. Uncertainties in respect of duration can be expressed through probability distributions. These uncertainties may originate from an uncertain amount of available equipment, personnel, or relief units, for example, or targets of the measures. In particularly, concurrently implemented measures may lead to delays during the implementation of a strategy, since, for example, concurrently implemented measures need to be finished before further measures can be implemented. Besides the duration of implementing a measure, the number of equipment, personnel, or relief units that potentially 'wait' because of delays during the implementation, is an interesting quantity as well, which can be expressed in the notion 'utilization'. Both, utilization and duration are quantities that result from simulations of strategies emphasizing the advantage of the strategy model that is based on Petri nets. Given an initial marking, simulations of Petri nets produce a sequence of markings aiming at, amongst others, analyses of quantitative aspects such as throughput times and costs (Oberweis, 1996). In the frame of this work, the costs of a strategy can be determined by JRodos.

The criterion 'robustness' considers uncertainties with regard to the extent of a disaster, changing environmental conditions, or insufficient information. One approach is to investigate different scenarios, to assess the different strategies and particularly the effectiveness under these varying conditions, and aggregate the scores for the different strategies over all scenarios (T. Comes et al., 2010). One may also demand a minimum score a strategy should achieve and count the frequency of achievement. The latter approach can be found in the industrial field in the course of assessing the robustness of a plan (Scholl, 2000). Evaluating the robustness of strategies is time-consuming and requires the cooperation of experts of different fields (M. Comes, 2011). Hence, an in-depth investigation is mainly possible in the later phases of a nuclear accident. For the early phases, a light version is conceivable by fixing decision-relevant factors that may be subject to variations, such as the source term or the weather category, and assessing different strategies under a predefined set of possible values of these factors. This step can particularly be automated.

The criterion 'confidence' refers to CBR and specifically the similarity values of the cases retrieved. In addition, a strategy that consists of measures that are part of other solutions retrieved may appear more trustworthy to the user than a complete new strategy. Hence, the deviation in the solution from other solutions is integrated in determining the confidence as well. Of course, further approaches exist to evaluate a CBR solution as introduced in chapter 2.1.4. For demonstration purposes, values associated to retrieval and reuse, respectively, are chosen to measure the criterion 'confidence'.

6.2.1 Example

Assume a release where 300 inhabitants are endangered and two strategies are provided by the decision support method after merging (Figure 6.7).

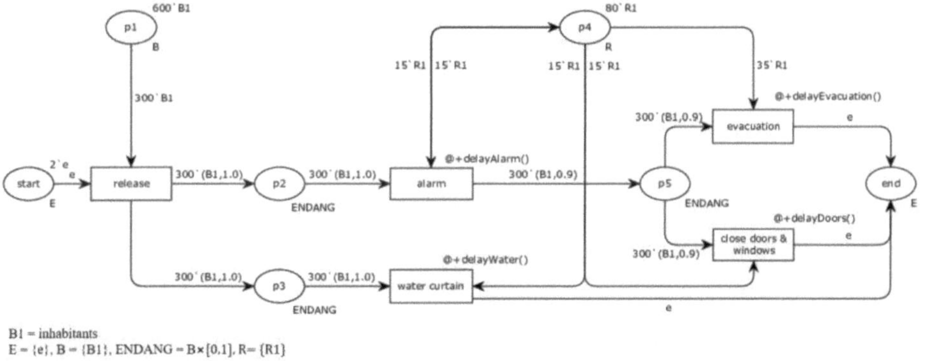

Figure 6.7: Strategies entering the assessment provided with delay functions to model uncertainty

The first strategy (A) suggests, after giving alarm, to ask the inhabitants in the surrounding area to close their doors and windows. Meanwhile, a water curtain should be established. The second strategy (B) suggests an evacuation instead of closing doors and windows. For the durations of the measures a normal distribution $N(\mu, \sigma^2)$ is assumed with the following means (μ) and variances (σ^2): 'alarm' $N(2, 0.2)$, 'close doors and windows' $N(4, 0.4)$, 'water curtain' $N(8, 3)$, 'evacuation' $N(13, 9)$. Values for the mean and variance are understood as relative time used for comparison. Strategy A needs 30 relief units, which are divided into two groups. Strategy B needs 50 relief units where 35 relief units are needed for alarm and evacuation and 15 relief units establish the water curtain. The strategies include few measures and hence there are no real waiting relief units. Exemplarily, the different durations of the concurrently implemented measures 'alarm' and 'close doors and windows' and 'water curtain' as well as 'alarm' and 'evacuation' and 'water curtain' are regarded as source for a potential delay. In particular, the ratio between the average time differences between the completion of 'water curtain' and 'close doors & windows' and 'water curtain' and 'evacuation', multiplied with the number of waiting relief units and the average duration of the entire strategy, multiplied with the number of all relief units, is determined. Table 6.1 shows the average values received by simulating each strategy 1000 times with CPN Tools. Assume the strategies are based on long releases causing medium contamination. For assessing the robustness of the strategies, two scenarios are considered: long release with first high and second low contamination. For each scenario, the effectiveness and costs of each strategy is estimated (Table 6.2) to get an average score for each strategy over both scenarios where the probability value for the first scenario is set 0.7 and for the second scenario 0.3. The attribute values are aggregated according to the weighted sum. The weights can be chosen between 0 and 10 where 0 is interpreted as 'unimportant' and 10 as 'most important'. Furthermore, a minimal value is demanded each strategy should achieve and is set exemplarily to 0.4. To make the alternatives comparable, the attribute values are mapped lineally to the interval [0,1] where the upper and lower bounds as shown in Table 6.3 are worst and best attribute values, respectively. Values of dose reduction, utilization, similarity, and deviation in solution are already in the interval [0,1]. Public acceptance is mapped to 1 and 0 for the values 'high' and 'low', respectively. In order to maintain the correct interpretability, inverse value functions such as for dose reduction, waste, costs, average duration, and deviation in solution are applied to maintain the interpretation: the higher the value, the better. It is assumed that Strategy A results from a retrieved case with similarity 0.6 whereas the case Strategy B results from has similarity 0.9. Since there are only two strategies to choose from, the deviation in solution only reflects the differences between them, which is set to 0.33 to show that only one measure differs.

Table 6.1: Attribute values included in the assessment

	Strategy A	Strategy B	Unit	Weight
Factor of dose reduction	0.8	0.1	-	9
Waste	1000	1000	Liter	1
Public acceptance	high	low	-	5
Average utilization	0.823	0.812	-	1
Average duration	7.59	19.833	-	2
Costs	100000	300000	Euro	1
Average assessment	0.492	0.552	-	3
Achievement of minimum assessment	1	1	-	3
Similarity	0.6	0.9	-	8
Deviation in solution	0.33	0.33	-	6

Table 6.2: Attribute values for assessing the robustness of the strategies

		Factor of dose reduction	Waste	Public acceptance	Costs	Strategy assessment
Scenario 1	Strategy A	0.9	2000	High	300000	0.45
	Strategy B	0.2	2000	Low	500000	0.52
Scenario 2	Strategy A	0.7	800	High	100000	0.59
	Strategy B	0.05	800	Low	300000	0.63
Unit		-	Liter	-	Euro	-
Weight		9	1	5	1	

Table 6.3: Upper and lower bounds for determining the value functions

Attribute	Upper bound	Lower bound
Waste	5000	0
Costs	1000000	0
Average duration	24	6

Strategy A and B are assessed with the MCDA Tool developed at KIT[2]. Figure 6.8 depicts the result of the strategy assessment where strategy B is identified as more appropriate for achieving the overall objective. The stacked-bar chart illustrates the

[2] https://portal.iket.kit.edu/projects/MCDA/

contributions of each attribute to the final result. Sensitivity analyses show the solutions' stability with regard to changes in the attribute weights, which may result in a change in ranking. For example, change in the attribute weight of 'costs' would not alter the ranking (Figure 6.9) whereas a decrease of the attribute weight for 'factor of dose reduction' leads to an increase of the assessment value for strategy A up to a ranking change of strategy A and B (Figure 6.10).

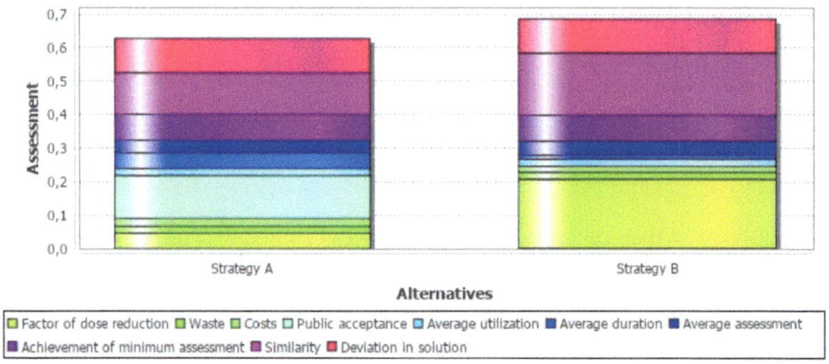

Figure 6.8: Assessment of strategies illustrated as stacked-bar chart

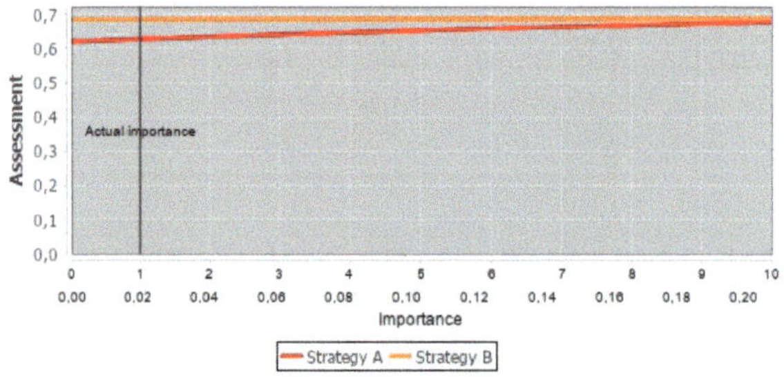

Figure 6.9: Stability of result according to changes in the weight of 'costs'

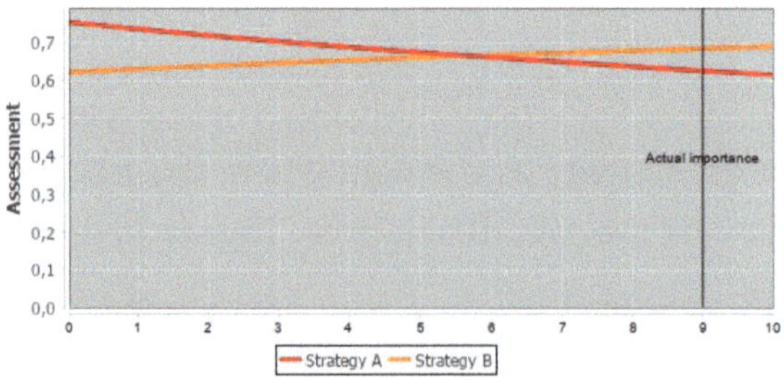

Figure 6.10: Stability of result according to changes in the weight of 'factor of dose reduction'

6.3 Summary and Discussion

The reuse step of the case-based decision support method includes (i) numerical adaptations for the number of affected people, area size as well as amount of waste and costs, (ii) merging of several strategies to cover a large set of currently targets, and (iii) strategy assessment, in case several strategies are available. Numerical adaptations utilize the relations between the number of affected people and costs for the release phase, and the area size and the amount of waste and costs for the later phases. Missing values can be determined with the help of the population distribution category or the population density.

The idea of merging is to merge the common active components of the Petri nets, which are common events leading to endangerment and measures reducing the endangerment as well as their pre- and post-mappings. The latter are enhanced to both preserve the original runs and identify possible new runs for newly combined targets, which essentially results from preserving all possibilities each net is offering. In particular, the sets of transition modes are unified, the pre- and post-mappings of common transition modes can be chosen from the original mappings, and for non-common transition modes, the original mappings are maintained. The objectives are to identify strategies that cover all targets specified in the query and clearly reveal where a choice of measures is available. Besides the type that specifies the targets with its degree of endangerment, the examples introduce a further type, which is the target solely. This way of modeling enables to specifically analyze new combinations of targets and the proposed combination of measures.

The basic idea of strategy assessment is to integrate commonly discussed approaches in the literature that refer to performance measures and investigating robustness. A new approach is to integrate CBR related values that reflect the trustworthiness of the solutions proposed. MAVT is suggested to bring together the different views on strategy assessment providing a wide discussion basis for the user where each contribution of the attributes values to the overall result becomes visible. MAVT not only provides a way to rank different strategies but also offers a structured and transparent procedure of strategy assessment taking into account users' preferences and uncertainties. With a suitable tool, the users can discuss and analyze the results according to their sensitivity in respect of the weights or attribute values set. The multi-criteria assessment proposed particularly considers current conditions, possible future developments, utilizes simulations to account for current constraints and uncertainties with regard to time, for example, and facilitates users' trust and understanding in the mechanism of the decision support method by integrating confidence values.

The reuse of prepared strategies aims at offering an appropriate strategy to counter the current problem situation. Besides numerical adaptations to match current measurable or assessable quantities, a challenge is to determine a strategy that takes into account all targets currently endangered. Constructing scenarios intends to cover a wide range of possible problem descriptions. However, working with similarities allows deviations that may demand several strategies from different cases to be combined. This chapter proposes how the combination can be realized and emphasizes the added value the Petri net approach offers. The subsequent multi-criteria assessment integrates different approaches ranging from evaluating the effectiveness and robustness, parameters deduced from simulations to method-specific quantities. Hence, reuse includes discussing possible strategies with the help of different criteria as well, preferably in a structured way with visual support as the proposed approach and tool enables. This chapter finalizes the methodical background of the case-based decision support. The following chapter is dedicated to implementation and evaluation by means of a specific example.

7 Implementation and Evaluation

This chapter presents the prototypical implementation of the case-based decision support method as well as its evaluation. The 'Case-based reasoning application software' (CBR application in the following)[1] resulted from joint work within the working group 'Accident Management Systems' at the Institute for Thermal Energy Technology and Safety of the Karlsruhe Institute of Technology (KIT) and was presented at the NERIS workshop[2] in Dublin in 2018 (Moehrle et al., 2018, 2019). The implementation focuses on the core method CBR with its case base and the graphical user interface and can be improved in following directions: (i) Modeling of strategies as Petri nets and integrating them in the case base; (ii) Extending the merging step to process Petri nets; (iii) Building the connections between CPN Tools, CBR Application, and the MCDA Tool developed at KIT. With regard to the latter, information exchange is realized via XML files and hence the CBR Application can be enhanced accordingly. Since the method CBR is not restricted to nuclear emergencies only, research has been conducted in various directions as well. The application is set up in a flexible way to be expandable to other event types. In the following, the current state of the application is presented that goes beyond nuclear emergencies. The integration of different event types in a decision support application is especially interesting in disaster management (Moehrle et al., 2019).

7.1 Architecture Overview

The CBR application is embedded in a web-based client server architecture. Over the last decades, web technologies have entered the development of decision support systems resulting in many successful application examples (Bhargava, Power, & Sun, 2007). Besides the access to decision supporting tools via a web browser, web technologies particularly facilitate communication and decision-making in distrib-

1 http://portal.iket.kit.edu/CBR/

2 https://www.eu-neris.net/activities/workshops/dublin-2018.html

uted teams (Power, 2000). Moreover, analysis and computation are platform-independent, remote, and distributed which facilitates information exchange. Also, system maintenance is simplified and centralized (Bhargava et al., 2007).

The management process of nuclear emergencies is complex involving various activities and corresponding responsibilities (Carter & French, 2005). Particularly, the institutions providing support and advice to the decision-makers may be located at different places. Therefore, a system that is accessible from different locations where the input and results can be synchronized and shared between the persons in charge is of great value. A web-based application is well suited to fulfill this task, greatly simplifying the requirements of software and hardware as only a mobile device with a web browser is needed. Furthermore, besides the general usefulness of CBR in the frame of disaster management, a web-based access particularly facilitates knowledge sharing (Otim, 2006). As some of the scientific discussions revolve around emergency management handling multiple disaster types at the same time new challenges in the system's architecture arise. In particular, after the Fukushima Daiichi nuclear power plant accident, one discussion topic was emergency preparedness with a special focus on severe accidents possibly linked to natural disasters (International Atomic Energy Agency (IAEA), 2015b). This chapter proposes a generic system design allowing easy expandability of existing structures as well as integration of new event types.

Figure 7.1 illustrates the web-based client server architecture and the information exchange of the single components: the frontend GUI, the backend CBR application, and the knowledge database (KDB) where the scenarios and historical accidents as well as general information for decision support are stored.

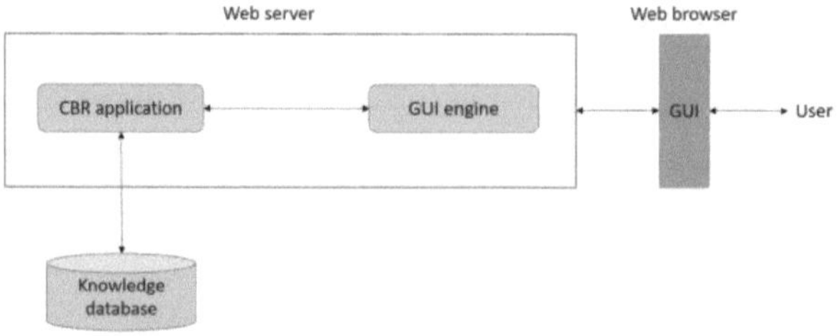

Figure 7.1: Overview of the architecture

7.1.1 Knowledge Database

So far, natural events such as earthquakes and storms and nuclear accidents are stored in different schemes in the KDB. An excerpt of the scheme for storing the cases reported in this thesis has already been illustrated (Chapter 4.5, Figure 4.4). The KDB was enhanced within the subsequent project HARMONE (Bai, Staudt, Kaiser, & Raskob, 2018) focusing on remediation strategies for inhabited areas and food production systems for long-term management according to another scheme. In the following, 'HARMONE event' particularly refers to scenarios developed during this project. Furthermore, research on natural disasters was conducted in the frame of CEDIM's (Center for Disaster Management and Risk Reduction Technology) Forensic Disaster Analysis (FDA) that was concerned with near-real time analyses of disasters and their impacts (Möhrle & Raskob, 2014). In the course of this project, earthquake events from the CATDAT damaging earthquake database (Daniell, Khazai, Wenzel, & Vervaeck, 2011) were integrated into the KDB which primarily focus on resulting damages. Multiple disaster types may occur at the same time promoting the development of a system capable of analyzing different event types. So far, the database is populated with 512 cases of which 178 are nuclear events and 334 are natural events, mainly earthquakes.

7.1.2 CBR Application

The CBR application of this thesis is developed on the basis of jCOLIBRI2 (Recio-García, González-Calero, & Díaz-Agudo, 2014) that is further enhanced in several application-specific directions, such as the structure of the solution description and the reuse step allowing combinations of measures. Each event type has its own configuration directory storing information on database access and classes building a case.

The CBR application is started when a new event is specified and a corresponding XML document with information about the event type and its characteristics is loaded. Accordingly, the application is configured. With regard to nuclear accidents, the application distinguishes project-dependent events and PREPARE and HARMONE, respectively. The latter particularly does not regard accident phases and covers always the long-term post-accident phase. The cases are loaded and accessed subsequently for the similarity calculation. In case of a nuclear accident (PREPARE), similar cases are retrieved for each phase involving a configuration of the similarity function, respectively. Depending on the accident phase again, cases are either adapted only or adapted and merged, if necessary. For the pre-release phase, no adaptation steps are conducted since the strategies consist of rule-based measures without any quantities. After calculating suggested solutions, the results are written in an XML document. If there is a triggering event such as an earthquake event, similar triggering events and their damages are determined to be added to the final result XML document. Figure 7.2 gives a brief overview of the main program flow.

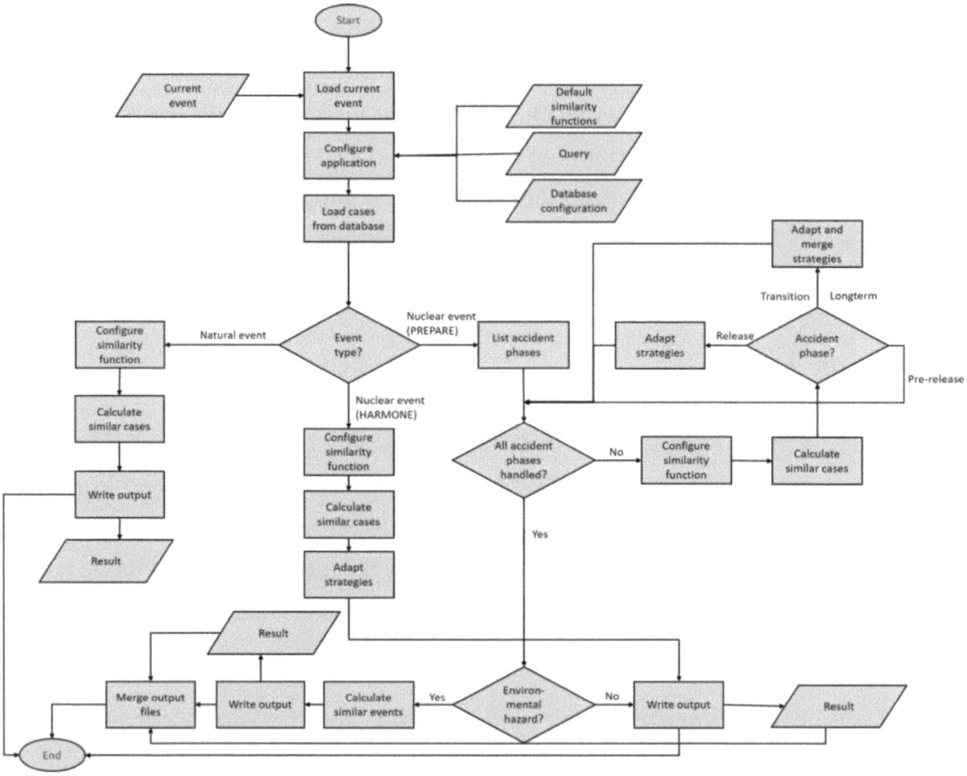

Figure 7.2: Flow chart of the main class of the CBR application

Interaction of CBR Application and GUI Engine

The information exchange between the CBR application and the GUI engine as well as generation of the event type dependent input mask is realized in a generic and flexible manner. When accessing the start page of the user interface, one may select the event type for which a query is to be formulated. The GUI engine generates the corresponding input mask based on a pre-defined XML document that contains information on the attributes, their domains, and their domain formats such as multiple lists or text fields. The user may then specify the query and send a request with the current event description as well as configurations on retrieval and the similarity function. In case of earthquakes and storms, the user may select the desired information on damages of past events as well.

With the user requests, an XML document is created and passed on to the CBR application by the GUI engine. The CBR application has now information on the event type, attributes selected, their specified values, attribute weights, and realization of the two-step retrieval and, in case of earthquakes and storms, information of past events the user is interested in. The two-step retrieval particularly enables to first filter the set of problem descriptions and calculate the similarities between the query and the remaining cases afterwards. The user may select the corresponding filter attributes and may state a similarity threshold or the number of desired cases, respectively. In case of nuclear events, the accident phase is specified as well, for which possible solutions are needed. According to the event type, the CBR application connects to the corresponding database schemes and determines solutions, which are damages or measures. The results are stored in an XML document and passed on to the GUI engine for displaying the results to the user.

In addition to the exchange of XML documents between the CBR application and the GUI engine, the latter can import and export XML documents from and to other sources as well. Furthermore, each query is stored with a time stamp and can be opened again later.

Figure 7.3 sums up the basic information exchange. The grey boxes depict the different steps from selecting an event type to illustrating the results. The dotted arrows show the processing of information specified via the GUI by the GUI engine.

The solid arrows indicate the exchange of XML documents. CBR application and KDB connect via XML documents as well.

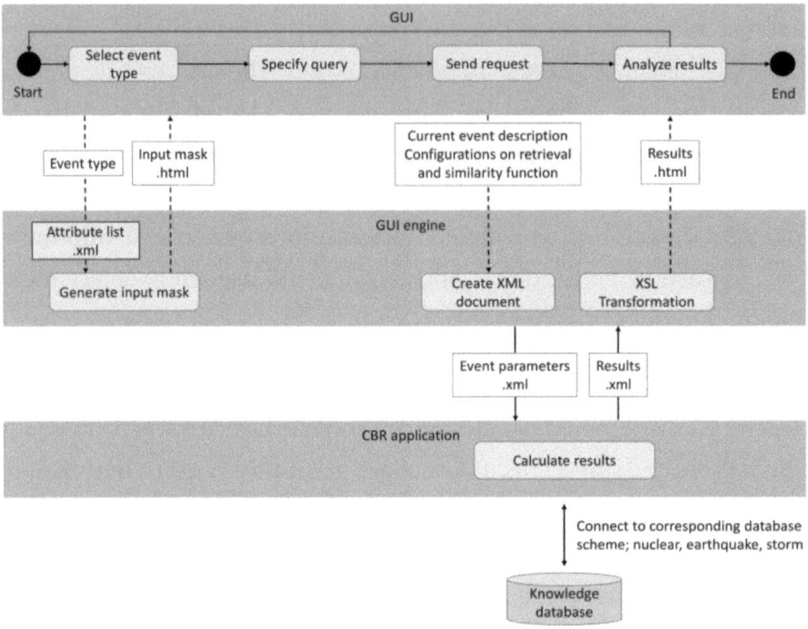

Figure 7.3: Interaction between CBR application and GUI engine

Enhancing Existing Structures and Integrating New Event Types

Since knowledge is stored in a database, current tables and structures may be enhanced easily and if necessary, new schemes can be created, particularly if a new event type should be integrated into the decision supporting software. On the CBR application side, corresponding classes and configuration files need to be updated. Since the GUI is generated by the GUI engine on the basis of an XML document, further attributes can be easily integrated. Here, the name of the attribute, the type and domain as well as default local similarity function characteristics can be specified (Figure 7.4).

```
<attribute>
        <name> population distribution</name>
        <type>List</type>
        <value>metropolitan,rural,urban</value>
        <localSim>true</localSim>
        <weight>5.</weight>
        <active>true</active>
        <outName>populationDistribution</outName>
</attribute>
```

Figure 7.4: Excerpt of the GUI generating XML document

Regarding the CBR application, assigning local similarity functions to attributes is configured in an event-type independent document. Possibly, as new event types imply new attributes, new local and global similarity functions need to be implemented and assigned. Depending on the type of event to be included, the package structure of the CBR application needs to extended, accordingly. Currently, natural and nuclear events are distinguished whereas structures for problem and solution describing classes are defined. Possibly, new adaptation mechanisms need to be included. The configuration directory of the CBR application is structured to different event types and needs to be enhanced accordingly. Figure 7.5 depicts the database configuration document. The main class of the CBR application realizes the CBR cycle whereas different actions are triggered by the event type. Further enhancements concern the event type dependent presentation of the final results being prepared by the GUI engine.

```
<DataBaseConfiguration>
    <HibernateConfigFile>nuclearEvent/hibernate.cfg.xml</HibernateConfigFile>
    <DescriptionMappingFile>nuclearEvent/eventDescription.hbm.xml</DescriptionMappingFile>
    <DescriptionClassName>dss.eventDescription.nuclear.NuclearEvent</DescriptionClassName>
    <SolutionMappingFile>nuclearEvent/strategy.hbm.xml</SolutionMappingFile>
    <SolutionClassName>dss.solutionDescription.nuclear.Solution</SolutionClassName>
    <JustificationOfSolutionClassName>dss.justificationDescription.nuclear.GeneralJustification
    </JustificationOfSolutionClassName>
    <JustificationOfSolutionMappingFile>nuclearEvent/justification.hbm.xml
    </JustificationOfSolutionMappingFile>
</DataBaseConfiguration>
```

Figure 7.5: Database configuration of the CBR application

7.1.3 Graphical User Interface

The web-based user interface is a comfortable way to access the CBR application, in particular to obtain first suggestions on reasonable strategies in an emergency, without any pre-required software installations except of a web browser. Users can specify and configure the similarity calculation individually and hence integrate their preferences and expertise.

Different event types and their corresponding input masks are prepared and can be chosen from a drop-down list. Moreover, besides default interfaces for each event type, already calculated events can be retrieved and selected or imported from another location.

In case of nuclear events, different tabs are prepared to structure the event specification, particularly according to different accident phases. The attributes types range from numerical values to symbols, whereas for the latter combo boxes with single or multiple selection options are provided. Weights from 1 (almost not important) to 10 (highly important) can be entered in a text field and checkboxes activate filter attributes, if desired. Figure 7.6 shows the input mask. The user can choose different event types for which different input masks are prepared.

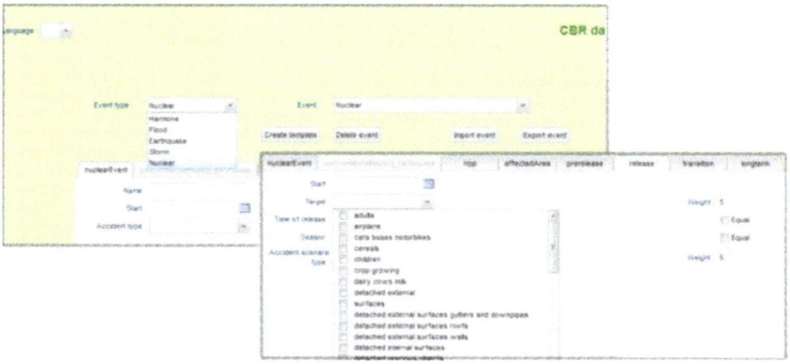

Figure 7.6: Input mask of the CBR application

After specifying query and similarity functions, the calculation can be launched. The user can set a similarity threshold or fixed number of cases considered for the final result. The results are shown in a newly generated tab assigned with a timestamp. For the nuclear cases, a condensed strategy, combining measures, targets, and further information is provided. Moreover, information on the chosen cases as well as effectiveness values or results from simulated strategies in inhabited areas or food production systems are displayed. The retrieved cases can also be analyzed more in detail and can be expanded and collapsed for better clarity. Figure 7.7 depicts some example results for nuclear events.

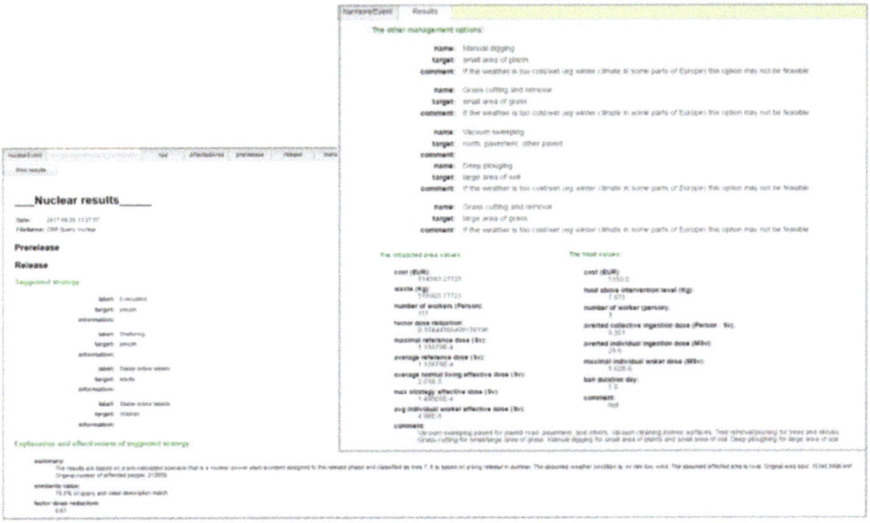

Figure 7.7: Result tab exemplarily on the basis of a nuclear query

7.1.4 Open Points

As stated before and as can be seen in the screenshots of the results (Figure 7.7), the strategies are not yet modeled as Petri nets but the measures are stored in a list with a defined course of action. The merging class rather focuses on (i) sorting the measures from the cases according to different exposure pathways, (ii) keeping measures that are directed towards current targets, and (iii) filtering measures according to the soil type. The latter is particularly an attribute that may be specified by the user in the input mask and which is for adaptation only. The implementation of the merging approach presented in this thesis can be realized by processing XML or PNML documents, the formats CPN Tools provides for storing the strategies.

Furthermore, the scenarios are subject of reuse only and the historical events are provided as additional information to learn from since they rather demonstrate issues in emergency management than being positive examples. As stated before, the connections between the CBR application, CPN Tools, and the MCDA Tool have to be closely established. To be more precise, the CBR application needs to be enhanced in several ways, in particular to better process the simulation results from CPN Tools, and consider the analysis results according to robustness, CBR related quantities as well as effectiveness values from the retrieved cases. Thereby the user is offered a broader decision basis. Figure 7.8 illustrates how the application can be extended accordingly. The solid arrows indicate exchanges of documents. Basically, further classes that are concerned with the strategy evaluation need to be integrated where separate classes for each criterion are suggested.

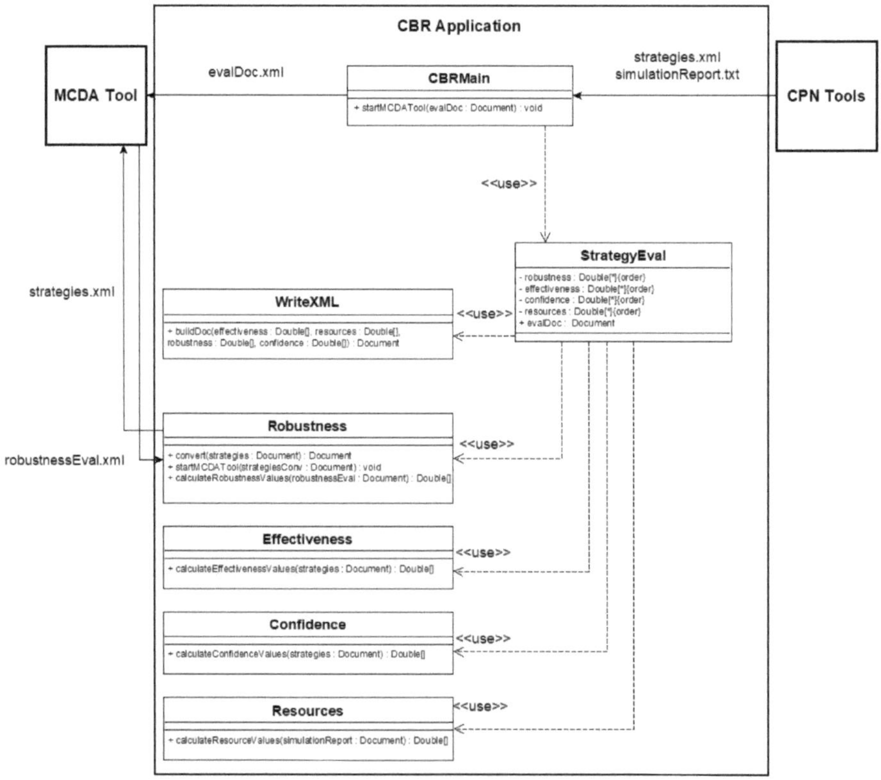

Figure 7.8: Overview of necessary connections between the MCDA Tool, CBR Application, and CPN Tools

7.2 Evaluation of the Developed Method

This chapter presents the evaluation of the decision support method by means of a case study that is derived from the Fukushima Daiichi nuclear power plant accident. The evaluation aims at examining the achievement of the objectives formulated in Chapter 1.2. The approach is to analyze the Fukushima Daiichi nuclear power plant accident, to identify points in time the developed method could be applied, to compare the results with the strategies that were implemented in reality, and discuss the provided decision support. The evaluation particularly should demonstrate the added value of applying the elaborated method in emergency management. Hence, the **objectives** pursued are to evaluate if the developed method

(i) provides decision support for all phases of a nuclear accident and in particular identifies coherent strategies as discussion basis,

(ii) suggests how to handle with the crucial issue of uncertainty in nuclear emergency management

(iii) integrates experience and expert knowledge for decision support,

(iv) takes into account different stakeholders with partially conflicting objectives,

(v) supports the harmonization work in Europe, also by supporting the interaction with other tools for emergency management, and

(vi) is applicable, especially by means of the prototypical implementation.

The case study for evaluating the method is oriented towards the Fukushima Daiichi nuclear power plant accident (Bundesamt für Strahlenschutz, 2012; Gesellschaft für Anlagen- und Reaktorsicherheit (GRS), 2016; International Atomic Energy Agency (IAEA), 2015a, 2015b) that was triggered by the Tohoku earthquake occurred at 14:46 local time on 11 March 2011 and the subsequent tsunami at the northeast coast of Japan. The tsunami reached the Japanese coast approximately 40 minutes after the earthquake. The main wave reaching the nuclear power plant arrived about 50 minutes after the earthquake with a height of more than 14 meters, exceeding the tsunami barrier seawalls that were designed to protect against a maximum tsunami height of 5.5 m.

At the time of the earthquake, units 1-3 were in operation and units 4-6 were shut down due to revisions. The earthquake led to the loss of off-site power and all operating reactors to be shut down. The units at the power plant responded as intended by the designers and as stipulated in the operating procedures. However, the tsunami flooded emergency diesel generators and batteries resulting in a station blackout[3]. Hence water injection and cooling of the fuel rods and monitoring of the reactors were not possible anymore. Amongst others, destroyed infrastructure complicated the injection with fresh water and the missing cooling of the fuel rods led to core meltdowns in units 1, 2, and 3 resulting in damages in the containment. Consequently, radioactive fission products were released. Oxidizing cladding tube material produced additional heat and hydrogen gas and units 1, 3, and 4 were severely damaged due to hydrogen explosions. In total, several 100 Petabequerel iodine equivalent were released, mainly iodine 131 and cesium 137. The amount of discharged radioactive materials to the environment is approximately 10 percent of the Chernobyl accident where an explosion of the reactor threw material such as strontium and plutonium in the environment. Moreover, fire carried radioactive material in great heights and distances. However, the oceanic release from the Fukushima Daiichi nuclear power plant was the largest release of radionuclides from a nuclear accident into an ocean, mainly due to direct release of radioactive liquid effluents and atmospheric deposition. During the first days of the accident, most of the particles were blown out over the pacific. On the 15 and 16 March 2011, wind from southeast in combination with precipitation carried the particles to northwest in range of several dozen kilometers. Contrasting to the Chernobyl accident, the contaminated area around the Fukushima Daiichi power plant is smaller, even if the highest measured doses are similar in both accidents..

Table 7.1 highlights some events and implemented measures and particularly points in time when the developed decision support method (which is referred to

[3] A station blackout occurred if there is no power supply via electricity network nor emergency diesel generators. In this case, selected components are supplied by batteries which last 10 h for Unit 1, for example.

as 'CBR method' in the following) could be applied. The complex accident sequence is therefore reduced for the purpose of this evaluation. Furthermore, published INES classifications are depicted. With regard to the long-term post-accident phase, the focus is on the remediation of contaminated areas excluding the stabilization of the reactors and preparation for eventual decommissioning, waste management, and rehabilitation of the communities, which are tasks of recovery as well (International Atomic Energy Agency (IAEA), 2015c). Remediation is defined as "any measures that may be carried out to reduce the radiation exposure from existing contamination of land areas through actions applied to the contamination itself (the source) or to the exposure pathways to humans […]" (International Atomic Energy Agency (IAEA), 2007, p. 166). Due to the limited scenarios for the long-term post-accident phase, the focus is especially on decontamination measures. The division of the accident phases and particularly the beginning of the transition phase cannot be declared globally but needs to be defined area-wise. In particular, areas where first decontamination measures were planned and implemented might be assigned to the transition phase. In general, defining the start and end points of the various phases clearly can be difficult and different accident phases may coexist in different areas (International Atomic Energy Agency (IAEA), 2018). The division in Table 7.1 is based on the definition in Chapter 3.1 as well as the divisions provided by the IAEA (International Atomic Energy Agency (IAEA), 2015c, 2018).

Table 7.1: Timeline of the Fukushima Daiichi Nuclear Power Plant Accident. Selected points in time are illustrated. CBR *x* indicates points in time to apply the CBR method.

Date		Event	Ordered measures	Official accident classification	Accident phase
2011	11 Mar	Tsunami		Nuclear emergency (Japanese Government)	Pre-release CBR 1
		Starting to plan venting	Evacuation in a 2 km radius around the plant		
		Core of unit 2 predicted to become uncovered	▪ Evacuation in a 3 km radius around the plant ▪ Sheltering within 3-10 km radius		

Date		Event	Ordered measures	Official accident classification	Accident phase
		without cooling			
	12 Mar	Primary containment vessel of unit 1 exceeds max. design pressure; Venting was delayed	Evacuation in a 10 km radius		CBR 2
		Venting at unit 1		INES 4 (Unit 1; NISA)[4]	Release CBR 3 CBR 4
		Explosion at unit 1			
			Extension of the evacuation area to a 20 km radius		
	13 Mar	Venting at units 2 and 3			
		Explosion at unit 3			
	15 Mar	Explosion at unit 4		INES 6 (ISIS)[5]	
		Wind from southeast to northwest with precipitation; Increased radioactive releases	Sheltering within a 20-30 km zone around the power plant		CBR 5 CBR 6
	15-22 Mar		▪ Permission of flights in a radius of 30 km around the plant		

4 Nuclear and Industrial Safety Agency (NISA), 2011a - Japan

5 Institute for Science and International Security, 2011 - USA

Date	Event	Ordered measures	Official accident classification	Accident phase
		▪ Evacuation of ships in 10 km radius in costal water		
17 Mar		Publication of contamination limits for food to restrict the consumption of food		
18 Mar			INES 5 (Units 1-3; NISA)[6]	
20 Mar	Power supply of units 1 and 2 established again			
21 Mar		Prevention of disseminating and selling of contaminated food		
22 Mar	Power supply of block 3 established again			
23 Mar			INES 7 (H. Hirsch)[7]	
25 Mar		Recommendation to leave the 30 km zone		
Apr	Publication of dose measurements	▪ Extension of the 20 km zone in the northwest direction (='Deliberated evacuation area'); People were asked to leave the zone until the end of May 2011. ▪ 20 km zone announced as restricted zone	INES 7 (Units 1-3; NISA)[8]	Transition phase and subsequent long-term post-accident phase for areas where people should live further

[6] Nuclear and Industrial Safety Agency (NISA), 2011b

[7] Classification is based on first assessments of Institut de Radioprotection et de Sûreté Nucléaire (IRSN) and Zentralanstalt für Meteorologie und Geodynamik (ZAMG) (Hirsch, 2011)

[8] Nuclear and Industrial Safety Agency (NISA), 2011a

Date		Event	Ordered measures	Official accident classification	Accident phase
			▪ Outside the 20 km zone: 'Evacuation prepared area' (corresponds to 30 km zone): lifestyle habits were restricted and pregnant women, children, and sick people should not stay in the area. Kindergartens and schools were closed and it was recommended to deliberately leave the zone. ▪ Decontamination measures outside the evacuation zone at schools and kindergartens		CBR 7 CBR 8
	May		Topsoil removal from playgrounds		
	June		'Specific spots recommended for evacuation' were announced exceeding the effective dose of 20 mSv in the first year. Precautionary measures as well as evacuation was recommended. Until end of 2012 260 spots that means 282 households were affected.		
			'Health Management for the Residents in Fukushima Prefecture' started to observe possible long-term effects.		
	July				Transition (Restricted zone and

Date		Event	Ordered measures	Official accident classification	Accident phase
					Deliberate Evacuation Area)
	Sept		Lifting of 'Evacuation prepared area'		
	16 Dec	Cold Shut-down[9] for units 1-3	Restructuring of evacuation and restriction zones due to predicted doses per year. ▪ Doses < 20mSv/a: lifting evacuation forbidding overnight stay; decontamination (cleaning roofs and gutters, removing surfaces) with the aim of 1 mSv/a. ▪ Doses > 20mSv/a: entering with restriction of deliberate evacuation area		Long-term post-accident
2012	Jan		Enacting of decontamination law Decontamination measures: See Table 7.2		
2014	Apr		Some evacuation orders were lifted after decontamination.		

[9] The end of the accident state is defined by the Government of Japan as 'cold shutdown': achievement of significant suppression of radiological release and steady decline of radiation dose rates.

Table 7.2: Commonly implemented remediation measures in Japan since the accident (International Atomic Energy Agency (IAEA), 2015c, Table 5.2-3)

Target	Remediation measures
Houses, buildings	Removal of deposits from the roof, gutters and any decking
	Wiping roofs and walls
	Vacuum sanding
	High pressure washing
Schoolyards, gardens and parks	Topsoil removal
	Weed/grass/pasture removal
Roads	Removal of deposits in ditches
	High pressure washing
Gardens and trees	Mowing
	Removal of fallen leaves
	Removal of topsoil
	High pressure washing
	Paring of fruit trees
Farmlands	Tillage reversal
	Topsoil removal
	Soil treatment (e.g. enhanced application of fertilizer)
	Soil hardening and removal
	Weed/grass/pasture removal
Animal production	Control of radiocaesium levels in animal feed
Forests and woodland	Removal of fallen leaves and lower twigs
	Pruning

For each point in time that is identified for applying the CBR method, the problem description is provided (see Table 7.3-Table 7.10). The attributes are organized thematically belonging either to a general event description, the description of the nuclear power plant, the area affected, release characteristics, or for characterizing an accident phase. In the course of time, more information becomes available. Attribute values that are defined and do not change are not repeated throughout the tables. However, these values are included in the similarity calculations. After each description, the results gained from the CBR method are discussed and particularly compared to the implemented measures in Fukushima. If not further specified, the measures are assumed to be implemented concurrently such as evacuation and sheltering. The application of the Petri net based strategy model as well as the multi-criteria strategy assessment is particularly used in the transition and long-term post-accident phase when time pressure is not as dominant as in the emergency phase.

CBR 1

Table 7.3: Query at 'CBR 1'

CBR 1		Solution
General description		Strategy ▪ Evacuation and Iodine Thyroid Blocking within a 5 km distance in a zone of 360 degrees around the installation. ▪ Sheltering and Iodine Thyroid Blocking from 5 to 20 km distance in a zone of 360 degrees around the installation.
Name	Fukushima Demonstration	
Begin	11 March 2011 15:42 local time	
Accident type	Nuclear power plant accident	
Event description	Earthquake and Tsunami on the east coast of Japan. Four power plants are threatened. Severe accident might happen. Venting might be necessary.	
Nuclear power plant		
Name	Fukushima Daiichi	
Nuclear Power Plant type	Boiling water reactor	
Average thermal power	2812	
Affected area		
Name	Fukushima	
Area type	Prefecture	
Population distribution	Urban	
Pre-release characteristics		
Risk of core melt	Yes or unknown	
Maintaining of containment integrity	Yes or unknown	
Wind direction	Variable or unknown	
Estimated release time	Unknown	

Discussion of the solution

The result obtained by the CBR method is based on the 'HERCA-WENRA approach' (HERCA & WENRA, 2014) supporting rapid decisions on measures in the early phase when very little is known about the situation. The method suggests evacuation and iodine thyroid blocking in a 5 km radius as well as sheltering and iodine thyroid blocking up to 20 km. Since the weather conditions are uncertain, the implementation is suggested in a zone of 360 degrees around the nuclear power plant. In Japan, measures were implemented around the plant as well, successively increasing the radius from 2 to 3 and then to 10 km. The successive extension of the evacuation zones led, amongst others, to distrust in the public and multiple evacuations. Furthermore, at this time, iodine thyroid blocking agents were not pre-distributed in Japan, although stockpiles were available within the 10 km emergency zone (Callen & Homma, 2017). The national government provided advice on implementing iodine thyroid blocking on 16 March (Callen & Homma, 2017), which reduced the effectiveness of this measure. The intake of stable iodine should be implemented shortly before and maximum 24 h after the intake of radioactive iodine (Strahlenschutzkommission, 2011).

Decision support provided

The CBR method indicates the intake of stable iodine as well as a larger evacuation zone from the early beginning when a severe accident is suspected. Even though the HERCA-WENRA approach was developed after the Fukushima Daiichi nuclear power plant accident, there was awareness on the risk of a total outage of electricity at the power plant in case a tsunami exceeds the barrier seawalls (The Fukushima Nuclear Accident Independent Investigation Commission, 2012). Hence, the generic HERCA-WENRA approach might have been developed earlier before the accident if the small probability of occurrence would have been earlier carefully considered.

In summary, the larger evacuation radius the CBR method suggests, helps to avoid repeated evacuation. Furthermore, iodine thyroid blocking is suggested before the release of radioactive substances.

The advisories of different countries expressed a great uncertainty and varied according to the area that should be left and the point in time when to leave (Investigation Committee on the Accident at Fukushima Nuclear Power Stations of Tokyo Electric Power Company, 2012b). The recommendations on the distribution and intake of stable iodine tablets were not harmonized as well. The CBR method supports a harmonized response by referring to transnational recommendations.

CBR 2

Table 7.4: Query at 'CBR 2'

<table>
<tr><td colspan="2">CBR 2</td><td>Solution</td></tr>
<tr><td colspan="2">General description</td><td rowspan="4">Strategy
▪ Evacuation and Iodine Thyroid Blocking up to 20 km distance in a zone of 360 degrees around the installation.
▪ Sheltering and Iodine Thyroid Blocking up to 100 km distance in a zone of 360 degrees around the installation.</td></tr>
<tr><td>Event description</td><td>... Primary containment vessel of unit 1 exceeds max. design pressure; Venting was delayed</td></tr>
<tr><td colspan="2">Pre-release characteristics</td></tr>
<tr><td>Maintaining of containment integrity</td><td>No</td></tr>
</table>

Discussion of the solution

The exceedance of the maximum design pressure in unit 1 may indicate a loss of the containment integrity suggesting a second application of the CBR method at this point in time. The suggested evacuation zone corresponds to the restricted area around the nuclear power plant in Japan. In particular, on 12 March, the evacuation radius was extended again from 10 to 20 km. The CBR method suggests iodine thyroid blocking up to 100 km around the plant, earlier than the official recommendation from the national government.

Decision support provided

The method indicates the larger 20 km evacuation zone earlier than ordered in Japan. Furthermore, sheltering and iodine thyroid blocking is suggested in a large area, which is owed to the instable conditions of the nuclear power plant. Furthermore, the method points out again iodine thyroid blocking in a timely manner. Although the CBR method initially suggest evacuation in radius of 5 km (CBR 1) and now a radius of 20 km, the extension is suggested within a few hours. In Japan, the radius was extended three times over 2 days. The last extension to 20 km was ordered after radioactive substances were released. However, evacuation is most effective, before the radioactive plume reaches the affected area.

In summary, the CBR method identifies an effective strategy and particularly indicates a larger evacuation zone and iodine thyroid blocking before any radioactive material is released. Again, the suggestion is based on transnational recommendations and helps foreign governments to provide harmonized advices to their nationals.

CBR 3

Table 7.5: Query at 'CBR 3'

CBR 3		Solution
General description		Do nothing.
Iodine equivalent	4	
Event description	…Venting at unit 1 initiated.	
Release characteristics		
Begin	12 March 2011 14:00 local time	
Target	People	
Time of day of release	Day	
Season	Spring	
Weather at release	No rain	
Release duration category	Short	
Cause	Deliberate	

Discussion of the solution

With the deliberate venting of unit 1 the release phase starts. At this time, the Nuclear and Industrial Safety Agency in Japan classified the event as INES 4. Based on this classification and further outline data, the CBR method would suggest to do nothing, which clearly contradicts to the results before. Here, the user is obliged to review the classification as the condition of the plant indicates a severe accident. The CBR method could then be applied again with a new classification.

Decision support provided

The method reveals the contradictions between the official classification of the accident and the results retrieved before. The user is now demanded to reclassify the accident and reapply the CBR method with the same problem description so far and a new classification.

CBR 4

Table 7.6: Query at 'CBR 4'

CBR 4		Solution
General description		Strategy ▪ Evacuation of an area of 22.4 km² where about 6713 people would be affected. ▪ Sheltering in an area of 709.5 km² where 212850 people would be affected. ▪ Iodine thyroid blocking for adults in an area of 202.7 km² where 54665 adults would be affected. ▪ Iodine thyroid blocking for children in an area of 2641.4 km² where 80034 children would be affected. Other similar scenarios with similar weather condition and season.
Iodine equivalent	7	

CBR 4		Solution
		Chernobyl accident: Experiences with measures applied in Prypyat

Discussion of the solution

The result is based on an INES 7 scenario in spring in an urban[10] area, where the weather condition is 'no rain stable wind'. The similarity between the current problem description and the description of the scenario retrieved is 0.639, which is owed to an imbalance between scenario describing attributes and the general availability of different attributes for describing a problem. Throughout data collection and building of the database, the used attributes for describing the problems differ, depending on whether scenarios were generated or information on historical events were elicitated. Especially for describing historical events, many attributes were used, where for scenario generation the first approach was to roughly categorize the possible accidents with few attributes. The scenarios are mainly used for suggesting strategies where the historical events provide general hints on the implementation. Hence, the imbalance of the number of describing attributes and resulting low similarity values are not regarded as crucial.

JRodos determines specific sectors for implementing measures, depending on the predicted wind direction and precipitation. Hence, instead of suggesting an implementation in a circular area, a more concrete and also smaller area (in contrast to the result of CBR 3) size is displayed now.

Decision support provided

The CBR method may initiate discussions on a partly revocation of the order 'sheltering and iodine thyroid blocking up to 100 km distance in a zone of 360 degrees around the installation'. In general, prolonged sheltering can lead to serious disruptions in people's lives, as could be observed in Japan (International Atomic Energy Agency (IAEA), 2015b). Furthermore, the user may now run a simulation system such as JRodos to get a clearer picture concerning the areas affected. Especially in

[10] Assumes a population density of 300 people per km^2. For comparison: Germany: 232 people/km^2 (state: 2018), Fukushima: 376 people/km^2 (state: 2018).

the early phase, the CBR method complements the existing decision support systems such as JRodos. However, simulation-based systems need the source term and predicted weather data for their calculations and the CBR method, amongst others, gives first hints when the source term is not yet estimated such as in Japan on 12 March. However, at this point in time, the user may simulate the dispersion and deposition of radionuclides based on an INES 7 source term and a loss-of-coolant accident from a source term library (Löffler et al., 2012).

Again, the method helps foreign governments to decide on measure advices to their nationals in the country where the accident occurred. The CBR method helps to roughly classify the accident, also according to the feasibility of measure implementation.

As additional decision support, experiences made in Prypyat during the Chernobyl accident are retrieved. The similarity is 0.573. Some problems with regard to evacuation are pointed out such as the choice of the evacuation route. People were taken off in a preplanned direction that increased the already accumulated dose. In Japan, the evacuation route posed a problem as well.

In summary, the method provides a strategy and an estimation of the extent of the accident according to the people affected by measures. Past experiences help to avoid potential pitfalls. The results retrieved support the review and possibly revocation of measures retrieved before and helps to give advices to the nationals staying in the country affected. As mentioned before, during the accident, the advisories of the foreign government diverged.

For completion, simulation systems that determine potential affected areas in a more detailed way are expected to run.

CBR 5

Table 7.7: Query at 'CBR 5'

<table>
<tr><td colspan="2">CBR 5</td><td>Solution</td></tr>
<tr><td colspan="2">General description</td><td rowspan="11">Strategy
▪ Evacuation of an area of 1.1 km^2 where about 338 people would be affected
▪ Sheltering in an area of 53.5 km^2 where 16050 people would be affected.
▪ Iodine thyroid blocking for adults in an area of 3.1 km^2 where 826 adults would be affected.
▪ Iodine thyroid blocking for children in an area of 96.2 km^2 where 2915 children would be affected.

Further similar scenario with varied season.

Further similar scenario with INES 7 classification.</td></tr>
<tr><td>Iodine equivalent</td><td>6</td></tr>
<tr><td>Event description</td><td>… Wind from southeast to northwest with precipitation; Increased radioactive releases.</td></tr>
<tr><td colspan="2">Affected area</td></tr>
<tr><td>Size</td><td>3900 km^2 (half circle with radius 50 km^2)</td></tr>
<tr><td>Target</td><td>People</td></tr>
<tr><td colspan="2">Release characteristics</td></tr>
<tr><td>Weather at release</td><td>Rain</td></tr>
<tr><td>Release duration category</td><td>Long</td></tr>
<tr><td>Cause</td><td>Accidental</td></tr>
<tr><td>Accident scenario type</td><td>Loss-of-coolant accident</td></tr>
</table>

Discussion of the solution

Three days later, the Institute for Science and International Security re-classified the event as INES 6, which triggers a re-application of the CBR method due to a changed prognosed weather situation and particularly a change of wind direction and precipitation.

The strategy and implementation areas of the measures are based on a JRodos scenario that is classified as INES 6 and simulates a long release in spring with rainy weather conditions where an urban area is affected. The similarity between the problem description and the scenario description is 0.638.

The smaller areas in comparison to the areas retrieved at 'CBR 4' is owed to the INES classification. Although being classified as serious accident (INES 6), the areas are, for example, much smaller than for accidents classified as INES 7. As indicated before, the accident might have been classified as INES 7 before, promoting a re-application of the method with current weather prognosis and a classification of INES 7. Note that an INES 7 scenario is also listed in the similar cases.

Decision support provided

The result of the method shows the changed area sizes due to modified weather prognosis. These results may be used to compare them with results gained in the following and particularly calculations with an iodine equivalent of INES 7, which is already listed in the results here.

CBR 6

Table 7.8: Query at 'CBR 6'

CBR 6		Solution
General description		Strategy
Iodine equivalent	7	▪ Evacuation of an area of 192.8 km² where about 57844 people would be affected. ▪ Sheltering in an area of 4123.7 km² where 1237106 people would be affected. ▪ Iodine thyroid blocking for adults in an area of 254.8 km² where 68706 adults would be affected. ▪ Iodine thyroid blocking for children in an area of 2465.4 km² where 74701 children would be affected. Further similar scenarios with varied season.

Discussion of the solution

The results of CBR 6 are based on a scenario describing an INES 7 accident with long release in spring and rainy weather conditions where the affected area is urban. The similarity between the scenario retrieved and the problem description of CBR 6 is 0.678.

The area size for evacuation is smaller than the real evacuation area in Japan. The areas determined by JRodos are sectors where measures should be implemented. The weather forecast assumes specific wind directions, which makes sector-wise considerations possible. In Japan, the restricted zone is about a semicircle with 20 km radius and the deliberate evacuation area corresponds to a 45° sector when regarding a circle with 40-50 km radius. The sheltering area is larger when comparing INES 6 and INES 7 results under the same rainy weather conditions. This is primarily owed to the accident classification. Again, the user may run a simulation system taking into account the changed weather forecast.

In contrast to INES 7 calculations in CBR 4, the area size for iodine thyroid blocking for children is smaller, which is owed to the rain that wash out contaminants from the plume and particularly transport them to the ground. However, the main exposure pathway for iodine is inhalation.

Decision support provided

The extent of the accident is updated according to changed weather conditions and expressed by the area sizes for measures and the number of affected people. One may map the area sizes for evacuation and sheltering to a 6th of a circular area and calculate the corresponding radii. For evacuation the radius is 20 km and for sheltering 100 km. Hence, the suggestions in the pre-release phase are confirmed according to the distance from the nuclear power plant. The difference is that a weather prognosis is available, which limits the affected area. At this point in time, the method would suggest to maintain the strategy suggested before. From now on, discussions on relocation, particularly with the help of measurements begin. In April 2011, the criterion of 20mSv dose projected to be received within one year from the date to the accident is announced from the national government to determine areas beyond the 20 km zone from which people might need to be relocated

(International Atomic Energy Agency (IAEA), 2015b). In contrast to evacuation, relocation is "the non-urgent removal or extended exclusion of people from a contaminated area to avoid chronic exposure [...]" (International Atomic Energy Agency (IAEA), 2007, p. 166). Scenarios concerning relocation are not yet integrated in the case base and hence no suggestions can be made accordingly.

CBR 7

Table 7.9: Query at 'CBR 7'

<table>
<tr><td colspan="2">CBR 7</td><td>Solution</td></tr>
<tr><td colspan="2">Specific characteristics of the transition phase</td><td rowspan="5">Strategy
▪ Milk: Clean feeding to 90 days followed by the use of sorbents[11] from 90 days up to 540 days
▪ Meat: Use sorbents for 90 days, after which apply clean feed (also for about 90 days) up to the time of slaughter to bring the activity concentration levels in meat below the MPL. The timing of the strategy depends on the slaughter time of the cattle. Use live monitoring to ensure the target concentration is achieved before slaughter.
▪ Green vegetables: Disposal of plants that were subject to direct deposition. No strategy required for plants sown after deposition.

Further similar scenarios.</td></tr>
<tr><td>Begin</td><td>April 2011</td></tr>
<tr><td>Contamination</td><td>Cs 134; Cs 137</td></tr>
<tr><td>Target</td><td>Dairy cows milk; Meat; Vegetables</td></tr>
<tr><td>Exposure pathway</td><td>Ingestion</td></tr>
</table>

[11] The official name is ,addition of AFCF to concentrate ration' and refers to a radiocaesium binder, added to the diet of, for example, dairy cows or meat producing animals, to reduce the activity concentrations in meat or milk below maximum permitted levels (MLPs).

Discussion of the solution

At this point in time, the transition phase might start for specific areas where people should live further. With regard to the exposure pathway 'ingestion', strategies in the early phase concentrate mainly on food restriction and disposal or removal of certain targets such as milk or cereals. In the course of time, further strategies aiming at preventing the intake of contaminants through the food chain, are required. Exemplarily, three targets, namely milk, meat, and vegetables are regarded. The results are based on a deposition in spring of the amount of 10^5 Bq/m^2 of Cs134 and Cs137. The similarity value is 0.661. The regarded scenario and especially the developed strategies resulted from the European project HARMONE (Harmonising Modelling Strategies of European Decision Support Systems for Nuclear Emergencies) (Bai et al., 2018). In particular, strategies were recommended for continuing the production of milk, meat, and green vegetables by decreasing the activity concentrations below the Maximum Permitted Levels (MLP) specified in Council Regulations (Euratom, 2016).

Decision support provided

During release, the mainly applied measures to avoid the intake of contaminants is the restriction of specific food entering the food chain. With the beginning of the transition phase, additional measures and especially intermediate- and long-term strategies that are oriented towards the exposure pathway 'ingestion', are important to reduce the radiation exposure in areas where people live further. The CBR method suggests studied strategies and shows experiences with the implementation of specific measures.

The suggested strategy is exemplarily modeled with CPN Tools (Figure 7.9) offering further analysis possibilities. In particular, the following points could be investigated: (i) Implementation duration of the measures. A generic approach for the target milk would be clean feeding for 90 days and the use of sorbents from 90 days up to 540 days. If clean feed is not available in spring and alternative uncontaminated feed cannot be brought to the area, an earlier use of sorbents is recommended. The implementation duration as well as uncertainties concerning this matter, can be integrated in the Petri net model. (ii) Available resources. The amount of affected cows and area size of affected vegetables as well as required resources can be adapted in the Petri net model too, for example, to discuss the feasibility of the strategy. (iii) General time schedule. With regard to milk, the strategy must ensure that activity concentrations are consistently below the MPL, since milk enters the food chain on a continuous basis. With regard to meat, the strategy needs to focus on the period before slaughter. Sorbents should be used for 90 days and for about 90 days, clean feed should be applied to bring the activity concentrations below the MPL. If no clean feeding is possible, extended use of sorbents should be implemented for an extended period. Hence, the time shift up to the period before slaughter as well as uncertainties with regard to clean feed, can be integrated in the Petri net model as well.

In summary, the CBR method suggests a strategy that is based on a similar validated scenario supporting decisions on appropriate strategies when there is little experience. Modeled as Petri nets, further analysis possibilities beyond dose reduction and waste are offered. The latter is particularly covered by simulation systems such as JRodos. However, in the later phases of an accident, more criteria enter decision-making. The CBR method particularly supports decision-making from identifying appropriate strategies to assessing them.

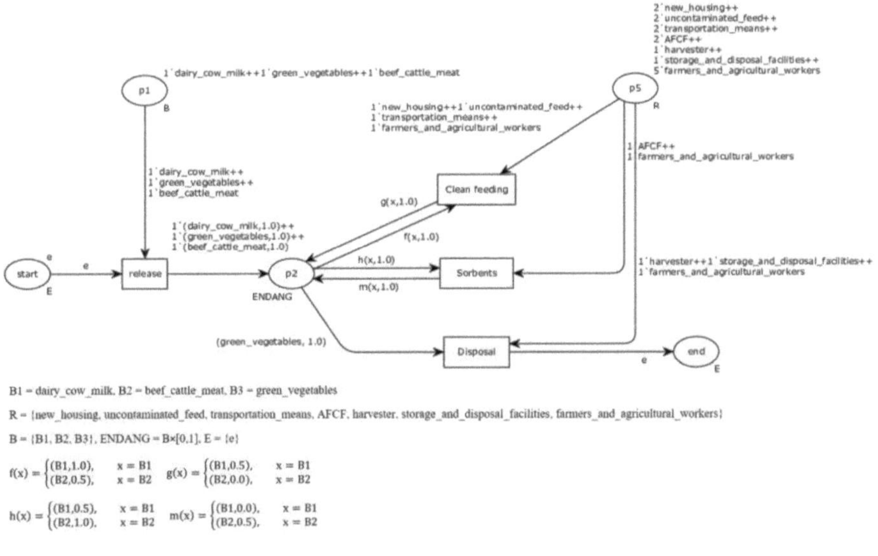

Figure 7.9: Suggested strategy of 'CBR 7'. The strategy addresses the ingestion of contaminated food by humans.

CBR 8

Table 7.10: Query at 'CBR 8'

<table>
<tr><td colspan="2">CBR 8</td><td>Solution</td></tr>
<tr><td colspan="2">Specific characteristics of the long-term post-accident phase</td><td rowspan="5">Strategy
▪ Roofs: Roof brushing or roof cleaning with pressurized hot water
▪ Internal Surfaces: Vacuum cleaning
▪ Paved other: Turning paving slabs
▪ Small area of grass: Grass cutting and removal and rotovating or triple digging
▪ Large area of grass: Grass cutting and removal and rotovating or deep ploughing
▪ Small area of plants: Plant and shrub removal and rotovating or triple digging
▪ Trees and shrubs: Tree and shrub pruning/removal

Similar cases the solution is based on.</td></tr>
<tr><td>Begin</td><td>April 2011</td></tr>
<tr><td>Contamination</td><td>Cs 134; Cs 137</td></tr>
<tr><td>Target</td><td>Multi-storey external surfaces roofs; Multi-storey internal surfaces; Paved other; Small area of grass; Large area of grass; Small area of plants; Trees and shrubs;</td></tr>
<tr><td>Exposure pathway</td><td>External radiation ground</td></tr>
</table>

Discussion of the solution

The strategy obtained results from two similar scenarios in the case base that suggest strategies for dry depositions in summer in an urban area. They differ with respect to the targets and propose different measures for some of them. The similarity value of the first scenario is 0.571 with a factor of dose reduction of 0.227 whereas the second case has a similarity value of 0.464 and a factor of dose reduction of 0.214. Hence, their effectiveness with regard to dose reduction is similar. The small similarity values are again owed to the different number of attributes used for describing the problems. The scenarios assigned to the long-term accident phase are particularly described with few attributes.

The choice of placing the 8th run of the CBR application at this point in time has following reason: The transition phase has, amongst others, the task to prepare for the long-term accident phase and particularly develop appropriate strategies. Here, areas where people should live further and which are less contaminated are regarded, justifying the reuse of the strategies that are based on (i) an INES 6 event and a scenario assuming a contamination of $1 \cdot 10^6$ Bq/m^2 of Cs137 and Cs134 and $1 \cdot 10^7$ Bq/m^2 I131, which corresponds to effective doses to adults in a range of 10-20mSv/y, respectively and (ii) the reuse of dry deposition scenarios, since the areas in Japan with wet deposition, were more contaminated. Regarding deposition in summer is less crucial, since major differences in the measure selection and implementation would arise when regarding deposition during winter months. For example, due to missing leaves, the dose from trees is smaller during winter months. Hence, for a winter scenario, trees are unlikely to be taken into account in the measure selection. Furthermore, the strategies retrieved are expected to be implemented as early as possible being consistent with the point in time chosen for re-applying the CBR method. For example, some measures are less effective the later they are applied, such as grass cutting that should be implemented before rain occurs, since after rain more activity would be at the base of the grass and in the soil.

The IAEA considers the months from around July to December 2011 as the transition phase, in which policies and arrangement for recovery were established (International Atomic Energy Agency (IAEA), 2018). However, in April, first decontamination activities started in Japan. Furthermore, for identifying remediation measures, experimental and field based demonstration projects were carried out in 2011 in Japan (Hardie & McKinley, 2014; International Atomic Energy Agency (IAEA), 2015c). The reasons were amongst others the need to identify effective and applicable measures suitable for the site specific conditions in Japan, the lack of experience in dealing with remediation of large areas and inhabited areas or to train work force on the use of different equipment (International Atomic Energy Agency (IAEA), 2015c). Besides the demonstration projects, information on past nuclear and radiological accidents formed the basis on decisions on remediation measures. Consequently, the CBR application might be run earlier than the 'official' beginning of the transition phase for identifying early decontamination strategies. July 2011 could be a further point in time for identifying long-term recovery strategies. However, due to a lack of scenarios addressing long-term recovery, a further run is not pursued in the framework of this evaluation.

Figure 7.10 illustrates the strategy of the first similar case retrieved. The function *f* reflects that the measure 'grass cutting and removal' is directed towards the targets 'small area of grass' and 'large area of grass'. The function *h* reflects that rotovating can be applied to 'small area of grass', 'large area of grass', and 'small area of plants'.

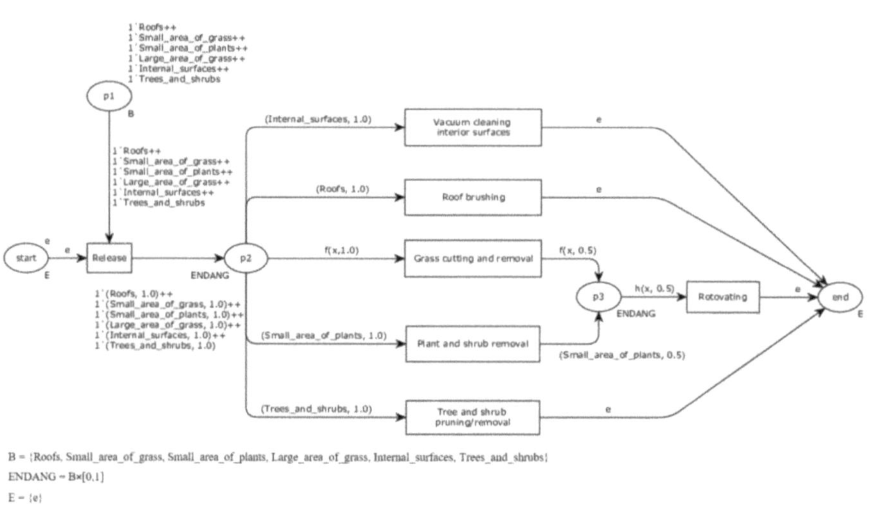

Figure 7.10: First decontamination strategy for a dry deposition in summer

Figure 7.11 illustrates the strategy of the second similar case retrieved. Here, one measure is directed towards one target. The function *k* reflects that 'vacuum sweeping paved' can be applied to 'paved road' and 'paved pavement'. The function *g* reflects that 'triple digging' can be applied to 'small area of grass', 'small area of plants', and 'small area of soil'. The function *l* reflects that 'deep ploughing' can be applied to 'large area of plants', 'large area of soil', and 'large area of plants'. Both decontamination strategies are merged to cover all targets specified in 'CBR 8' (Figure 7.12). The function *f* reflects that 'grass cutting and removal' can be applied to 'small/large area of grass', *g* reflects that 'triple digging' can be applied to 'small area of grass/plants', and *h* reflects that 'rotovating' can be applied to 'large/small area of grass' and 'small area of plants'.

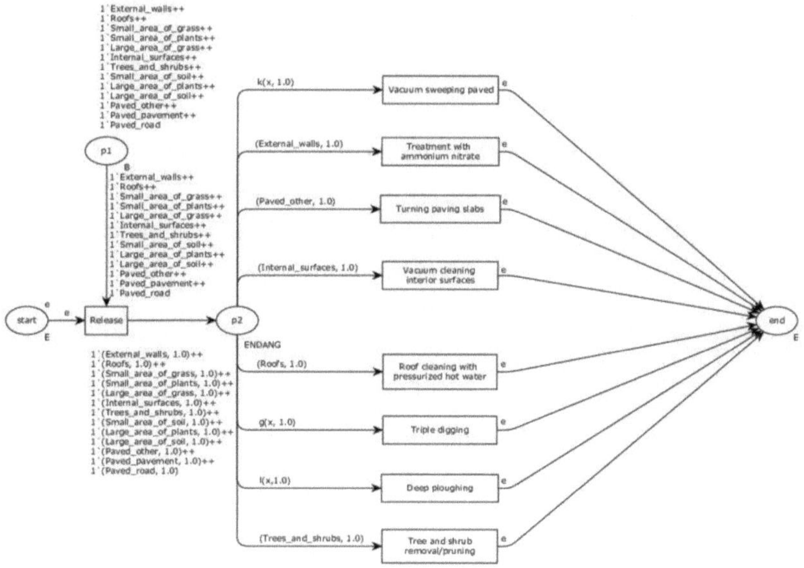

B = {External_walls, Roofs, Small_area_of_grass, Small_area_of_plants, Large_area_of_grass, Internal_surfaces, Trees_and_shrubs, Small_area_of_soil, Large_area_of_plants, Large_area_of_soil, Paved_other, Paved_pavement, Paved_road}

ENDANG = B×[0,1]

E = {e}

Figure 7.11: Second decontamination strategy for a dry deposition in summer

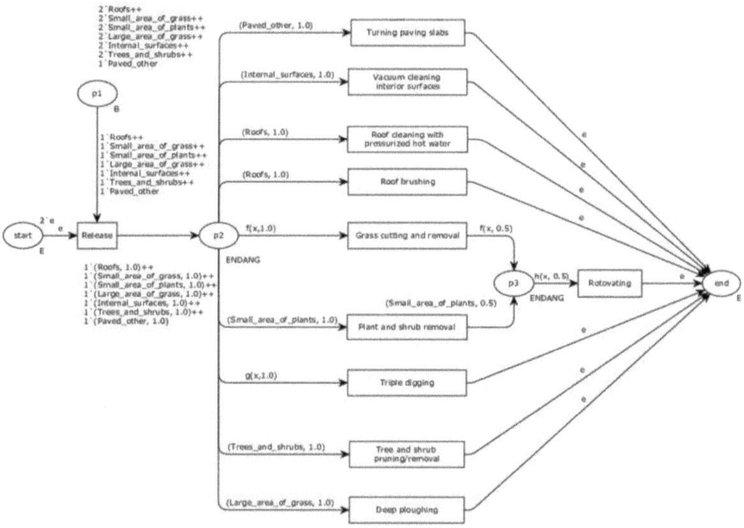

B = {Roofs, Small_area_of_grass, Small_area_of_plants, Large_area_of_grass, Internal_surfaces, Trees_and_shrubs, Paved_other}

ENDANG = B×[0,1]

E = {e}

Figure 7.12: Strategy based on merging strategies of Figure 7.10 and Figure 7.11

For example, the suggested strategy (Figure 7.12), which results from merging two strategies, includes alternative measures for the targets 'small area of grass' and 'large area of grass'. For 'small area of grass' either 'triple digging' or 'grass cutting and removal' and 'rotovating' is possible whereas for 'large area of grass' the measures 'deep ploughing' or 'grass cutting and removal' and 'rotovating' are offered. This is surely not satisfactory for decision-making and hence, a multi-criteria assessment can now help to investigate the four possibilities in a structured manner. For illustration purposes, a sub-set of used criteria is sufficient. Furthermore, it is assumed that the targets can be investigated independently from each other and that the choice of one measure has no direct effect on the effectiveness of another measure that is directed towards a different target. Table 7.11 displays the different possible strategies excluding the other targets.

Table 7.11: Different possible strategies with regard to small and large area of grass

Strategy A	Small area of grass: Triple digging Large area of grass: Grass cutting and removal and rotovating
Strategy B	Small area of grass: Grass cutting and removal and rotovating Large area of grass: Grass cutting and removal and rotovating
Strategy C	Small area of grass: Grass cutting and removal and rotovating Large area of grass: Deep ploughing
Strategy D	Small area of grass: Triple digging Large area of grass: Deep ploughing

Table 7.12 displays effectiveness values of the measures with regard to dose reduction. These values are determined in the course of the HARMONE project (Bai et al., 2018) and are the basis of the factors of dose reduction in Table 7.13. The amount of waste and costs of each measure are gained with the help of JRodos. Public acceptance is estimated according to a perceived effectiveness of the measures. The removal of contamination instead of dilution by, for example, rotovating, is assumed to have higher public acceptance.

Table 7.12: Dose reduction values for grass areas. These values are determined during the HARMONE project.

Target	Average external gamma effective dose with no option applied (Sv)	Measure applied	Average external gamma effective dose with option applied (Sv)	Dose reduction (Sv)
Small area of grass	$4.0\ 10^{-3}$	Grass cutting and removal	$2.0\ 10^{-3}$	$2.0\ 10^{-3}$
		Rotovating	$2.1\ 10^{-3}$	$1.9\ 10^{-3}$
Large area of grass	$9.9\ 10^{-4}$	Grass cutting and removal	$5.0\ 10^{-4}$	$4.9\ 10^{-4}$
		Rotovating	$5.1\ 10^{-4}$	$4.8\ 10^{-4}$

Table 7.13: Attribute values of the strategies to be assessed. These values are per m² assuming 50 % small area of grass and 50% large area of grass.

	Strategy A	Strategy B	Strategy C	Strategy D	Weight
Factor of dose reduction	0.24	0.2	0.2	0.1	9
Waste[12]	0.05	0.1	0.05	0	6
Costs[13]	20.012	0.212	0.206	20.006	5
Public acceptance	low	high	low	low	8
Similarity	0.5175	0.571	0.5175	0.464	5

For the strategy assessment, the weights as displayed in Table 7.13 assume higher preferences in generating highly effective strategies producing a small amount of waste and having high public acceptance. Table 7.14 lists the used normalization functions enabling to compare the different attribute values with each other.

[12] Waste: Grass cutting: 0.1 kg/m².

[13] Cost: Triple digging 20 EUR/m², Deep ploughing 0.006 EUR/m², Grass cutting and removal/ Rotovating 0.2 EUR/m² (small area), 0.012 EUR/m² (large area).

Table 7.14: Normalization functions of the different attributes

Attribute	Normalization function f	Comment
Factor of dose reduction	$f(x) = 1 - x$	It is assumed that a factor of dose reduction 1 is the worst case meaning that no dose reduction is achieved.
Waste	$f(x) = (60 - x)/60$	Mechanical top soil and turf or plant removal and soil replacement is taken for comparison (60 kg/m²)
Cost	$f(x) = (22 - x)/22$	The measure 'roof cleaning with pressurized hot water' costs 22 EUR/m² and is used as reference for a measure with high costs.
Public acceptance	$f(x) = x$	High acceptance = 1, low acceptance = 0
Similarity	$f(x) = x$	

Figure 7.13 illustrates the result of strategy assessment recommending strategy B for decontamination.

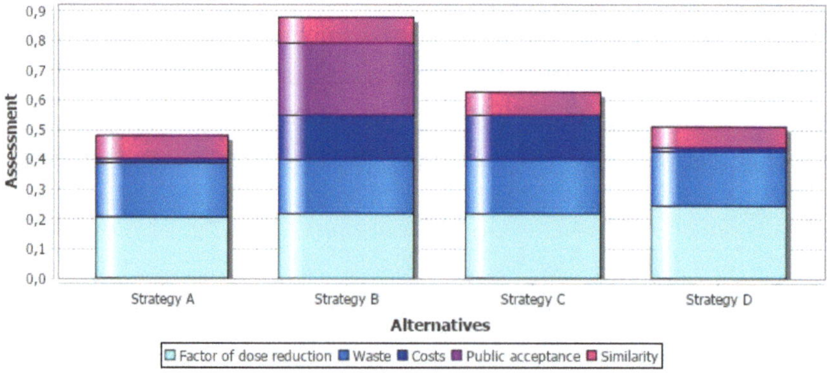

Figure 7.13: Stacked-bar chart of the result of strategy assessment

Decision support provided

As mentioned before, decision on measures in Japan were based on experimental and field based demonstration projects as well as investigations on former nuclear and radiological accidents. Table 7.2 shows the commonly implemented measures that do not rely on a specific order. Furthermore, as an expert reported during the PREPARE project, implementation was not done consistently over large areas and a further review of strategies might have reduced the waste problem. The CBR method (i) identifies a strategy that is based on similar problem descriptions and their developed effective strategies, (ii) shows the original strategies and alternative measures with side effects (such as more waste), (iii) provide means to analyze different available strategies in a structured manner according to different criteria. Furthermore, modeled as Petri nets, the strategies can be subject to further investigations according to resources. The CBR method includes historical knowledge and particularly experience with implementing measures as well. At this point in time, the method indicates the large amount of waste as well as a timely implementation of specific measures. For example, the measure 'grass cutting and removal' that is also suggested by the CBR method, should be implemented as early as possible to be effective.

7.2.1 Achievement of the Evaluation Objectives

The example in the section before is derived from a real accident and demonstrates the basic capabilities of the developed method. In the following, the evaluation objectives are discussed in more detail.

Decision support for all phases of a nuclear accident

The method is intended to be applied several times and particularly in each phase throughout an accident. The case study shows that appropriate strategies are suggested for each phase taking into account the implementation order of measures. Moreover, historical accidents and especially experiences made with implementing measures as well as already compiled expert knowledge such as handbooks help to avoid pitfalls. The type of decision support slightly varies throughout the phases. During the pre-release and release phases the focus is on (i) identifying appropriate strategies in a fast and timely manner to be effective, (ii) categorizing an accident according to its scale and particularly size of affected area and number of affected people and (iii) to assess the feasibility of strategies. The added value of the CBR method particularly lies in countering the acute time pressure and uncertainty the decision-makers are faced with by referring to knowledge that was already compiled before an accident in a structured manner. As soon as more information on the source term and weather prognosis are available, the method indicates running a simulation system to obtain more exact results on the area size and number of affected people. With reference to the case study, the CBR method indicates earlier a larger evacuation radius, which helps to avoid repeated evacuation. Furthermore, the CBR method suggests to implement evacuation and sheltering together with iodine thyroid blocking. The real advice of the national government on implementing iodine thyroid blocking came a few days later and hence lead to a reduced effectiveness. Furthermore, the foreign governments did not agree on iodine thyroid blocking. In addition, the CBR method reveals false official event classifications, helps to categorize the accident, and also refers to transnational recommendations, which is helpful for foreign countries to give harmonized advice to their nationals.

During the transition and long-term post-accident phases the focus is on (i) identifying appropriate strategies and particularly taking into account the implementation order of measures for different exposure pathways, (ii) providing analysis capabilities according to duration and required resources and particularly their uncertainties, and (iii) providing means to compare different strategies according to several criteria in a structured manner. In contrast to other multi-criteria approaches in nuclear emergency management in the literature, already developed strategies of similar problem descriptions are reused in the analysis. Furthermore, as also could be seen in the case study, there is a lack of knowledge on coherent strategies, especially in respect of decontamination. The CBR method fills this gap by promoting the development of scenarios in advance of an accident and by reusing these scenarios for decision support in emergency management. The added value of the method lies in suggesting measures and their implementation order as well as indicating potential pitfalls on the basis of validated scenarios, multi-criteria assessment, and historical accidents. This approach particularly counters the lack of experience and multitude of decision criteria the decision-makers are faced with.

Suggesting strategies throughout an accident requires sufficient cases in the case base. As a starting point, the different defined weather, population distribution, and scale categories as well as season for different accident phases can be used as basis for scenario construction. Furthermore, targets with high contributions to the dose can be taken into account in the first instance. The potential of enriching the case base by refining the categories defined so far, is especially discussed in the summary and outlook chapter of this thesis.

Handling uncertainty in nuclear emergency management

The issue of uncertainty is addressed in several ways. First of all, the core method, CBR has an inherent way to handle uncertainty by working with similarities and especially approximate reasoning. This approach implies that decisions cannot be made straightaway but draw upon similar problematic situations and their solutions. The main sources of uncertainty in nuclear emergency management are the source term and the weather prognosis. The first is owed to the uncertain conditions in the nuclear power plant and triggering events whose consequences are difficult to assess. The rare occurrences and hence lack of experience complicate the handling of the uncertainty as well. The approach is to integrate attributes in the retrieval that describe information that is reflected by the source term: the substances that are to be released and the consequences that are to be expected by such a release. The iodine equivalent, the accident scenario type, characteristics of the nuclear power plant, as well as release duration and category can be regarded as compensating attributes. A further approach is, also having time pressure in mind, to work with categories instead of demanding exact numerical values. This applies, for instance, for the weather condition that can be assigned to a predefined category. The characteristics of these categories are particularly taken into account in the local similarity functions of the retrieval step. In addition, preparedness and in particular elaborating scenarios in advance of an accident are means to handle uncertainty as well by referring to accidents and appropriate strategies that have already been thought through and particularly taking these as starting point for further discussions. As in the beginning of the Fukushima Daiichi nuclear power plant accident, the source term was not available and the output of simulation systems were not taken into account in the decisions on strategies. Furthermore, source term estimations in the European countries were not harmonized in the beginning. The developed method, as shown in the case study, particularly provides support without the exact knowledge of the source term in terms of area sizes and number of affected people and particularly for roughly categorizing the entire accident. The method cannot predict exact areas for the early measures but which is left to the simulation systems.

Besides uncertainty in the beginning of such an accident, the method provides means to conduct analyses concerning possibly uncertain parameters in respect of strategy implementation. Due to a lack of experience with regard to selecting and implementing measures during the later phases, simulations taking into account uncertainty as well as a structured assessment of several possible strategies are offered as additional decision support. The strength of the CBR method particularly lies in an integrated approach to handle various characteristics of uncertainty.

Integrating experience and expert knowledge for decision support

Experience and expert knowledge are integrated in the case base through historical accidents provided by experts, scenarios confirmed by experts, knowledge compiled of handbooks or project results as well as results of the task force in Europe set up after the Fukushima Daiichi nuclear power plant accident. Retrieval and reuse partly result from discussions with experts during the PREPARE project as well. To name a few, in terms of distinguishing between release by day and night or by integrating the accident scenario type as well as by taking into account waste storage possibilities in the decisions on decontamination strategies.

Taking into account different stakeholders with partially conflicting objectives

The combination of CBR and MCDA enables to assess different possible strategies taking into account various criteria. As an advantage, the strategies gained by CBR are further used for the multi-criteria assessment. Hence, strategies do not have to be developed to be then further assessed. Instead, strategies that are based on similar problematic situations are reused to be assessed additionally to radiological quantities and are aligned to current circumstances. The latter refers, for instance, to public acceptance, which may vary for different countries and affected areas and which may contrast to cost and the amount of waste produced by certain measures.

As mentioned before, soil removal may give the public a better feeling in terms of reducing contamination than diluting contamination by digging or ploughing and hence transporting contamination to deeper soil layers. The multi-criteria assessment helps to structure the problem, reduce its complexity, and promotes discussions of the stakeholders involved. The advantage of this approach is particularly emphasized in several publications (Papamichail & French, 2013) but which is in the framework of this thesis, particularly combined with CBR and embedded in an entire decision support method addressing all phases of a nuclear accident.

Supporting harmonization work in Europe and the interaction with other tools for emergency management

The harmonization work in Europe is particularly addressed by integrating the HERCA-WENRA approach and results from European projects such as PREPARE and HARMONE. The generic scenarios developed are independent of specific country regulations and take into account international recommendations such as recommendations of the IAEA. As shown in the case study, the method complements existing simulation systems. However, the latter are also used to determine effectiveness values of certain strategies. Hence, for a comprehensive multi-criteria analysis, especially in the later phases, the interaction with other tools such as JRodos are necessary. Figure 7.14 gives an overview of the interaction with other tools.

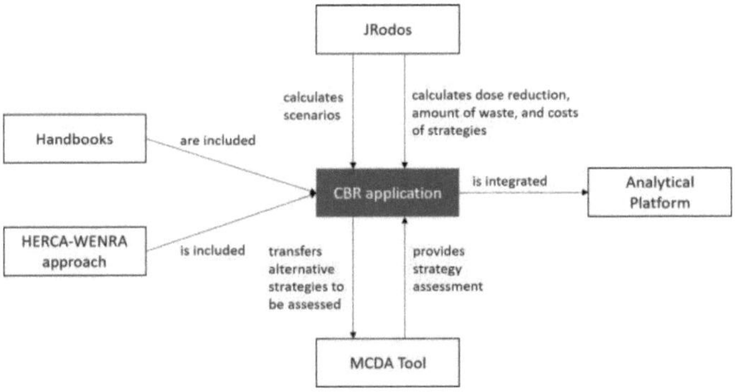

Figure 7.14: Interaction of the CBR application with other tools in emergency management

Demonstrating applicability by means of a prototypical implementation

The basic components of the method are implemented as illustrated in chapter 7.1. The prototype is capable of configuring the retrieval step and calculating similar cases from the case base as well as combine several strategies to address all targets of interest. The application can be accessed via a web browser and hence is independent of any local installations. This design is particularly interesting for nuclear emergency management where several advisory bodies do not need to be located at the same place. The application particularly supports the exchange of results.

As mentioned in Chapter 1 the results of this thesis have been elaborated in the framework of the PREPARE project and particularly have partly been integrated in the 'Analytical Platform' to be used by experts for analyses and information exchange and the public community to obtain information about an incident. Experts particularly should discuss their preliminary conclusions aiming at getting a common picture transcending national borders.

The Analytical Platform was evaluated according to perceptions and expectations of potential users about the usefulness, trustworthiness, interaction with other users and governance offered by the system as well as the willingness and interest to join and contribute with expertise (Montero, Sala, Trueba, & Baudé, 2016). The persons interviewed were part of the NERIS community and partner of PREPARE (73 organizations) where 47% responded. The system was regarded as more useful for experts than public to be used in a distant accident or after the emergency phase to centralize information and enhancing collaboration and exchange between experts. In general, the interest to participate was great where clear rules for operating shared information was demanded. Furthermore, political support from organizations involved clearly contribute to the success of such a system.

7.2.2 Discussion of the Evaluation Method

The evaluation has been conducted in the frame of a case study to demonstrate the achievement of the objectives. Due to a limited time frame, an evaluation including experts has not been conducted. To assess the strategies and the decision support provided by the CBR method, papers and reports dealing with emergency management during the Fukushima Daiichi nuclear power plant accident have been used. They present the strategies implemented as well as the difficulties in deciding on them. The evaluation particularly demonstrates how the CBR method overcomes some of the issues in decision-making namely the time pressure and uncertainty in the beginning of an accident and the large number of possible measures in the later phases and their reasonable combination to a strategy taking into account partially diverging preferences. The added value of the CBR method is particularly shown by comparing the identified strategies with real implemented strategies as well as by discussing how issues that arose can be overcome. However, the saving of time is not expressed numerically, for example. For this purpose, experiments with experts need to be conducted. Furthermore, the general suggestions for handling uncertainty are to (i) work with rough classifications rather than demanding exact numerical values to (ii) prepare scenarios in advance of an accident to better handle upcoming uncertainties, and to (iii) make use of similar already developed scenarios in the course of an accident. The evaluation of this thesis does not include an expert survey in respect of this issue aiming at measuring numerically how uncertainty decreased. However, the added value of these approaches is argumented with the help of related studies that either investigate directly decision-making in nuclear emergency management (T. Comes et al., 2015; French et al., 2017) or investigate generally experts in situations in which the stakes are high (Klein, 2008; Meso et al., 2002; Paton & Flin, 1999; Riesbeck & Schank, 1989).

With regard to the later phases, the lack of cases does not make comprehensive experiments possible, since cases in the case base, which are confirmed by experts, just cover few possible accidents. However, the importance of such an approach is underpinned by the various studies after the Fukushima Daiichi nuclear power plant accident and by the specific case study presented in the chapter before.

It is important to note that although the method has been developed after the Fukushima Daiichi nuclear power plant accident, the scenarios referred to in the case study, represent knowledge that was available before the accident. Hence, the accident itself has been excluded for demonstrating the achievement of the objectives defined in this thesis.

8 Conclusions and Outlook

Decision-making in the course of nuclear disasters is challenging due to uncertainty in respect of decisive information, a short time frame available for identifying appropriate strategies as well as a multitude of possible measures and stakeholders with partially conflicting objectives. Hence, developing decision support methods and tools requires diverse approaches for countering the just as diverse issues in disaster management. This thesis presents a novel approach in nuclear emergency management that builds upon experience and expert knowledge, where the decision consists in choosing one or several appropriate measures and to combine them to a strategy.

To achieve the objective of developing a decision support method that identifies appropriate strategies throughout a nuclear accident taking into account uncertainty and multiple stakeholders, case-based reasoning (CBR) is enhanced by the development of scenarios. CBR is oriented towards the decision-making behavior of experts under time pressure and uncertainty and provides a framework for storing and reusing experience in a structured manner. The main idea is to reuse solutions of similar problems to solve a current problem whereas similar problems also help to avoid mistakes. CBR can be applied in domains that are not fully understood being advantageous in respect of the exceptionality of nuclear accidents. Furthermore, strategies can be identified more quickly and do not need to be generated from scratch. Besides many applications examples in the general disaster management domain, the transparent process of deriving a strategy is advantageous for the later success in practice. Scenarios are fictitious nuclear accidents and appropriate strategies. Their development supports preparedness in general and enhances the case base by possible nuclear accidents. Developing scenarios and reusing them in the course of an incident saves time and helps to avoid mistakes by thinking through possible consequences in advance. The development of scenarios is an important research field in nuclear emergency management. The new approach in this thesis is particularly the structured integration for later reuse in the framework of a decision support method. Scenarios are particularly results of simulations building a bridge between elaborated decision support systems such as JRodos and the new approach of this thesis.

Furthermore, a strategy model based on High-level Petri nets (HLPNs) is developed for capturing combinations of measures and particularly their order of implementation. Petri nets are used in a variety of emergency management applications and are suitable to model strategies in a structured and unambiguous manner. Furthermore, they enable an automated reuse in the framework of CBR and have analysis capabilities of structure and dynamic behavior and allow for analyses with regard to the feasibility of a strategy. The latter is particularly useful if several strategies are available for selection. The strategy model developed is generic and allows for enhancements in various directions such as according to time and uncertainty in available resources, for example. Further decisive factors, such as the radionuclides involved, can be integrated as well.

CBR is also combined with multi-criteria decision analysis (MCDA) to particularly address various preferences that need to be respected in the final decision. MCDA supports a transparent and structured decision-making process taking into account various objectives. Being subject of current research in nuclear emergency management and successfully combined with CBR in related areas, MCDA is integrated in the reuse step of CBR within the framework of this thesis. The aim is to assess several strategies by means of diverse criteria that have become established in terms of strategy assessment. The novel approach in this thesis is to integrate these different perspectives taking into account possible future developments, effectiveness, resources as well as confidence in the strategies retrieved by the decision support method.

This chapter is structured as follows: At first, the achievement of the objectives is discussed in more detail (Chapter 8.1). Chapter 8.2 points out some open questions and directions for future research.

8.1 Key Findings and Conclusions

Decision-making in the course of nuclear disasters is complex, since the release of radioactive substances may lead to long-term and transnational health risks for humans and environmental contamination. Decisions on strategies define the fundamental procedures of protecting the public and have to be made in balance with intervening in people's life and in a societal consensus. Besides the multitude of possible measures, measures need to follow a specific order to be effective and their selection needs to be aligned to the current frame conditions that change with each accident. Current decision support methods and tools help in constructing a strategy by ad hoc projections of the radiological situation and analyses in respect of measure combinations, for example with regard to their effectiveness – either computer-based or with the help of handbooks. The latter particularly indicates possible side effects and constraints. However, strategies need to be newly constructed with each new event and results of simulation systems are subject to uncertainties as well, amongst others, due to uncertain input parameters. Further research focuses on MCDA and the development of scenarios for supporting long-term decisions and preparedness. However, there is no mechanism that makes this already elaborated knowledge reusable. This thesis proposes a new approach building upon current research and insights gained after the Fukushima Daiichi nuclear power plant accident and pursues a completely new direction in terms of the core, particularly experience-based, problem-solving paradigm. The objective of developing a decision support method consists of several sub-objectives where the following section briefly shows how each of these objectives has been achieved.

Providing a decision support method that can be applied throughout an accident supports consistent decision-making since information already integrated for describing the current problem situation and deriving a solution can be directly utilized. Information on the release, for example, is important for decisions in the long-term as well. The comprehensive decision support method of this thesis uses information included in the initial phases for the long-term phases as well, notably with updates, if available. The method is particularly developed to be applied several times during an accident *providing decision support for all accident phases*. The distinction into accident phases addresses phase-specific issues and supports elaborating appropriate strategies for each accident phase. The type of decision support slightly varies throughout the phases in alignment with the changing issues. During the pre-release and release phases the focus is on (i) identifying appropriate strategies in a *fast* and *timely manner to be effective*, (ii) *categorizing* an accident *according to its scale* and particularly size of affected area and number of affected people and (iii) to *assess the feasibility* of strategies. The latter two points particularly address the issues of a non-harmonized response of foreign countries observed in the past. During the transition and long-term post-accident phases the focus is on (i) identifying appropriate strategies and particularly taking into account the *implementation order of measures* for different exposure pathways, (ii) providing *analysis capabilities* according to required resources and particularly their uncertainties, and (iii) providing means to *compare different strategies according to several criteria* in a structured manner. The decision support provided for the later phases particularly counters the present lack of experience concerning long-term strategies. In general, the CBR method not only provides decision support by means of suggesting strategies but also by indicating potential pitfalls and experiences made in the past with implementing strategies. The *strategy model* developed enables to capture strategies in a structured and unambiguous manner taking into account their *order of implementation*. Besides a reasonable combination of measures to a strategy, the order of implementation directly influences the effectiveness of the entire strategy. The strategy model is generic, integrating events causing the endangerment of a target and effects resulting from implementing a measure making an automated reuse and adaptation possible. The latter especially refers to the problem statement how to *combine several strategies* where each strategy only covers a part of the problem. The proposed *merging* approach focuses on the commonalities of the strategies and merges several Petri nets at a syntactical level. The strategy model particularly offers further analysis possibilities which, embedded in the entire decision support approach, takes a completely new direction in nuclear emergency management.

Uncertainty in nuclear emergency management is still a crucial issue and current research focuses on enhancing methods and tools to enable robust decision-making. The *core method* proposed by this thesis has an inherent way to handle uncertainty by working with approximate reasoning and without demanding complete knowledge on the current problem situation. The main sources of uncertainty are the source term and the weather prognosis. The approach of this thesis is to integrate *compensating attributes* in the retrieval such as the iodine equivalent, the accident scenario type, characteristics of the nuclear power plant, as well as release duration and category. Furthermore, *symbolic attributes* and categories, respectively, are integrated instead of demanding exact numerical values. This applies, for instance, for the weather condition that can be assigned to a predefined category. The characteristics of these categories are particularly taken into account in the local similarity functions of the retrieval step. In addition, preparedness and in particular *elaborating scenarios* in advance of an accident are means to handle uncertainty as well by referring to accidents and appropriate strategies that have already been thought through and particularly taking these as starting point for further discussions. Furthermore, besides initial uncertainties, the developed provides means to conduct *analyses* concerning possibly *uncertain parameters in respect of strategy implementation*. The strength of the CBR method particularly lies in an integrated approach to handle various characteristics of uncertainty.

Experience and expert knowledge build the core of the entire decision support method consisting of *historical accidents* provided by experts, *scenarios* confirmed by experts, knowledge compiled of *handbooks*, as well as *acknowledged results* such as general frameworks for decision-making established by international task forces. The CBR method reflects and integrates current practice in a structured manner providing appropriate knowledge in a suitable form.

Especially in the later phases, *multiple stakeholders* enter the decision process. Decisions on long-term strategies that may affect property rights and have consequences on the willingness to return, have to be made in a societal consensus. Particularly, decisive criteria may now conflict or manifest very individually for different countries. The multi-criteria assessment helps to structure the problem, reduce its complexity, and promotes discussions of the stakeholders involved. In particular, the case-based strategies are further used for the multi-criteria assessment where several perspectives are integrated. In particular, the trust in the suggested strategies are reflected by means of a *confidence* value. In contrast to criteria defined in the literature that purely refer to decision objectives, the underlying decision support method is taken into account as well. Furthermore, *effectiveness*, *resources*, and *robustness* are objectives regarded. The latter particularly considers possible future uncertainties. The multi-criteria assessment is mainly developed for the later phases but can also be applied in the early phases of an accident with appropriate preparations that accelerate the assignment of attribute values.

The CBR method integrates different methods but also results from other decision support methods and systems, such as a rule-based approach *supporting the harmonization work in Europe* or simulation results of JRodos promoting the *interaction with other tools for emergency management*. The latter particularly refers to the exchange of results with an MCDA tool as well. The *prototype* particularly demonstrates the *applicability of the developed method* where the user can configure retrieval and similarity calculation individually. The application can be accessed via a web browser and hence is independent of any local installations. This design is particularly interesting for nuclear emergency management where several advisory bodies do not need to be located at the same place.

8.2 Directions for Future Research

The case-based decision support method takes a new path and provides the basis for further exploring experience-based decision-making in nuclear emergency management. Consequently, the single components developed and shaped in the framework of this thesis, open up new research directions for further extensions and enhancements. These refer to enhancing merging at a semantic level, extending the problem model and the case base, and transferring the decision support method developed to other disaster types.

8.2.1 Enhancing Merging at a Semantic Level

Merging aims at suggesting a comprehensive strategy solving the entire problem at hand where partially solving strategies are retrieved from the case base. Here, 'solving' refers to the set of targets that are specified in the query. Merging is realized at a syntactical level where equally labeled transitions and their corresponding pre- and post-mappings are merged. Here, the sets of types and transition modes of the single Petri nets are united. Hence, the merging preserves the original runs of the Petri nets and identifies possible new runs for newly combined targets. The latter particularly refers to choices of possible measures, also. The pre- and post-mappings for common transition modes can be chosen from the pre-and post-mappings of the respective Petri nets that are merged. An application example is the choice of resources that would arise if the single strategies imply different resources for the same measure. The pre- and post-mappings of transitions that are not merged remain unchanged. The merging approach is generic and neither linked to a specific event nor measure type. So far, the strategy model integrates two decisive factors for measure selection i.e., the targets and the resources needed for implementation. For example, enhancements are possible through additional types. However, the merging so far does not detect inappropriate combinations of measures or inappropriate orders of implementation. Inappropriate combinations refer to measures whose targets are of different sensibility such as playgrounds or industrial areas and possible impacts on neighboring targets are crucial. Furthermore, inappropriate combinations make measures redundant such as cleaning indoor surfaces and removing indoor objects. Inappropriate orders of implementation refer to orders that make measures not implementable such as mechanical digging before grass cutting. Hence, the focus here is on (i) combinations of measures, whose possible impacts are crucial for targets being located next to each other, (ii) combinations of measures, whose targets depend on each other, and (iii) orders of implementation that are not possible due to logical inconsistencies.

Merging assumes that if at least one transition corresponds in different Petri nets, the nets can be merged. Furthermore, if not explicitly modeled, merging assumes a concurrent implementation of measures. Hence, merging states what *may be possible,* which can be justified, on the one hand, through the common transition(s), but also through the similarity value, which is a determining factor for a strategy to be included in the merging. A possible approach is to explicitly capture inappropriate combinations or implementation orders of measures and to restrict possible runs of the merged net. Related research areas are, for example, history-dependent process dynamics in Petri nets by means of transition guards (van Hee, Serebrenik, Sidorova, Voorhoeve, & van der Werf, 2007), to explicitly forbid certain behavior during merging and particularly by run-time adaptation of process dynamics (Fahland & Woith, 2009), or rule-based Petri net transformations for constructing system behavior from single components (Hartmut Ehrig et al., 2008). Thus, enhancements of the merging approach as well as adaptations after merging are possible future research directions. In summary, merging at a syntactical level allows local considerations whereas merging at a semantic level requires a global approach.

8.2.2 Extending the Problem Model and the Case Base

The problem model comprises finitely many attributes, which are defined as pairs of unique label and domain. The chosen attributes are comprehensive and especially in respect of the symbolic attributes, domains are defined to enable fast reasoning in times of time pressure and uncertainty. The decision support method developed is notably useful for understanding and categorizing an event in a foreign country and thus particularly assuming that very little information is available. The domains of the symbols resulted from the project and served as basis for the scenarios generated with the help of JRodos. However, further investigations are important to extend the domain of certain symbolic attributes to retrieve more precise solutions. For example, weather categories can be refined by applying learning algorithms to simulation results of JRodos. Weather data over an extended period, different source terms, and different sites may serve as input for JRodos, which determines area sizes of early measures, for example. The learning algorithm may now identify appropriate categories for a weather situation aiming at classifying an event according to the implementation size for specific early measures. In this connection, one may detect subtler differences of possible consequences of a release by night and by day or in different types of areas. So far, urban, rural, and metropolitan areas are distinguished. However, the installation site and the surrounding area, which are respected in the simulations of JRodos, have consequences on the dispersion and deposition of radioactive substances. Thus, refining the categories defined so far facilitates more appropriate results.

The core of the decision support method is the case base storing problem descriptions and appropriate solution descriptions to be reused to solve a current problem. As Figure 4.5 illustrates, the distribution over the accident phases is not balanced. Hence, as also indicated in Chapter 7.2, problems referring to relocation or remediation in general, cannot be handled so far, since the corresponding cases are missing in the case base. From a methodical point of view, this thesis is not limited to specific problems assigned to release or decontamination, for example. However, the concrete implementation and application of the decision support method requires enough cases particularly referring to the competence of a CBR system (Chapter 2.1.4), which is particularly important with regard to the maintenance of the case base where knowledge is added, deleted, or modified. Furthermore, collecting cases for the transition and long-term post-accident is challenging and requires a close cooperation of experts. Strategies cannot be generated automatically but need to be reviewed by experts for approval. In general, scenario-based analyses are important for handling the various uncertainties in the course of a nuclear accident and particularly to take into account variations in the weather prognosis and the source term (French et al., 2017). This thesis especially suggests to *store* this knowledge and to *elaborate appropriate strategies* in the course of uncertainty analyses. Future research must particularly be devoted to the topic *knowledge elicitation*.

8.2.3 Transferring to Further Disaster Types

The case-based decision support method that integrates CBR, the development of scenarios, HLPNs, and MCDA, is, from a methodical point of view, transferrable to other disaster types, since the approach of identifying appropriate strategies experience-based is independent of the underlying triggering event. However, one may not directly transfer the method developed without (i) clearly define the objectives of decision support and (ii) adapt the models to the disaster type to be investigated. With regard to the first point, the overarching objective in nuclear emergency management is to protect public and environment, where the measures chosen need to be commensurate and decided in a societal consensus. Thus, decision support particularly aims at helping in identifying *strategies* that define a *fundamental procedure* to achieve the overarching objective. Hence, the decision support method developed can be transferred to further application examples, where, generally speaking, a course of actions is searched for. However, as indicated before, the models that are part of the decision support method need to be adapted to the new disaster type. This refers to the problem model and the choice of attributes describing a problem as well as the solution model and the attributes reflecting the effectiveness of a solution. In this context, similarity functions need to be adapted too, since domain properties need to be investigated for each attribute individually. The attribute-based representation of cases is very flexible whereas for each new event, appropriate attributes need to be elaborated with domain experts. The case base has a flat organization facilitating the transfer to other disaster types. However, this form of representation does also mean that problems are solved locally as the assumptions in Chapter 1 indicate: The *whole problem* in the course of a (potential) nuclear accident, not knowing which strategy is appropriate to protect public and environment from a possible radiation exposure, is divided into several *sub-problems* that particularly focus on specific areas during specific accident phases. Thus, although being part of an accident, an aspect that is particularly captured in the database, each case in the case base describes a stand-alone problem and regarding this, retrieval is organized. Accordingly, the method developed supports solving problems locally but, for example, does not indicate conflicting solutions in neighboring areas. To compensate, an approach is re-organizing the case base and deliberately link cases through case characteristics and enhance retrieval respectively. However, this kind of case base representation would imply complex scenario construction and thus has been excluded in the framework of this thesis. Another approach is to determine strategies locally and then to merge them for analyzing the gained solution affecting a larger area. Here, it is important to remain in one accident phase since solutions for different accident phases cannot be combined.

In summary, the reason for focusing on nuclear accidents is, besides the scientific relevance, the possibilities given for elaborating the models in more detail. From a methodical point of view, the case-based method is transferrable to other decision problems, where a decision consists in choosing one or several measures and to combine them appropriately. However, the method derives first possible solutions *heuristic-based* to be analyzed according to several criteria afterwards. Hence, transferability has to be judged according to validity of the main assumption that similar problems have similar solutions. The new decision support method in this thesis particularly facilitates decision-making in complex situations where diverse issues prevail, notably by combining intuitive with analytical approaches

Bibliography

Aamodt, A., & Plaza, E. (1994). Case-based reasoning: Foundational issues, methodological variations, and system approaches. *AI Communications*, *7*(1), 39–59. https://doi.org/10.3233/AIC-1994-7104

Agerwala, T., & Choed-Amphai, Y.-C. (1978). A Synthesis Rule for Concurrent Systems. In *15th Design Automation Conference* (pp. 305–311). Las Vegas, NV, USA: IEEE. https://doi.org/10.1109/DAC.1978.1585190

Ahn, H., Kim, K., & Han, I. (2006). Global optimization of feature weights and the number of neighbors that combine in a case-based reasoning system. *Expert Systems*, *23*(5). https://doi.org/10.1111/j.1468-0394.2006.00410.x

Alptekin, G. I., & Büyüközkan, G. (2011). An integrated case-based reasoning and MCDM system for Web based tourism destination planning. *Expert Systems with Applications*, *38*(3), 2125–2132. https://doi.org/10.1016/j.eswa.2010.07.153

Althoff, K.-D. (1995). Evaluating Case-Based Reasoning Systems. In A. Aamodt, K.-D. Althoff, R. Magaldi, & R. Milne (Eds.), *Case-Based Reasoning: A New Force In Advanced Systems Development*. Unicom Seminars & AI Intelligence.

Amailef, K., & Lu, J. (2013). Ontology-supported case-based reasoning approach for intelligent m-Government emergency response services. *Decision Support Systems*, *55*(1), 79–97. https://doi.org/10.1016/j.dss.2012.12.034

Aoki, M., & Rothwell, G. (2013). A comparative institutional analysis of the Fukushima nuclear disaster: Lessons and policy implications. *Energy Policy*, *53*, 240–247. https://doi.org/10.1016/j.enpol.2012.10.058

Arjona, E., Bueno, G., & López-Mellado, E. (2010). Synthesis of Coloured Petri Nets from Natural-like Language Descriptions. In *Advances in Petri Net Theory and Applications.* IntechOpen. https://doi.org/10.5772/10293

Armaghan, N., & Renaud, J. (2012). An application of multi-criteria decision aids models for Case-Based Reasoning. *Information Sciences*, *210*, 55–66. https://doi.org/10.1016/j.ins.2012.04.033

Assali, A. A., Lenne, D., & Debray, B. (2009). Case retrieval in ontology-based CBR systems. In B. Mertsching, M. Hund, Z. Aziz (Eds.) *KI 2009: Advances in Artificial Intelligence. KI 2009. Lecture Notes in Computer Science* (Vol. 5803, pp. 564–571). Springer Berlin Heidelberg. https://doi.org/10.1007/978-3-642-04617-9_71

Auriol, E., Clark, M., Cox, P., Diamond, B., Hunn, M., Koemmerer, C., ... Ward, B. (2004). *Learning from critical incidents: knowledge management methods and technologies for supporting critical incident managers*. (A. Lewis, Ed.). [S.l.]: Les éditions Sapientia.

Avesani, P., Perini, A., & Ricci, F. (2000). Interactive Case-Based Planning for Forest Fire Management. *Applied Intelligence, 13*, 41–57. https://doi.org/10.1023/A:1008327312956

Bai, S., Staudt, C., Kaiser, J. C., & Raskob, W. (2018). Knowledge Database and Regionalization of JRODOS for the HARMONE Project. In *4th NERIS Workshop, Adapting nuclear and radiological emergency preparedness, response and recovery to a changing world*. Dublin, Ireland.

Bammidi, P., & Moore, K. L. (1994). Emergency Management Systems: A Systems Approach. In *IEEE International Conference on Systems, Man and Cybernetics*. San Antonio, TX, USA: IEEE. https://doi.org/10.1109/ICSMC.1994.400070

Barbarosoğlu, G., Özdamar, L., & Cevik, A. (2002). An Interactive Approach for Hierarchical Analysis of Helicopter Logistics in Disaster Relief Operations. *European Journal of Operational Research*, 140(1), 118–133. https://doi.org/10.1016/S0377-2217(01)00222-3

Beamon, B. M., & Balcik, B. (2008). Performance measurement in humanitarian relief chains. *International Journal of Public Sector Management, 21*(1), 4–25. https://doi.org/10.1108/09513550810846087

Belton, V., & Stewart, T. J. (2002). *Multiple Criteria Decision Analysis An Integrated Approach*. Kluwer Academic Publishers. https://doi.org/10.1007/978-1-4615-1495-4

Bergmann, R. (2002). *Experience Management: Foundations, Development Methodology, and Internet-Based Applications. Lecture Notes in Computer Science (Vol. 2432)*. Springer-Verlag Berlin Heidelberg. https://doi.org/10.1007/3-540-45759-3

Bergmann, R., Kolodner, J., & Plaza, E. (2006). Representation in case-based reasoning. *The Knowledge Engineering Review, 20*(3), 209–213. https://doi.org/10.1017/S0269888906000555

Bergmann, R., Muñoz-Avila, H., & Veloso, M. M. (1996). General-Purpose Case-Based Planning: Methods and Systems. *AI Communications, 9(3)*, 128-137.

Bergmann, R., Wilke, W., Vollrath, I., & Wess, S. (1996). Integrating General Knowledge with Object-Oriented Case Representation and Reasoning. In H.-D. Burkhard & M. Lenz (Eds.), *4th German Workshop: Case-Based Reasoning - System Development and Evaluation* (pp. 120–127). Berlin, Germany.

Bertsch, V. (2007). *Uncertainty Handling in Multi-Attribute Decision Support for Industrial Risk Management*. Universität Karlsruhe (TH).

Bertsch, V., Treitz, M., Geldermann, J., & Rentz, O. (2007). Sensitivity analyses in multi-attribute decision support for off-site nuclear emergency and recovery management. *International Journal of Energy Sector Management, 1*(4), 342–365. https://doi.org/10.1108/17506220710836075

Betke, H., & Seifert, M. (2017). BPMN for Disaster Response Processes – A methodical extension. In M. Eibl & M. Gaedke (Eds.), *INFORMATIK 2017, Lecture Notes in Informatics, Gesellschaft für Informatik* (pp. 1311-1324). Bonn, Germany. https://doi.org/10.18420/in2017_132

Bhargava, H. K., Power, D. J., & Sun, D. (2007). Progress in Web-based decision support technologies. *Decision Support Systems, 43*(4), 1083–1095. https://doi.org/10.1016/j.dss.2005.07.002

Bishop, P., Hines, A., & Collins, T. (2007). The current state of scenario development: an overview of techniques. *Foresight, 9*(1), 5–25. https://doi.org/10.1108/14636680710727516

Bogaerts, S., & Leake, D. B. (2004). Facilitating CBR for incompletely-described cases: Distance metrics for partial problem descriptions. In P. Funk & P. A. González Calero (Eds.), *Advances in Case-Based Reasoning. ECCBR 2004. Lecture Notes in Computer Science* (Vol. 3155, pp. 62–76). Springer, Berlin, Heidelberg. https://doi.org/10.1007/978-3-540-28631-8_6

Bonisoli, A., Gerevini, A. E., Saetti, A., & Serina, I. (2015). Effective plan retrieval in case-based planning for metric-temporal problems. *Journal of Experimental and Theoretical Artificial Intelligence, 27*(5), 603–647. https://doi.org/10.1080/0952813X.2014.993506

Bonissone, P. P., & Cheetham, W. (1997). Financial applications of fuzzy case-based reasoning to residential property valuation. In *Proceedings of 6th International Fuzzy Systems Conference*. Barcelona, Spain: IEEE. https://doi.org/10.1109/FUZZY.1997.616341

Bonzano, A., Cunningham, P., & Smyth, B. (1997). Using introspective learning to improve retrieval in CBR: A case study in air traffic control. In D. B. Leake & E. Plaza (Eds.), *Case-Based Reasoning Research and Development. ICCBR 1997. Lecture Notes in Computer Science (Lecture Notes in Artificial Intelligence)* (Vol. 1266, pp. 291–302). Springer, Berlin, Heidelberg. https://doi.org/10.1007/3-540-63233-6_500

Borges, A. P., Dordal, O. B., Ribeiro, R., Ávila, B. C., & Scalabrin, E. E. (2015). Generation of Economical Driving Plans Using Continuous Case-Based Planning. In S. Hammoudi, L. Maciaszek, E. Teniente, O. Camp, & J. Cordeiro (Eds.), *Enterprise Information Systems. ICEIS 2015. Lecture Notes in Business Information Processing* (Vol. 241, pp. 192–213). Springer, Cham. https://doi.org/10.1007/978-3-319-29133-8

Boriah, S., Chandola, V., & Kumar, V. (2008). Similarity Measures for Categorical Data: A Comparative Evaluation. In *Proceedings of the SIAM International Conference on Data Mining,* (pp. 243–254). Atlanta, Georgia, USA. https://doi.org/10.1137/1.9781611972788.22

Börjeson, L., Höjer, M., Dreborg, K.-H., Ekvall, T., & Finnveden, G. (2006). Scenario types and techniques: Towards a user's guide. *Futures, 38*(7), 723–739. https://doi.org/10.1016/j.futures.2005.12.002

Borrajo, D., Roubíčková, A., & Serina, I. (2015). Progress in Case-Based Planning. *ACM Computing Surveys, 47*(2), 1–39. https://doi.org/10.1145/2674024

Bouafia, M., & Zahari Khairi, R. (2017). Naturalistic Decision-Making in Natural Disasters: An Overview. *Journal of Geography & Natural Disasters, 7*(1), 1–5. https://doi.org/10.4172/2167-0587.1000186

Bradfield, R., Wright, G., Burt, G., Cairns, G., & Van Der Heijden, K. (2005). The origins and evolution of scenario techniques in long range business planning. *Futures, 37*(8), 795–812. https://doi.org/10.1016/j.futures.2005.01.003

Bradley, M. M. (2007). NARAC: an emergency response resource for predicting the atmospheric dispersion and assessing the consequences of airborne radionuclides. *Journal of Environmental Radioactivity, 96*(1-3), 116–121. https://doi.org/10.1016/j.jenvrad.2007.01.020

Brown, J., Watson, S., Nisbet, A. (2015). *UK Recovery Handbooks for Radiation Incidents 2015 Drinking Water Supplies Handbook* (4.2). Retrieved June 7, 2017, from https://www.gov.uk/government/publications/uk-recovery-handbooks-for-radiation-incidents-2015

Brown, D. E., & Robinson, D. C. (2005). Development of Metrics to Evaluate Effectiveness of Emergency Response Operations. In *10th International command and Control Research and Technology Symposium The Future of C2*. University of Virginia, Charlottesville, VA, USA.

Brown, J., Hammond, D. J., & Kwakman, P. (2009). *Generic handbook for assisting in the management of contaminated drinking water in Europe following a radiological emergency Version 2*. Retrieved May 5, 2018, from https://euranos.iket.kit.edu/index.php?action=euranos&title=products

Bruland, T., Aamodt, A., & Langseth, H. (2011). A hybrid CBR and BN architecture refined through data analysis. In *11th International Conference on Intelligent Systems Design and Applications, ISDA* (pp. 906–913). Cordoba, Spain: IEEE. https://doi.org/10.1109/ISDA.2011.6121773

Bulanov, P., Lazovik, A., & Aiello, M. (2011). Business process customization using process merging techniques. In *IEEE International Conference on Service-Oriented Computing and Applications (SOCA)*. Irvine, CA, USA: IEEE. https://doi.org/10.1109/SOCA.2011.6166255

Bundesamt für Strahlenschutz. (2012). *Die Katastrophe im Kernkraftwerk Fukushima nach dem Seebeben vom 11.März 2011*. Retrieved February 4, 2019, from http://www.bfs.de

Burkhard, H.-D., & Richter, M. M. (2001). On the Notion of Similarity in Case Based Reasoning and Fuzzy Theory. In Sankar Kumar Pal, T. S. Dillon, & D. S. Yeung (Eds.), *Soft Computing in Case Based Reasoning* (pp. 29–46). Springer London. https://doi.org/10.1007/978-1-4471-0687-6_2

Callen, J., & Homma, T. (2017). Lessons Learned in Protection of the Public for the Accident at the Fukushima Daiichi Nuclear Power Plant. *Health Physics, 112*(6), 550–559. https://doi.org/10.1097/HP.0000000000000666

Carrick, C., Yang, Q., Abi-Zeid, I., & Lamontagne, L. (1999). Activating CBR Systems through Autonomous Information Gathering. In K.-D. Althoff & L. K. Branting (Eds.), *Case-Based Reasoning Research and Development. ICCBR 1999. Lecture Notes in Computer Science (Lecture Notes in Artificial Intelligence)* (Vol. 1650, pp. 74–88). Springer, Berlin, Heidelberg. https://doi.org/10.1007/3-540-48508-2_6

Carter, E., & French, S. (2005). Nuclear Emergency Management in Europe: a Review of Approaches to Decision Making. In B. Van de Walle & B. Carlé (Eds.), *2nd International Conference on Information Systems for Crisis Response and Management (ISCRAM 2005)* (pp. 247–259). Brussels, Belgium.

CEN. (2009a). CWA 15931-1 Disaster and emergency management - Shared situation awareness - Part 1: Message structure. Retrieved May 5, 2013, from https://www.oasis-open.org/committees/download.php/42411/CWA_15931-1

CEN. (2009b). CWA 15931-2 Disaster and emergency management - Shared situation awareness - Part 2: Codes for the message structure. Retrieved May 5, 2013, from https://www.oasis-open.org/committees/download.php/42412/CWA_15931-2.pdf

Center for Disaster Management and Risk Reduction Technology (CEDIM). (2005). *Glossary Terms and definitions of risk sciences*. Retrieved May 3, 2018, from https://www.cedim.kit.edu/download/glossar-gesamt-20050624.pdf

Chakraborty, B., Ghosh, D., Maji, R. K., Garnaik, S., & Debnath, N. (2010). Knowledge Management with Case-Based Reasoning Applied on Fire Emergency Handling. In *8th IEEE International Conference on Industrial Informatics* (pp. 708–713). Osaka, Japan: IEEE. https://doi.org/10.1109/indin.2010.5549654

Cheetham, W. (2000). Case-Based Reasoning with Confidence. In E. Blanzieri & L. Portinale (Eds.), *Advances in Case-Based Reasoning. EWCBR 2000. Lecture Notes in Computer Science (Lecture Notes in Artificial Intelligence)* (Vol. 1898, pp. 15–25). Springer, Berlin, Heidelberg. https://doi.org/10.1007/3-540-44527-7_3

Cheetham, W., & Price, J. (2004). Measures of Solution Accuracy in Case-Based Reasoning Systems. In Peter Funk & P. A. González-Calero (Eds.), *Advances in Case-Based Reasoning. ECCBR 2004. Lecture Notes in Computer Science, vol 3155.* (pp. 106–118). Springer, Berlin, Heidelberg. https://doi.org/10.1007/978-3-540-28631-8_9

Cheminod, M., Bertolotti, I. C., Durante, L., & Valenzano, A. (2013). Modeling Emergency Response Plans with Coloured Petri Nets. In B. Hämmerli, N. Kalstad Svendsen, & J. Lopez (Eds.), *Critical Information Infrastructures Security. Lecture Notes in Computer Science* (Vol. 7722, pp. 106–117). Springer, Berlin, Heidelberg. https://doi.org/10.1007/978-3-642-41485-5_10

Chen, Y., Kilgour, D. M., & Hipel, K. W. (2011). A case-based distance approach to multiple criteria ranking. In *8th International Conference on Service Systems and Service Management - Proceedings of ICSSSM'11*. Tianjin, China: IEEE. https://doi.org/10.1109/ICSSSM.2011.5959466

Cheng, W., & Hüllermeier, E. (2008). Learning similarity functions from qualitative feedback. In K.-D. Althoff, R. Bergmann, M. Minor, & A. Hanft (Eds.), *Advances in Case-Based Reasoning. ECCBR 2008. Lecture Notes in Computer Science* (Vol. 5239, pp. 120–134). Springer, Berlin, Heidelberg. https://doi.org/10.1007/978-3-540-85502-6_8

Chino, M., Ishikawa, H., & Yamazawa, H. (1993). SPEEDI and WSPEEDI: Japanese emergency response systems to predict radiological impacts in local and worldwide areas due to a nuclear accident. *Radiation Protection Dosimetry, 50*(2–4), 145–152.

Chua, J. J., & Tischer, P. E. (2004). Determining the Trustworthiness of a Case-Based Reasoning Solution. In M. Mohammadian (Ed.) *Proceedings of the 2004 International Conference on Computational Intelligence for Modelling, Control and Automation - CIMCA '2004* (pp. 952-962). University of Canberra.

Clemen, R. T., & Reilly, T. (2001). *Making Hard Decisions with Decision Tools®.* Cengage Learning.

Comes, M. (2011). *Decision Maps for Distributed Multi-Criteria Decision Support*. Karlsruhe Institute of Technology (KIT).

Comes, T., Hiete, M., Wijngaards, N., & Schultmann, F. (2010). Enhancing Robustness in Multi-criteria Decision-Making: A Scenario-Based Approach. In *2nd International Conference on Intelligent Networking and Collaborative Systems, INCoS 2010* (pp. 484–489). Thessaloniki, Greece: IEEE. https://doi.org/10.1109/INCOS.2010.16

Comes, T., Wijngaards, N., & Van de Walle, B. (2015). Exploring the future : Runtime scenario selection for complex and time-bound decisions. *Technological Forecasting & Social Change, 97*, 29–46. https://doi.org/10.1016/j.techfore.2014.03.009

Cortadella, J., Kishinevsky, M., Lavagno, L., & Yakovlev, A. (1995). Synthesizing Petri Nets from State-Based Models. In *Proceedings of IEEE International Conference on Computer Aided Design (ICCAD)* (pp. 164–171). San Jose, CA, USA: IEEE. https://doi.org/10.1109/ICCAD.1995.480008

Craw, S., Wiratunga, N., & Rowe, R. C. (2006). Learning adaptation knowledge to improve case-based reasoning. *Artificial Intelligence, 170*(16–17), 1175–1192. https://doi.org/10.1016/j.artint.2006.09.001

Cunningham, P. (1998). CBR : Strengths and Weaknesses. In A. P. del Pobil, J. Mira, & M. Ali (Eds.), *Tasks and Methods in Applied Artificial Intelligence. IEA/AIE 1998. Lecture Notes in Computer Science (Lecture Notes in Artificial Intelligence)* (Vol 1416, pp. 517-524). Springer, Berlin, Heidelberg. https://doi.org/10.1007/3-540-64574-8_437

D'Aquin, M., Badra, F., Lafrogne, S., Lieber, J., Napoli, A., & Szathmary, L. (2007). Case base mining for adaptation knowledge acquisition. In *20th International Joint Conference on Artificial Intelligence IJCAI'07* (pp. 750–755). Hyderabad, India.

Daniell, J. E., Khazai, B., Wenzel, F., & Vervaeck, A. (2011). The CATDAT damaging earthquakes database. *Natural Hazards and Earth System Science, 11*(8), 2235–2251. https://doi.org/10.5194/nhess-11-2235-2011

Davenport, T. H., & Prusak, L. (1998). *Working Knowledge: How Organizations Manage What They Know*. Harvard Business School Press.

de Brito, M. M., & Evers, M. (2016). Multi-criteria decision-making for flood risk management: A survey of the current state of the art. *Natural Hazards and Earth System Sciences, 16*(4), 1019–1033. https://doi.org/10.5194/nhess-16-1019-2016

Dharani, B., & Geetha, T. V. (2013). Adaptive Learning Path Generation using Colored Petri Nets based on Behavioral Aspects. In *International Conference on Recent Trends in Information Technology (ICRTIT)* (pp. 459–465). Chennai, India : IEEE. https://doi.org/10.1109/icrtit.2013.6844247

Dijkman, R. (2007). A Classification of Differences between Similar Business Processes. In *11th IEEE International Enterprise Distributed Object Computing Conference (EDOC 2007)* (pp. 37–37). Annapolis, MD, USA: IEEE. https://doi.org/10.1109/EDOC.2007.24

Dilmaghani, R. B., & Rao, R. R. (2009). A Systematic Approach to Improve Communication for Emergency Response. In *42nd Hawaii International Conference on System Sciences*. Big Island, HI, USA: IEEE. https://doi.org/10.1109/hicss.2009.39

Ding, Z.-J., Wang, J.-L., & Jiang, C.-J. (2008). An Approach for Synthesis Petri Nets for Modeling and Verifying Composite Web Service. *Journal of Information Science and Engineering, 24*(5), 1309–1328.

Dvir, G., Langholz, G., & Schneider, M. (1999). Matching attributes in a fuzzy case based reasoning. In *18th International Conference of the North American Fuzzy Information Processing Society - NAFIPS* (pp. 33–36). New York, NY, USA: IEEE. https://doi.org/10.1109/NAFIPS.1999.781647

Ehrhardt, J., & Weis, A. (Eds). (2000). *RODOS : Decision support system for off-site nuclear emergency management in Europe, Final report of the RODOS project, European Commission, Brussels. Report EUR 19144*. Retrieved May 5, 2013, from https://publications.europa.eu/en/publication-detail/-/publication/4750bb8c-b9c6-4761-a4fd-3c553230d340

Ehrig, Hartmut, Hoffmann, K., Padberg, J., Ermel, C., Prange, U., Biermann, E., & Modica, T. (2008). Petri Net Transformations. In V. Kordic (Ed.), *Petri Net,Theory and Applications*. IntechOpen. https://doi.org/10.5772/5310

El-Sappagh, S. H., & Elmogy, M. (2015). Case Based Reasoning : Case Representation Methodologies. *International Journal of Advanced Computer Science and Applications*, *6*(11), 192–208. https://doi.org/10.14569/IJACSA.2015.061126

ENCO for European Commission DG ENER. (2014). *Review of Current Off-site Nuclear Emergency Preparedness and Response Arrangements in EU Member States and Neighbouring Countries*. https://doi.org/10.2833/20298

Euratom. (2016). Council Regulation (Euratom) 2016/52. *Official Journal of the European Union*. Retrieved February 4, 2019, from https://eur-lex.europa.eu/legal-content/EN/TXT/?uri=uriserv:OJ.L_.2016.013.01.0002.01.ENG

Fahland, D. (2009). Oclets - Scenario-based modeling with Petri nets. In G. Franceschinis & K. Wolf (Eds.), *Applications and Theory of Petri Nets. PETRI NETS 2009. Lecture Notes in Computer Science* (Vol. 5606, pp. 223–242). Springer, Berlin, Heidelberg. https://doi.org/10.1007/978-3-642-02424-5_14

Fahland, D., & Woith, H. (2009). Towards Process Models for Disaster Response. In *Business Process Management Workshops. BPM 2008. Lecture Notes in Business Information Processing* (Vol. 17, pp. 254–265). Springer, Berlin, Heidelberg. https://doi.org/10.1007/978-3-642-00328-8_25

Fan, Z.-P., Li, Y.-H., Wang, X., & Liu, Y. (2014). Hybrid similarity measure for case retrieval in CBR and its application to emergency response towards gas explosion. *Expert Systems with Applications*, *41*(5), 2526–2534. https://doi.org/10.1016/j.eswa.2013.09.051

Federal Office of Civil Protection and Disaster Assistance. (2011). Method of Risk Analysis for Civil Protection. Retrieved May 5, 2013, from http://www.bbk.bund.de/SharedDocs/Downloads/BBK/EN/booklets_leaflets/Method_of_ Risk_Analysis.pdf?__blob=publicationFile

Fernández-Riverola, F., Díaz, F., & Corchado, J. M. (2007). Reducing the Memory Size of a Fuzzy Case-Based Reasoning System Applying Rough Set Techniques. *IEEE Transactions on Systems, Man, and Cybernetics - Part C: Applications and Reviews*, *37*(1), 138–146. https://doi.org/10.1109/tsmcc.2006.876058

Franke, J., Charoy, F., & Ulmer, C. (2010). A Model for Temporal Coordination of Disaster Response Activities. In S. French, B. Tomaszewski, & C. Zobel (Eds.), *7th International Conference on Information Systems for Crisis Response and Management (ISCRAM 2010)*. Seattle, USA.

French, S. (1997). Uncertainty Modelling, Data Assimilation and Decision Support for Management of Off-Site Nuclear Emergencies. *Radiation Protection Dosimetry, 73*(1-4), 11–15. https://doi.org/10.1093/oxfordjournals.rpd.a032110

French, S. (2003). Modelling, making inferences and making decisions: The roles of sensitivity analysis. *Top, 11*, 229–251. https://doi.org/10.1007/BF02579043

French, S, Argyris, N., Haywood, S., Hort, M., & Smith, J. Q. (2017). Uncertainty Handling during Nuclear Accidents. In T. Comes, F. Bénaben, C. Hanachi, M. Lauras, & A. Montarnal (Eds.), *14th International Conference on Information Systems for Crisis Response and Management (ISCRAM 2017)*. Albi, France.

French, S, & Niculae, C. (2005). Believe in the Model: Mishandle the Emergency. *Journal of Homeland Security & Emergency Management, 2*(1), 1–16. https://doi.org/10.2202/1547-7355.1108

Gallego, E., Brittain, J. E., Håkanson, L., Heling, R., Hofman, D., & Monte, L. (2000). MOIRA : A Computerised Decision Support System for the Restoration of Radionuclide Contaminated Freshwater Ecosystems. In *10th International Congress of the International Radiation Protection Association*. Hiroshima, Japan.

García, F. A., Orozco, J., Gonzàlez, J., & Arcos, J. L. (2007). Assessing Confidence in Cased Based Reuse Step. In *10th International Conference of the Catalan Association for Artificial Intelligence, CCIA 2007*. Sant Julià de Lòria, Andorra.

Garrido, A., Morales, L., & Serina, I. (2016). On the use of case-based planning for e-learning personalization. *Expert Systems with Applications, 60*, 1–15. https://doi.org/10.1016/j.eswa.2016.04.030

Geldermann, J., Bertsch, V., Treitz, M., French, S., Papamichail, K. N., & Hämäläinen, R. P. (2009). Multi-criteria decision support and evaluation of strategies for nuclear remediation management. *Omega, 37*(1), 238–251. https://doi.org/10.1016/j.omega.2006.11.006

Georgiadou, P. S., Papazoglou, I. A., Kiranoudis, C. T., & Markatos, N. C. (2010). Multi-objective evolutionary emergency response optimization for major accidents. *Journal of Hazardous Materials*, *178*(1-3), 792–803. https://doi.org/10.1016/j.jhazmat.2010.02.010

German Commission on Radiological Protection. (2014). Basic Radiological Principles for Decisions on Measures for the Protection of the Population against Incidents involving Releases of Radionuclides. Retrieved May 5,2018, from https://www.ssk.de/SharedDocs/Beratungsergebnisse_PDF/2014/RadiologischeGrundlagen_e.html

Gervasio, M. T., Iba, W., & Langley, P. (1998). Case-Based Seeding for an Interactive Crisis Response Assistant.In D. W. Aha & J. Daniels (Eds.), *Case-Based Reasoning Integrations: Papers from the 1998 Workshop (Technical Report WS-98-15)*. AAAI Press.

Gesellschaft für Anlagen- und Reaktorsicherheit (GRS). (2016). *Fukushima Daiichi - Unfallablauf, radiologische Folgen*. Retrieved February 4, 2019, from https://www.grs.de/publikation/grs-s-56

Gomes, P. (2004). Software Design Retrieval Using Bayesian Networks and WordNet. In P. Funk & P. A. González Calero (Eds.), *Advances in Case-Based Reasoning. ECCBR 2004. Lecture Notes in Computer Science* (Vol. 3155, pp. 184–197). Springer, Berlin, Heidelberg. https://doi.org/https://doi.org/10.1007/978-3-540-28631-8_15

Gottschalk, F., van der Aalst, W. M. P., & Jansen-Vullers, M. H. (2008). Merging Event-Driven Process Chains. In R. Meersman & Z. Tari (Eds.), *On the Move to Meaningful Internet Systems: OTM 2008. OTM 2008. Lecture Notes in Computer Science* (Vol. 5331, pp. 418–426). Springer, Berlin, Heidelberg. https://doi.org/10.1007/978-3-540-88871-0_28

Greco, Salvatore, Matarazzo, B., & Slowinski, R. (2006). Dominance-Based Rough Set Approach to Case-Based Reasoning. In V. Torra, Y. Narukawa, A. Valls, & J. Domingo-Ferrer (Eds.), *Modeling Decisions for Artificial Intelligence. MDAI 2006. Lecture Notes in Computer Science* (Vol. 3885, pp. 7–18). Springer, Berlin, Heidelberg. https://doi.org/https://doi.org/10.1007/11681960_3

Greene, D., Freyne, J., Smyth, B., & Cunningham, P. (2010). An Analysis of Current Trends in CBR Research Using Multiview Clustering. *AI Magazine*, *31*(2), 45–62. https://doi.org/10.1609/aimag.v31i2.2243

Gruber, T. R. (1993). A translation approach to portable ontology specifications. *Knowledge Acquisition*, *5*(2), 199–220. https://doi.org/10.1006/knac.1993.1008

Guillen-Scholten, J., Arbab, F., de Boer, F., & Bonsangue, M. (2006). Modeling the Exogenous Coordination of Mobile Channel-based Systems with Petri Nets. *Electronic Notes in Theoretical Computer Science*, *154*(1), 121–138. https://doi.org/10.1016/j.entcs.2005.12.036

Guo, L., Liu, Y., Wang, P., Meng, X., Jiang, J., Wang, Y., … Sun, H. (2009). Emergency Decision-Making Case Base System for River Region Based on CBR-AHP. In *International Conference on Energy and Environment Technology (ICEET 2009)*. Guilin, Guangxi, China: IEEE. https://doi.org/10.1109/ICEET.2009.369

Guo, Y., Peng, Y., & Hu, J. (2013). Research on high creative application of case-based reasoning system on engineering design. *Computers in Industry*, *64*(1), 90–103. https://doi.org/10.1016/j.compind.2012.10.006

Gupta, A., & Shah, H. C. (1998). The strategy effectiveness chart. *Applied Geography*, *18*(1), 55–67. https://doi.org/10.1016/S0143-6228(97)00046-5

Hammond, K. J. (1986). CHEF: A model of case-based planning. In *Proceedings of the Fifth National Conference on Artificial Intelligence* (pp. 267–271). Philadelphia, PA, USA: AAAI Press.

Hanney, K., & Keane, M. T. (1996). Learning adaptation rules from a case-base. In I. Smith & B. Faltings (Eds.), *Advances in Case-Based Reasoning. EWCBR 1996. Lecture Notes in Computer Science (Lecture Notes in Artificial Intelligence)* (Vol. 1168, pp. 179–192). Springer, Berlin, Heidelberg. https://doi.org/10.1007/BFb0020610

Hansson, K., Larsson, A., Danielson, M., & Ekenberg, L. (2011). Coping with complex environmental and societal flood risk management decisions: An integrated multi-criteria framework. *Sustainability*, *3*(9), 1357–1380. https://doi.org/10.3390/su3091357

Hardie, S. M. L., & McKinley, I. G. (2014). Fukushima remediation: status and overview of future plans. *Journal of Environmental Radioactivity, 133*, 75–85. https://doi.org/10.1016/j.jenvrad.2013.08.002

HERCA, & WENRA. (2014). HERCA-WENRA Approach for a better cross-border coordination of protective actions during the early phase of a nuclear accident. Retrieved January 15, 2015, from http://www.wenra.org/archives/new-european-approach-cross-border-emergency-prepa/

Hild, J., Fischer, Y., Ott, J., & Glökler, C. (2010). Markov Based Decision Support for Cost-Optimal Response in Security Management. In S. French, B. Tomaszewski, & C. Zobel (Eds.), *7th International Conference on Information Systems for Crisis Response and Management (ISCRAM 2010)*. Seattle, USA.

Hill, J. C., & Wright, P. C. (1997). From text to Petri nets: the difficulties of describing accident scenarios formally. In M. D. Harrison & J. C. Torres (Eds.), *Design, Specification and Verification of Interactive Systems '97. Eurographics.* (pp. 161–176). Springer, Vienna. https://doi.org/10.1007/978-3-7091-6878-3_11

Hirsch, H. (2011). *Fukushima – Einstufung auf INES - Skala*. Retrieved February 4, 2019, from https://www.greenpeace.de/sites/www.greenpeace.de/files/HH_INES_Rating_Fukushima_23_03_2011.pdf

Hoe, S., McGinnity, P., Charnock, T., Gering, F., Schou Jacobsen, L. H., Havskov Sørensen, J., … Astrup, P. (2009). ARGOS Decision Support System for Emergency Management. In *12th International Congress of the International Radiation Protection Association*. Buenos Aires, Argentina.

Hofmann, M., Betke, H., & Sackmann, S. (2015). Process-Oriented Disaster Response Management: A Structured Literature Review. *Business Process Management Journal, 21*(5), 966–987. https://doi.org/10.1108/bpmj-07-2014-0069

Hollnagel, E., & Fujita, Y. (2013). The Fukushima Disaster - Systemic Failures as the Lack of Resilience. *Nuclear Engineering and Technology, 45*(1), 13–20. https://doi.org/10.5516/net.03.2011.078

Horsman, G., Laing, C., & Vickers, P. (2012). A Case Based Reasoning Framework for Improving the Trustworthiness of Digital Forensic Investigations. In *IEEE 11th International Conference on Trust, Security and Privacy in Computing and Communications*. Liverpool, UK: IEEE https://doi.org/10.1109/TrustCom.2012.18

Hsieh, F.-S., & Chiang, C. Y. (2011). Collaborative composition of processes in holonic manufacturing systems. *Computers in Industry*, *62*(1), 51–64. https://doi.org/10.1016/j.compind.2010.05.012

Huang, Chao, Huang, Q. Y., Zhong, S. B., & Chen, J. G. (2013). Case Reuse Based on Fuzzy Reasoning – Adaption for Emergency Management. *Applied Mechanics and Materials*, *333–335*, 1324–1327. https://doi.org/10.4028/www.scientific.net/AMM.333-335.1324

Huang, Chun-Che, & Tseng, T.-L. B. (2004). Rough set approach to case-based reasoning application. *Expert Systems with Applications*, *26(3)*, 369–385. https://doi.org/10.1016/j.eswa.2003.09.008

Huang, W., & Tong, Z. (2011). Research on Emergency Plan Business Process modeling based on colored Petri Nets. In *Eighth International Conference on Fuzzy Systems and Knowledge Discovery (FSKD)* (pp. 2086–2089). Shanghai, China: IEEE. https://doi.org/10.1109/FSKD.2011.6020000

Iba, W., & Gervasio, M. (2000). Adaptive Assistance for Crisis Response. In *AAAI Technical Report SS-00-01*. American Association for Artificial Intelligence.

ICRP. (2007). *The 2007 Recommendations of the International Commission on Radiological Protection. ICRP Publication 103. Annals of the ICRP* (Vol. 37). Retrieved January 20, 2018, from http://www.icrp.org/page.asp?id=5

ICRP. (2009). *Application of the Commission's Recommendations for the Protection of People in Emergency Exposure Situations. ICRP Publication 109. Ann. ICRP 39 (1).* Retrieved January 20, 2018, from http://www.icrp.org/page.asp?id=5

Ievdin, I., Trybushnyi, D., Zheleznyak, M., & Raskob, W. (2010). RODOS re-engineering: aims and implementation details. *Radioprotection*, *45*(5), S181–S189. https://doi.org/10.1051/radiopro/2010024

Institute for Science and International Security. (2011). ISIS Statement on Events at Fukushima Daiichi Nuclear Site in Japan. Retrieved February 4, 2019, from http://isis-online.org/isis-reports/detail/isis-statement-on-events-at-fukushima-daiichi-nuclear-site-in-japan/

International Atomic Energy Agency (IAEA). (2007). *IAEA Safety Glossary*. Retrieved May 5, 2018, from https://www-pub.iaea.org/MTCD/publications/PDF/Pub1290_web.pdf

International Atomic Energy Agency (IAEA). (2008). *The International Nuclear and Radiological Event Scale, User's Manual*. Retrieved May 5, 2018, from https://www.iaea.org/publications/10508/ines-the-international-nuclear-and-radiological-event-scale-users-manual

International Atomic Energy Agency (IAEA). (2015a). *The Fukushima Daiichi Accident: Description and Context of the Accident* (Vol. 1). Retrieved February 4, 2019, from https://www-pub.iaea.org/MTCD/Publications/PDF/AdditionalVolumes/P1710/Pub1710-TV1-Web.pdf

International Atomic Energy Agency (IAEA). (2015b). *The Fukushima Daiichi Accident: Emergency Preparedness and Response* (Vol. 3). Retrieved February 4, 2019, from http://www-pub.iaea.org/MTCD/Publications/PDF/AdditionalVolumes/P1710/Pub1710-TV3-Web.pdf

International Atomic Energy Agency (IAEA). (2015c). *The Fukushima Daiichi Accident: Post-accident Recovery* (Vol. 5). Retrieved February 4, 2019, from https://www-pub.iaea.org/MTCD/Publications/PDF/AdditionalVolumes/P1710/Pub1710-TV5-Web.pdf

International Atomic Energy Agency (IAEA). (2018). *Arrangements for the Termination of a Nuclear or Radiological Emergency*. Retrieved February 4, 2019, from https://www.iaea.org/publications/12269/arrangements-for-the-termination-of-a-nuclear-or-radiological-emergency

International Organization for Standardization. (2000). *High-level Petri Nets - Concepts, Definitions and Graphical Notation Final Draft International Standard ISO/IEC 15909 Version 4.7.1*.

International Organization for Standardization. (2004). ISO/IEC 15909-1:2004 Systems and software engineering -- High-level Petri nets -- Part 1: Concepts, definitions and graphical notation. Retrieved December 15, 2012, from https://www.iso.org/standard/38225.html

Investigation Committee on the Accident at Fukushima Nuclear Power Stations of Tokyo Electric Power Company. (2012). *IV. Emergency Response Measures Primarily Implemented outside the Fukushima Dai-ichi Nuclear Power Station in Response to the Accident*. Retrieved February 4, 2019, from https://www.cas.go.jp/jp/seisaku/icanps/eng/05IVfinal.pdf

Jaccard, P. (1901). Distribution de la flore alpine dans le Bassin des Dranses et dans quelques regions voisines. *Bulletin de La Société Vaudoise Des Sciences Naturelles, 37*(140), 241-272.

Jagannathan, R., & Petrovic, S. (2009). Dealing with Missing Values in a Clinical Case-Based Reasoning System. In *2nd IEEE International Conference on Computer Science and Information Technology*. Beijing, China: IEEE. https://doi.org/10.1109/ICCSIT.2009.5234442

Jalali, V., & Leake, D. B. (2013). On Deriving Adaptation Rule Confidence from the Rule Generation Process. In S. J. Delany & S. Ontañón (Eds.), *Case-Based Reasoning Research and Development. ICCBR 2013. Lecture Notes in Computer Science* (Vol. 7969, pp. 179–187). Springer, Berlin, Heidelberg. https://doi.org/10.1007/978-3-642-39056-2_13

Jansen, J. M., Lijnse, B., & Plasmeijer, R. (2010). Towards Dynamic Workflow Support for Crisis Management. In S. French, B. Tomaszewski, & C. Zobel (Eds.), *7th International Conference on Information Systems for Crisis Response and Management (ISCRAM 2010)*. Seattle, USA.

Jarmulak, J., Craw, S., & Rowe, R. (2001). Using case-base data to learn adaptation knowledge for design. In *Proceedings of the 17th International Joint Conference on Artificial Intelligence - Volume 2* (pp. 1011–1016). Seattle, WA, USA: Morgan Kaufmann Publishers Inc.

Jeng, M. D., & DiCesare, F. (1993). A review of synthesis techniques for Petri Nets with applications to automated manufacturing systems. In *IEEE Transactions on Systems, Man, and Cybernetics, 23*(1), 301–312. IEEE. https://doi.org/10.1109/21.214792

Jeng, M. D. (1995). Modular synthesis of Petri nets for modeling flexible manufacturing systems. *International Journal of Flexible Manufacturing Systems, 7*, 287–310. https://doi.org/10.1007/BF01325038

Jensen, K., & Kristensen, L. M. (2009). *Coloured Petri Nets Modelling and Validation of Concurrent Systems*. Springer-Verlag Berlin Heidelberg. https://doi.org/10.1007/b95112

Jensen, K., & Rozenberg, G. (Eds.). (1991). *High-level Petri Nets Theory and Application*. Springer-Verlag Berlin Heidelberg. https://doi.org/10.1007/978-3-642-84524-6

Jensen, F. V. (1996). *Introduction to Bayesian Networks*. Springer-Verlag Berlin, Heidelberg.

Jiang, Y., Chen, J., & Ruan, X. (2006). Fuzzy similarity-based rough set method for case-based reasoning and its application in tool selection. *International Journal of Machine Tools & Manufacture, 46*(2), 107–113. https://doi.org/10.1016/j.ijmachtools.2005.05.003

Jiang, Z., Jiang, Y., Wang, Y., Zhang, H., Cao, H., & Tian, G. (2016). A hybrid approach of rough set and case-based reasoning to remanufacturing process planning. *Journal of Intelligent Manufacturing, 30*, 19–32. https://doi.org/10.1007/s10845-016-1231-0

Ju, Y., Wang, A., & Che, H. (2007). Modeling and Analysis of Traffic Accident Rescue Process Using GSPN. In *International Conference on Wireless Communications, Networking and Mobile Computing* (pp. 6601–6604). Shanghai, China: IEEE. https://doi.org/10.1109/WICOM.2007.1620

Kailiponi, P. (2010). Analyzing evacuation decisions using multi-attribute utility theory (MAUT). *Procedia Engineering, 3*, 163–174. https://doi.org/10.1016/j.proeng.2010.07.016

Kar, D., Chakraborti, S., & Ravindran, B. (2012). Feature Weighting and Confidence Based Prediction for Case Based Reasoning Systems. In B. D. Agudo & I. Watson (Eds.), *Case-Based Reasoning Research and Development. ICCBR 2012. Lecture Notes in Computer Science* (Vol. 7644, pp. 211–225). Springer, Berlin, Heidelberg. https://doi.org/10.1007/978-3-642-32986-9_17

Karmakar, S., & Dasgupta, R. (2011). A Petri Net Representation of a Web-Service-Based Emergency Management System in Railway Station. *World Academy of Science, Engineering and Technology, Open Science Index 59, International Journal of Computer and Information Engineering,* 5(11), 1417–1423. https://doi.org/https://doi.org/10.5281/zenodo.1078751

Keeney, R. L., & Raiffa, H. (1976). *Decisions with multiple objectives–preferences and value tradeoffs*. John Wiley, New York.

Khazai, B., Bessel, T., Möhrle, S., Dittrich, A., Schröter, K., Mühr, B., … Kunz, M. (2013). Das Hochwasser im Juni 2013 in Deutschland - Teil 2: Auswirkungen und Hochwasserbewältigung. In *13. DKKV Forum Katastrophenvorsorge*. Hamburg, Germany.

Khazai, B., Bessel, T., Möhrle, S., Dittrich, A., Schröter, K., Mühr, B., … Kunz, M. (2014). Near real time Forensic Disaster Analysis of the central European flood in June 2013 in Germany: Impact and management. In *Geophysical Research Abstracts, EGU2014-6054, General Assembly European Geosciences Union 2014* (Vol. 16).

Kiker, G. A., Bridges, T. S., Varghese, A., Seager, T. P., & Linkov, I. (2005). Application of Multicriteria Decision Analysis in Environmental Decision Making. *Integrated Environmental Assessment and Management, 1*(2), 95–108. https://doi.org/10.1897/IEAM_2004a-015.1

Kim, K. N., & Choi, J. (2012). Breaking the vicious cycle of flood disasters: Goals of project management in post-disaster rebuild projects. *International Journal of Project Management, 31*(1), 147-160. https://doi.org/10.1016/j.ijproman.2012.03.001

Kinley, A. (2001). *Learning to improve case adaptation*. Indiana University.

Klein, G. A. (1993). A recognition-primed decision (RPD) model of rapid decision making. In G. A. Klein, J. Orasanu, R. Calderwood, & C. E. Zsambok (Eds.), *Decision Making in Action: Models and Methods* (pp. 138–147). Ablex Publishing.

Klein, G. A. (2008). Naturalistic Decision Making. *Human Factors, 50*(3), 456–460. https://doi.org/10.1518/001872008X288385

Klein, G. A., Calderwood, R., & Clinton-Cirocco, A. (2010). Rapid Decision Making on the Fire Ground: The Original Study Plus a Postscript. *Journal of Cognitive Engineering and Decision Making*, *4*(3), 186–209. https://doi.org/10.1518/155534310X12844000801203

Klink, S., Li, Y., & Oberweis, A. (2008). INCOME2010 - a Toolset for Developing Process-Oriented Information Systems Based on Petri Nets. In *Proceedings of the 1st International Conference on Simulation Tools and Techniques for Communications, Networks and Systems & Workshops*. Marseille, France: ICST (Institute for Computer Sciences, Social-Informatics and Telecommunications Engineering). https://doi.org/10.4108/ICST.SIMUTOOLS2008.3094

Koh, I., & DiCesare, F. (1991). Modular Transformation Methods for Generalized Petri Nets and Their Application to Automated Manufacturing Systems. *IEEE Transactions on Systems, Man, And Cybernetics*, *21*(6), 1512–1522. https://doi.org/10.1109/21.135693

Kolodner, J. L. (1992). An introduction to case-based reasoning. *Artificial Intelligence Review*, *6*, 3–34. https://doi.org/10.1007/BF00155578

Konoplev, A., Golosov, V., Laptev, G., Nanba, K., Onda, Y., Takase, T., … Yoshimura, K. (2016). Behavior of accidentally released radiocesium in soil-water environment: Looking at Fukushima from a Chernobyl perspective. *Journal of Environmental Radioactivity*, *151, Pt. 3*, 568–578. https://doi.org/10.1016/j.jenvrad.2015.06.019

Kou, G., & Wu, W. (2014). Multi-criteria decision analysis for emergency medical service assessment. *Annals of Operations Research*, *223*, 239–254. https://doi.org/10.1007/s10479-014-1630-6

Krasuski, A., Maciak, T., & Kreński, K. (2009). Decision Support System for Fire Service Based On Distributed Database and Case-Based Reasoning. *Studies in Logic, Grammar and Rhetoric*, *17*(30), 159–169.

Kreński, K., Krasuski, A., & Łazowy, S. (2011). Ontologies and their potential for knowledge representation layer for a CBR System in fire service. *Bezpieczeństwo i Technika Pożarnicza*, 93–98.

Krupka, J., Kasparova, M., & Jirava, P. (2009). Case-Based Reasoning Model in Process of Emergency Management. In K. Cyran, S. Kozielski, J. Peters, U. Stanczyk, & A. Wakulicz-Deja (Eds.), *Man-Machine Interactions. Advances in Intelligent and Soft Computing* (Vol. 59, pp. 77–84). Springer, Berlin, Heidelberg. https://doi.org/10.1007/978-3-642-00563-3_7

Küster, J. M., Gerth, C., Förster, A., & Engels, G. (2008). *Process Merging in Business-Driven Development. IBM Research Report RZ 3703, IBM Zurich Research Laboratory.*

La Rosa, M., Dumas, M., Uba, R., & Dijkman, R. (2010). Merging Business Process Models. In R. Meersman, T. Dillon, & P. Herrero (Eds.), *On the Move to Meaningful Internet Systems (OTM 2010). Lecture Notes in Computer Science* (Vol. 6426, pp. 96–113). Springer, Berlin, Heidelberg. https://doi.org/10.1007/978-3-642-16934-2_10

La Rosa, M., Dumas, M., Uba, R., & Dijkman, R. M. (2013). Business Process Model Merging: An Approach to Business Process Consolidation. *ACM Transactions on Software Engineering and Methodology (TOSEM), 22*(2). https://doi.org/10.1145/2430545.2430547

La Rosa, M., & Mendling, J. (2009). Domain-driven Process Adaptation in Emergency Scenarios. In D. Ardagna, M. Mecella, & J. Yang (Eds.), *Business Process Management Workshops. BPM 2008. Lecture Notes in Business Information Processing* (Vol. 17). Springer, Berlin, Heidelberg. https://doi.org/10.1007/978-3-642-00328-8_28

Labib, A., & Harris, M. J. (2015). Learning how to learn from failures: The Fukushima nuclear disaster. *Engineering Failure Analysis, 47, Pt. A,* 117–128. https://doi.org/10.1016/j.engfailanal.2014.10.002

Lamontagne, L., & Abi-Zeid, I. (2006). Combining Multiple Similarity Metrics Using a Multicriteria Approach. In T.R Roth-Berghofer, M.H. Göker, H.A. Güvenir (Eds.) *Advances in Case-Based Reasoning. ECCBR 2006. Lecture Notes in Computer Science* (Vol. 4106, pp. 415–428). Springer, Berlin, Heidelberg. https://doi.org/10.1007/11805816_31

Leake, D. B. (1996a). CBR in Context : The Present and Future. In D. B. Leake (Ed.), *Case-Based Reasoning: Experiences, Lessons, and Future Directions* (pp. 1–35). AAAI Press/MIT Press.

Leake, D. B. (1996b). Experience, introspection and expertise: Learning to refine the case-based reasoning process. *Journal of Experimental & Theoretical Artificial Intelligence, 8*(3–4), 319–339. https://doi.org/10.1080/095281396147357

Leake, D. B., Kinley, A., & Wilson, D. (1995). Learning to Improve Case Adaptation by Introspective Reasoning and CBR. In M. Veloso, A. Aamodt (Eds.) *Case-Based Reasoning Research and Development. ICCBR 1995. Lecture Notes in Computer Science (Lecture Notes in Artificial Intelligence)* (Vol. 1010, pp. 229–240). Springer, Berlin, Heidelberg. https://doi.org/10.1007/3-540-60598-3_21

Leake, D. B., & Wilson, M. (2011). How Many Cases Do You Need? Assessing and Predicting Case-Base Coverage. In A. Ram & N. Wiratunga (Eds.), *Case-Based Reasoning Research and Development. ICCBR 2011. Lecture Notes in Computer Science* (Vol 6880, pp.92-106). Springer, Berlin, Heidelberg. https://doi.org/10.1007/978-3-642-23291-6_9

Lee, R., Barcia, R., & Khator, S. (1995). Case-Based Reasoning for cash flow forecasting using fuzzy retrieval. In M. M. Veloso & A. Aamodt (Eds.), *Case-Based Reasoning Research and Development. ICCBR 1995. Lecture Notes in Computer Science (Lecture Notes in Artificial Intelligence)* (Vol. 1010, pp. 510–519). Springer, Berlin, Heidelberg. https://doi.org/10.1007/3-540-60598-3_47

Lenz, K., & Oberweis, A. (2003). Inter-organizational Business Process Management with XML Nets. In H. Ehrig, W. Reisig, G. Rozenberg, & H. Weber (Eds.), *Petri Net Technology for Communication-Based Systems. Lecture Notes in Computer Science* (Vol. 2472, pp. 243–263). Springer, Berlin, Heidelberg. https://doi.org/10.1007/978-3-540-40022-6_12

Lenz, M., Bartsch-Spörl, B., Burkhard, H.-D., & Wess, S. (Eds.). (2004). *Case-Based Reasoning Technology*. Springer-Verlag Berlin Heidelberg.

Lewis, A. (2004). RIMSAT DSS Project: Integrating Model-Based and Case-Based Reasoning. Retrieved March 7, 2018, from http://dssresources.com/papers/features/lewis/lewis04052004.html

Li, H., Li, X., Hu, D., Hao, T., Wenyin, L., & Chen, X. (2009). Adaptation rule learning for case-based reasoning. *Concurrency Computation Practice and Experience, 21*(5), 673–689. https://doi.org/10.1002/cpe.1368

Li, H., & Sun, J. (2009). Hybridizing principles of the Electre method with case-based reasoning for data mining: Electre-CBR-I and Electre-CBR-II. *European Journal of Operational Research, 197*(1), 214–224. https://doi.org/10.1016/j.ejor.2008.05.024

Liao, T. W., Zhang, Z., & Claude, R. (1998). Similarity measures for retrieval in case-based reasoning systems. *Applied Artificial Intelligence: An International Journal, 12*(4), 267–288. https://doi.org/10.1080/088395198117730

Liao, Z., Mao, X., Hannam, P. M., & Zhao, T. (2012). Adaptation methodology of CBR for environmental emergency preparedness system based on an Improved Genetic Algorithm. *Expert Systems with Applications, 39*(8), 7029–7040. https://doi.org/10.1016/j.eswa.2012.01.044

Liao, Z., Mao, X., Liu, Y., Xu, Z., & Hannam, P. M. (2011). CBR respond and preparedness system development for environmental emergency. *Civil Engineering and Environmental Systems, 28*(4), 301–323. https://doi.org/10.1080/10286608.2011.604416

Lim, J., Chae, M., Yang, Y., Park, I., Lee, J., & Park, J. (2016). Fast Scheduling of Semiconductor Manufacturing Facilities Using Case-Based Reasoning. *IEEE Transactions on Semiconductor Manufacturing, 29*(1), 22–32. https://doi.org/10.1109/tsm.2015.2511798

Lin, L., Brauner, F., Münzberg, T., Meng, S., & Moehrle, S. (2013). Prioritization of Security Measures Against Terrorist Threats to Public Rail Transport Systems Using a Scenario-Based Multi-Criteria Method and a Knowledge Database. In M. Lauster (Ed.), *Future Security 2013: 8th Security Research Conference* (pp. 195–204). Berlin, Germany.

Lin, L., Moehrle, S., Muenzberg, T., & Raskob, W. (2014). A Decision Support Approach: Evaluating the Effectiveness of Security Measures by Scenario-Based Multi-Criteria Analysis. In K. Thoma, I. Häring, & T. Leismann (Eds.), *Future Security 2014: 9th Security Research Conference,* (pp. 266–273). Berlin, Germany.

Lin, S. W., & Chen, S. C. (2011). Parameter tuning, feature selection and weight assignment of features for case-based reasoning by artificial immune system. *Applied Soft Computing Journal, 11*(8), 5042–5052. https://doi.org/10.1016/j.asoc.2011.05.054

Lipshitz, R., & Strauss, O. (1997). Coping with Uncertainty: A Naturalistic Decision-Making Analysis. *Organizational Behavior and Human Decision Processes, 69*(2), 149–163. https://doi.org/10.1006/obhd.1997.2679

Löffler, H., Mildenberger, O., Sogalla, M., & Stahl, T. (2012). *Ressortforschungsberichte zur kerntechnischen Sicherheit und zum Strahlenschutz Aktualisierung der Quelltermbibliothek des Entscheidungshilfesystems RODOS für Ereignisse im Leistungsbetrieb - Vorhaben 3609S60009*. Retrieved June 20, 2018, from http://doris.bfs.de/jspui/bitstream/urn:nbn:de:0221-201202067299/3/BfS_2012_3604S04460.pdf

Lopez De Mantaras, R., McSherry, D., Bridge, D., Leake, D. B., Smyth, B., Craw, S., … Watson, I. (2006). Retrieval, reuse, revision and retention in case-based reasoning. *The Knowledge Engineering Review, 20*(3), 215-240. https://doi.org/10.1017/S0269888906000646

Luo, J., Xu, L., Shi, Z., Jamont, J.-P., & Zeng, L. (2007). Flood Decision Support System on Agent Grid : Method and Implementation. *Enterprise Information Systems, 1*(1), 49–68. https://doi.org/http://dx.doi.org/10.1080/17517570601092184

Ma, L., Li, S., & Chen, L. (2011). Research on Process of Coal Mine Emergency Plan Based on Stochastic Petri Net. In *International Conference on Information Management Innovation Management and Industrial Engineering* (pp. 535–538). Shenzhen, China: IEEE. https://doi.org/10.1109/ICIII.2011.136

Marling, C., Rissland, E., & Aamodt, A. (2005). Integrations with case-based reasoning. *The Knowledge Engineering Review, 20*(3), 241-245. https://doi.org/10.1017/S026988890600066X

Massie, S., Craw, S., & Wiratunga, N. (2005). What is CBR Competence. *BCS-SGAI Expert Update, 8*(1), 7–10.

Matsuda, N., Mikami, S., Sato, T., & Saito, K. (2017). Measurements of air dose rates in and around houses in the Fukushima Prefecture in Japan after the Fukushima accident. *Journal of Environmental Radioactivity, 166, Pt. 3,* 427–435. https://doi.org/10.1016/j.jenvrad.2016.03.012

Mauser, S. (2010). *Synthese von Petrinetzen aus halbgeordneten Abläufen*. FernUniversität in Hagen.

McCall, S. (1973). Review: Selected Works By Jan Łukasiewicz; L. Borkowski. *Synthese, 26*(1), 165–171. Retrieved February 15, 2018, from www.jstor.org/stable/20111516

McInerney, C. (2002). Knowledge management and the dynamic nature of knowledge. *Journal of the American Society for Information Science and Technology, 53*(12), 1009–1018. https://doi.org/10.1002/asi.10109

Merz, M., Hiete, M., Bertsch, V., & Rentz, O. (2007). Decision support for managing interruptions in industrial supply chains. In *8. Forum DKKV/CEDIM: Disaster Reduction in Climate Change*. Karlsruhe, Germany.

Meso, P., Troutt, M. D., & Rudnicka, J. (2002). A review of naturalistic decision making research with some implications for knowledge management. *Journal of Knowledge Management, 6*(1), 63–73. https://doi.org/10.1108/13673270210417709

Michie, D., Spiegelhalter, D. J., & Taylor, C. C. (Eds.). (1994). *Machine Learning, Neural and Statistical Classification*. *Ellis Horwood series in artificial intelligence*. Ellis Horwood.

Mitra, R., & Basak, J. (2005). Methods of case adaptation: A survey. *International Journal of Intelligent Systems, 20*(6), 627–645. https://doi.org/10.1002/int.20087

Moehrle, S. (2012). Generic self-learning decision support system for large-scale disasters. In L. Rothkrantz, J. Ristvej, & Z. Franco (Eds.), *9th International Conference on Information Systems for Crisis Response and Management (ISCRAM 2012)*. Vancouver, Canada.

Moehrle, S. (2013a). Modeling of countermeasures for large-scale disasters using high-level petri nets. In T. Comes, F. Fiedrich, S. Fortier, J. Geldermann, & T. Müller (Eds.), *10th International Conference on Information Systems for Crisis Response and Management (ISCRAM 2013)*. Baden-Baden, Germany.

Moehrle, S. (2013b). Towards a decision support system for disaster management. In *Safety, Reliability and Risk Analysis: Beyond the Horizon - Proceedings of the European Safety and Reliability Conference, ESREL 2013* (pp. 239–246).

Moehrle, S. (2014). On the assessment of disaster management strategies. In S. R. Hiltz, M. S. Pfaff, L. Plotnick, & P. C. Shih (Eds.), *11th International Conference on Information Systems for Crisis Response and Management (ISCRAM 2014)*. Pennsylvania, USA.

Moehrle, S., Bai, S., Mueller, T., Munz, E., Trybushnyi, D., & Raskob, W. (2018). Web-based decision support system for emergency management – System architecture and enhancement possibilities. *4th NERIS Workshop, Adapting Nuclear and Radiological Emergency Preparedness, Response and Recovery to a Changing World*. Dublin, Ireland.

Moehrle, S., Bai, S., Mueller, T., Munz, E., Trybushnyi, D., & Raskob, W. (2019). Triggering Events and Distributed Responsibilities Capabilities of Web-based Decision Support in Nuclear Emergency Management. In *4th NERIS Workshop, Adapting Nuclear and Radiological Emergency Preparedness, Response and Recovery to a Changing World*. Dublin, Ireland.

Moehrle, S., & Raskob, W. (2015). Structuring and reusing knowledge from historical events for supporting nuclear emergency and remediation management. *Engineering Applications of Artificial Intelligence, 46, Pt. B*, 303–311. https://doi.org/10.1016/j.engappai.2015.07.010

Moehrle, S., & Raskob, W. (2019). Reusing Strategies for Decision Support in Disaster Management – A Case-based High-level Petri Net Approach. In S. Y. Yurish (Ed.), *Advances in Artificial Intelligence: Reviews, Vol. 1*. IFSA Publishing, S.L. (Barcelona, Spain).

Moellmann, S., Engelmann, H., Braun, D., & Raskob, W. (2011). Key Performance Indicator Based Calculations as a Decision Support for the Tactical Level. In *8th International Conference on Information Systems for Crisis Response and Management (ISCRAM 2011)*. Lisbon, Portugal.

Möhrle, S., & Mühr, B. (2015). Case-based damage assessment of storm events in near real-time. In *Geophysical Research Abstracts, EGU2015-12293, General Assembly European Geosciences Union 2015* (Vol. 17). Vienna, Austria.

Möhrle, S., & Raskob, W. (2014). Case-based analytical support for rapidly assessing natural disasters. In *14. Forum Katastrophenvorsorge*. Leipzig, Germany.

Möhrle, S., Schoknecht, A., Raskob, W., & Oberweis, A. (2015). Ontology-Based Retrieval for Cased-Based Decision Support in Nuclear Emergency Management. In *12th International Conference on Information Systems for Crisis Response and Management (ISCRAM 2015)*. Kristiansand, Norway.

Montani, S., & Jain, L. C. (Eds.). (2014). *Successful Case-based Reasoning Applications - 2* (Vol. 494). Springer-Verlag Berlin Heidelberg. https://doi.org/10.1007/978-3-642-38736-4

Montero, M., Sala, R., Trueba, C., & Baudé, S. (2016). Conditions and means for a useful and trustworthy engagement of experts in the PREPARE analytical platform – survey and interviews outcomes. *Radioprotection, 51(HS2)*, S195–S197. https://doi.org/10.1051/radiopro/2016072

Moore, R. E., Kearfott, R. B., & Cloud, M. J. (2009). *Introduction to Interval Analysis*. Society for Industrial and Applied Mathematics Philadelphia, PA, USA. https://doi.org/10.1137/1.9780898717716

Mousseau, T. A., & Møller, A. P. (2014). Genetic and ecological studies of animals in Chernobyl and Fukushima. *The Journal of Heredity, 105*(5), 704–709. https://doi.org/10.1093/jhered/esu040

Müller, T., Meng, S., Raskob, W., Wiens, M., & Schultmann, F. (2015). A Transparent Approach for Prioritising Security Measures. In J. Beyerer, A. Meissner, & J. Geisler (Eds.), *Future Security 2015: 10th Security Research Conference*. Berlin, Germany.

Muñoz-Avila, H., & Cox, M. T. (2008). Case-based plan adaptation: An analysis and review. *IEEE Intelligent Systems, 23*(4), 75–81. IEEE. https://doi.org/10.1109/MIS.2008.59

Murata, T. (1989). Petri Nets: Properties, Analysis and Applications. *Proceedings of the IEEE, 77*(4), 541–580. IEEE. https://doi.org/10.1109/5.24143

Nakamura, A., & Kikuchi, M. (2011). What We Know, and What We Have Not Yet Learned: Triple Disasters and the Fukushima Nuclear Fiasco in Japan. *Public Administration Review, 71*(6), 893–899. https://doi.org/10.1111/j.1540-6210.2011.02437.x

Narahari, Y., & Viswanadham, N. (1985). A petri net approach to the modelling and analsys of flexible manufacturing systems. *Annals of Operations Research, 3*, 449–472. https://doi.org/10.1007/BF02023780

NERIS. (2014). Strategic Research Agenda of the NERIS Platform. Retrieved June 6, 2018, from http://www.eu-neris.net/

Network of Social Studies in the Prevention of Disasters in Latin America. (2009). *DesInventar, Disaster Inventory System, Methodological Guide Version 8.1.9*. Retrieved May 5, 2013, from http://www.desinventar.org

Nisbet, A., Brown, J., Cabianca, T., Jones, A. L., Andersson, K. G., Hänninen, R., ... Hiete, M. (2010). *Generic handbook for assisting in the management of contaminated inhabited areas in Europe following a radiological emergency Version 2*. Retrieved May 5,2018, from https://euranos.iket.kit.edu/index.php?action=euranos&title=products

Nisbet, A., Jones, A., Turcanu, C., Camps, J., Andersson, K. G., Hänninen, R., ... Oughton, D. (2009). *Generic handbook for assisting in the management of contaminated food production systems in Europe following a radiological emergency Version 2* (2nd ed.). Retrieved May 5, 2018, from https://euranos.iket.kit.edu/index.php?action=euranos&title=products

Nisbet, A., & Watson, S. (2015a). *UK Recovery Handbooks for Radiation Incidents 2015 Food Production Systems Handbook* (4th ed.). Retrieved June 7, 2017, from https://www.gov.uk/government/publications/uk-recovery-handbooks-for-radiation-incidents-2015

Nisbet, A., & Watson, S. (2015b). *UK Recovery Handbooks for Radiation Incidents 2015 Inhabited Areas Handbook* (4th ed.). Retrieved June 7, 2017, from https://www.gov.uk/government/publications/uk-recovery-handbooks-for-radiation-incidents-2015

Nuclear and Industrial Safety Agency (NISA). (2011a). *INES Ratings on the Events in Fukushima Daiichi Nuclear Power Plant April 12 2011*. Retrieved February 4, 2019, from http://www.criirad.org/actualites/dossier2011/japon_bis/pdf/nisa_classement_ines_7.pdf

Nuclear and Industrial Safety Agency (NISA). (2011b). *INES Ratings on the Events in Fukushima Daiichi Nuclear Power Plant March 18 2011*. Retrieved February 4, 2019, from https://reliefweb.int/report/japan/japan-ines-ratings-events-fukushima-dai-ichi-nps-and-fukushima-dai-ni-nps-tohoku

Nývlt, O., Haugen, S., & Ferkl, L. (2015). Complex accident scenarios modelled and analysed by Stochastic Petri Nets. *Reliability Engineering and System Safety*, *142*, 539–555. https://doi.org/10.1016/j.ress.2015.06.015

Oberweis, A. (1996). *Modellierung und Ausführung von Workflows mit Petri-Netzen*. Vieweg+Teubner, Wiesbaden. https://doi.org/10.1007/978-3-322-81039-7.

Oberweis, A., & Sander, P. (1996). Information system behavior specification by high level Petri nets. *ACM Transactions on Information Systems, 14*(4), 380–420. https://doi.org/10.1145/237496.237498

Oehlmann, R. (1998). Evaluating a case-based discovery system: a case-study in content-oriented evaluation. *Artificial Intelligence in Medicine, 12*(1), 61–76. https://doi.org/10.1016/s0933-3657(97)00040-7

Ölçer, A. İ., & Majumder, J. (2006). A Case-based Decision Support System for Flooding Crises Onboard Ships. *Quality and Reliability Engineering International, 22*(1), 59–78. https://doi.org/10.1002/qre.748

Omoto, A. (2013). The accident at TEPCO's Fukushima-Daiichi Nuclear Power Station: What went wrong and what lessons are universal? *Nuclear Instruments and Methods in Physics Research Section A: Accelerators, Spectrometers, Detectors and Associated Equipment, 731*, 3–7. https://doi.org/10.1016/j.nima.2013.04.017

Otim, S. (2006). A Case-Based Knowledge Management System for Disaster Management : Fundamental Concepts. In B. Van de Walle & M. Turoff (Eds.), *3rd International Conference on Information Systems for Crisis Response and Management (ISCRAM 2006)* (pp. 598–604). Newark, NJ (USA).

Pal, Sankar K., & Shiu, S. C. K. (2004). *Foundations of Soft Case-Based Reasoning*. John Wiley & Sons, Inc., Hoboken, New Jersey.

Papamichail, K. N., & French, S. (2000). Decision support in nuclear emergencies. *Journal of Hazardous Materials, 71*(1-3), 321–342. https://doi.org/10.1016/s0304-3894(99)00086-2

Papamichail, K. N., & French, S. (2005). Design and evaluation of an intelligent decision support system for nuclear emergencies. *Decision Support Systems, 41*(1), 84–111. https://doi.org/10.1016/j.dss.2004.04.014

Papamichail, K. N., & French, S. (2013). 25 Years of MCDA in nuclear emergency management. *IMA Journal of Management Mathematics, 24*(4), 481–503. https://doi.org/10.1093/imaman/dps028

Park, C. S., & Han, I. (2002). A case-based reasoning with the feature weights derived by analytic hierarchy process for bankruptcy prediction. *Expert Systems with Applications, 23*(3), 255–264. https://doi.org/10.1016/S0957-4174(02)00045-3

Paton, D., & Flin, R. (1999). Disaster stress: an emergency management perspective. *Disaster Prevention and Management, 8*(4), 261–267. https://doi.org/10.1108/09653569910283897

Pawlak, Z. (1982). Rough Sets. *International Journal of Computer & Information Sciences, 11*(5), 341–356.

Pearl, J. (1988). *Probabilistic reasoning in intelligent systems: networks of plausible inference*. Morgan Kaufmann Publishers Inc.

Peng, Y., Zhang, Y., Tang, Y., & Li, S. (2011). An incident information management framework based on data integration, data mining, and multi-criteria decision making. *Decision Support Systems, 51*(2), 316–327. https://doi.org/10.1016/j.dss.2010.11.025

Peres, F., Berthomieu, B., & Vernadat, F. (2011). On the composition of time Petri nets. *Discrete Event Dynamic Systems, 21*, 395–424. https://doi.org/10.1007/s10626-011-0102-2

Peterson, J. L. (1981). *Petri Net Theory and the Modeling of Systems*. Prentice-Hall, Inc., Englewood Cliffs, N.J. 07632.

Peťko, I., & Hudák, Š. (2012). General composition for high level Petri nets and its properties. *Central European Journal of Computer Science, 2*(3), 222–235. https://doi.org/10.2478/s13537-012-0017-5

Petri, C. A. (1962). *Kommunikation mit Automaten*. Universität Bonn.

Pfotenhauer, S. M., Jones, C. F., Saha, K., & Jasanoff, S. (2012). Learning from Fukushima. *Issues in Science and Technology, 28*(3), 79–84.

Polanyi, M. (1958). *Personal Knowledge: Towards a Post-Critical Philosophy.* Routledge & Kegan Paul Ltd.

Power, D. J. (2000). Web-based and model-driven decision support systems : concepts and issues. In *AMCIS 2000, Americas Conference on Information Systems*. Long Beach, California, USA.

Public Health England. (2015). Radiation recovery record form (RRRF): food, inhabited areas and drinking water. Retrieved October 20, 2016, from https://www.gov.uk/government/publications/radiation-recovery-record-form-food-inhabited-areas-and-drinking-water

Rafferty, B. (2001). FORIA : Forest Impact Analysis: An interactive decision support software providing information on the secondary effects of radiological countermeasures applied in forests. *Journal of Environmental Radioactivity, 56*(1-2), 209–214. https://doi.org/10.1016/s0265-931x(01)00054-6

Raskob, W., & Möhrle, S. (2014). Knowledge databases as instrument for a fast assessment in nuclear emergency management. In *3rd International Conference on Radioecology & Environmental Radioactivity (ICRER 2014)*. Barcelona, Spain.

Raskob, W., Möhrle, S., & Bai, S. (2016). Knowledge database and case-based reasoning. *Radioprotection, 51*(HS2), S185–S186. https://doi.org/10.1051/radiopro/2016069

Raskob, W., Möhrle, S., Bai, S., & Müller, T. (2016). Overview and applicability of the analytical platform. *Radioprotection, 51*(HS2), S179–S180. https://doi.org/10.1051/radiopro/2016067

Raskob, W., Müller, T., Möhrle, S., & Bai, S. (2016). The Analytical Platform of the PREPARE project. In *14th Congress of the International Radiation Protection Association (IRPA)*. Cape Town, South Africa.

Recio-García, J. A., Díaz-Agudo, B., González-Calero, P., & Sánchez-Ruiz-Granados, A. (2007). Ontology based CBR with jCOLIBRI. In R. Ellis, T. Allen, & A. Tuson (Eds.) *Applications and Innovations in Intelligent Systems XIV* (pp. 149–162). Springer, London. https://doi.org/10.1007/978-1-84628-666-7_12

Recio-García, J. A., González-Calero, P. A., & Díaz-Agudo, B. (2014). jCOLIBRI2: A framework for building Case-based reasoning systems. *Science of Computer Programming, 79*, 126–145. https://doi.org/10.1016/j.scico.2012.04.002

Richter, M. M. (1995). The Knowledge Contained in Similarity Measures. Retrieved January 25, 2018, from https://kluedo.ub.uni-kl.de/frontdoor/index/index/docId/117

Richter, M. M. (2004). Logic and Approximation in Knowledge Based Systems. In W. Lenski (Ed.) *Logic versus Approximation. Lecture Notes in Computer Science* (Vol. 3075, pp. 184–203). Springer, Berlin, Heidelberg. https://doi.org/10.1007/978-3-540-25967-1_13

Richter, M. M., & Weber, R. O. (2013). *Case-Based Reasoning*. Springer, Berlin, Heidelberg. https://doi.org/10.1007/978-3-642-40167-1

Riesbeck, C. K., & Schank, R. (1989). *Inside case-based reasoning*. Lawrence Erlbaum Associates, Inc., Publishers. https://doi.org/10.4324/9780203781821

Ríos-Insua, S., Gallego, E., Jiménez, A., & Mateos, A. (2006). A Multi-Attribute Decision Support System for selecting intervention strategies for radionuclide contaminated freshwater ecosystems. *Ecological Modelling, 196*(1-2), 195–208. https://doi.org/10.1016/j.ecolmodel.2005.11.034

Rissino, S., & Lambert-Torres, G. (2009). Rough Set Theory – Fundamental Concepts, Principals, Data Extraction, and Applications. In J. Ponce & A. Karahoca (Eds.), *Data Mining and Knowledge Discovery in Real Life Applications*. IntechOpen. https://doi.org/10.5772/6440

Rollón, E., Isern, D., Agostini, A., & Cortés, U. (2003). Towards the Distributed Management of Emergencies: Forest Fires Case Study. In *1st IJCAI Workshop on Environmental Decision Support Systems* (pp. 77–82). Acapulco, México.

Rongier, C., Lauras, M., Galasso, F., & Gourc, D. (2012). Towards a crisis performance-measurement system. *International Journal of Computer Integrated Manufacturing, 26*(11), 1087-1102. https://doi.org/10.1080/0951192X.2012.684711

Rueppel, U., & Wagenknecht, A. (2007). Improving Emergency Management by Formal Dynamic Process-Modelling. In *24th Conference on Information Technology in Construction* (pp. 559–564).

Saaty, T. L. (1980). *The Analytic Hierarchy Process*. McGraw-Hill, New York.

Sackmann, S., & Betke, H. (2013). Towards a Model-Based Analysis of Place-Related Information in Disaster Response Workflows. In T. Comes, F. Fiedrich, S. Fortier, J. Geldermann, & T. Müller (Eds.), *10th International Conference on Information Systems for Crisis Response and Management (ISCRAM 2013)* (pp. 78–83). Baden-Baden, Germany.

Saji, G. (2014). Safety goals for seismic and tsunami risks: Lessons learned from the Fukushima Daiichi disaster. *Nuclear Engineering and Design, 280*, 449–463. https://doi.org/10.1016/j.nucengdes.2014.09.013

Salamó, M., & López-Sánchez, M. (2011). Rough set based approaches to feature selection for Case-Based Reasoning classifiers. *Pattern Recognition Letters, 32*(2), 280–292. https://doi.org/10.1016/j.patrec.2010.08.013

San Pedro, J., & Burstein, F. (2003). A Framework for Case-Based Fuzzy Multicriteria Decision Support for Tropical Cyclone Forecasting. In *Proceedings of the 36th Hawaii International Conference on System Sciences*. Big Island, HI, USA: IEEE. https://doi.org/10.1109/HICSS.2003.1174209

Scholl, A. (2000). *Robuste Planung und Optimierung : Grundlagen - Konzepte und Methoden - experimentelle Untersuchungen*. Darmstadt Technical University.

Schröter, K., Khazai, B., Mühr, B., Elmer, F., Bessel, T., Möhrle, S., … Merz, B. (2014). The Central European Flood in June 2013 : Experiences from a Near-Real Time Disaster Analysis in Germany. In *Geophysical Research Abstracts, EGU2014-6054, General Assembly European Geosciences Union 2014* (Vol. 16). Vienna, Austria.

Schwartz, D. G. (1991). A system for reasoning with imprecise linguistic information. *International Journal of Approximate Reasoning, 5*(5), 463–488. https://doi.org/10.1016/0888-613X(91)90002-4

Sell, C., & Braun, I. (2009). Using a Workflow Management System to Manage Emergency Plans. In J. Landgren & S. Jul (Eds.), *6th International Conference on Information Systems for Crisis Response and Management (ISCRAM 2009)*. Gothenburg, Sweden.

Shan, S., Wang, L., & Li, L. (2012). Modeling of emergency response decision-making process using stochastic Petri net: an e-service perspective. *Information Technology and Management, 13, 363-376*. https://doi.org/10.1007/s10799-012-0128-7

Shen, H., Huang, W. W., Zhao, J., & Jin, T. (2008). A Sequential Group Decision Process for Emergency Response. In *IEEE International Conference on Systems, Man and Cybernetics* (pp. 867–871). Singapore, Singapore: IEEE. https://doi.org/10.1109/ICSMC.2008.4811389

Shen, H., & Zhao, J. (2010). Decision-making Support Based on the Combination of CBR and Logic Reasoning. In S. French, B. Tomaszewski, & C. Zobel (Eds.), *7th International Conference on Information Systems for Crisis Response and Management (ISCRAM 2010)*. Seattle, USA.

Shi, H., Xin, M., & Dong, W. (2011). A kind of case similarity evaluation model based on case-based reasoning. In *International Conference on Internet of Things and 4th International Conference on Cyber, Physical and Social Computing* (pp. 453–457). Dalian, China: IEEE. https://doi.org/10.1109/iThings/CPSCom.2011.57

Shiba, K., Kitamura, Y., Kozaka, T., Uno, I., Shimizu, K., Masumoto, K., … Yanaga, M. (2013). Decontamination of radioactivity from contaminated vegetables derived from the Fukushima nuclear accident. *Radiation Measurements, 55*, 26–29. https://doi.org/10.1016/j.radmeas.2013.01.010

Shin, K., & Han, I. (1999). Case-based reasoning supported by genetic algorithms for corporate bond rating. *Expert Systems with Applications, 16*(2), 85–95. https://doi.org/10.1016/S0957-4174(98)00063-3

Sihver, L., & Yasuda, N. (2018). Causes and Radiological Consequences of the Chernobyl and Fukushima Nuclear Accidents. *ASME Journal of Nuclear Engineering and Radiation Science, 4*(2). https://doi.org/10.1115/1.4037116

Sinclair, H., Doyle, E. E. H., Johnston, D. M., & Paton, D. (2012). Decision-making training in local government emergency management. *International Journal of Emergency Services, 1*(2), 159–174. https://doi.org/10.1108/20470891211275939

Smiti, A. (2011). Overview of Maintenance for Case based Reasoning Systems. *International Journal of Computer Applications, 32*(2), 49–57. https://doi.org/10.5120/3881-5423

Smiti, A., & Elouedi, Z. (2013). Modeling Competence for Case Based Reasoning Systems Using Clustering. In *Proceedings of the Twenty-Sixth International Florida Artificial Intelligence Research Society Conference Modeling* (pp. 399–404).

Smyth, B., & McKenna, E. (1998). Modelling the Competence of Case-Bases. In B. Smyth & P. Cunningham (Eds.), *Advances in Case-Based Reasoning. EWCBR 1998. Lecture Notes in Computer Science* (Vol 1488, pp. 208-220). Springer, Berlin, Heidelberg. https://doi.org/10.1007/BFb0056334

Smyth, B., & McKenna, E. (1999). Building Compact Competent Case-Bases. In K.-D. Althoff, R. Bergmann, & L. Branting (Eds.), *Case-Based Reasoning Research and Development. ICCBR 1999. Lecture Notes in Computer Science (Lecture Notes in Artificial Intelligence)* (Vol. 1650, pp. 329–342). Springer, Berlin, Heidelberg. https://doi.org/10.1007/3-540-48508-2_24

Smyth, B., & McKenna, E. (2001). Competence models and the maintenance problem. *Computational Intelligence, 17*(2). https://doi.org/10.1111/0824-7935.00142

Song, J. H. (2018). An assessment on the environmental contamination caused by the Fukushima accident. *Journal of Environmental Management, 206*, 846–852. https://doi.org/10.1016/j.jenvman.2017.11.068

Spalazzi, L. (2001). A Survey on Case-Based Planning. *Artificial Intelligence Review, 16*, 3–36. https://doi.org/10.1023/A:1011081305027

Stahl, A. (2003). *Learning of Knowledge-Intensive Similarity Measures in Case-Based Reasoning*. Universität Kaiserslautern.

Stahl, A., & Gabel, T. (2006). Optimizing similarity assessment in case-based reasoning. In *Proceedings of the 21st National Conference on Artificial Intelligence* (AAAI 2006) (pp. 1667-1670).

Steinhauser, G., Brandl, A., & Johnson, T. E. (2014). Comparison of the Chernobyl and Fukushima nuclear accidents: a review of the environmental impacts. *Science of the Total Environment, 470–471*, 800–817. https://doi.org/10.1016/j.scitotenv.2013.10.029

Strahlenschutzkommission. (2011). *Verwendung von Jodtabletten zur Jodblockade der Schilddrüse bei einem kerntechnischen Unfall Empfehlung der Strahlenschutzkommission*. Retrieved February 4, 2019, from http://www.ssk.de

Strand, P., Sundell-Bergman, S., Brown, J. E., & Dowdall, M. (2017). On the divergences in assessment of environmental impacts from ionising radiation following the Fukushima accident. *Journal of Environmental Radioactivity, 169-170*, 159-173. https://doi.org/10.1016/j.jenvrad.2016.12.005

Sun, B., Xu, L. Da, Pei, X., & Li, H. (2003). Scenario-based knowledge representation in case-based reasoning systems. *Expert Systems, 20*(2), 92–99. https://doi.org/10.1111/1468-0394.00230

Sun, S., Kumar, A., & Yen, J. (2006). Merging workflows: A new perspective on connecting business processes. *Decision Support Systems, 42*(2), 844–858. https://doi.org/10.1016/j.dss.2005.07.001

Sushmita, S., & Chaudhury, S. (2007). Hierarchical Fuzzy Case Based Reasoning with Multi-criteria Decision Making for Financial Applications. In A. Ghosh, R. K. De, & S. K. Pal (Eds.), *Pattern Recognition and Machine Intelligence. PReMI 2007. Lecture Notes in Computer Science* (Vol. 4815, pp. 226–234). Springer, Berlin, Heidelberg. https://doi.org/10.1007/978-3-540-77046-6_28

Tavana, M. (2008). Dynamic process modelling using Petri nets with applications to nuclear power plant emergency management. *International Journal of Simulation and Process Modelling, 4*(2), 130–138. https://doi.org/10.1504/ijspm.2008.022074

Thatcher, A., Vasconcelos, A. C., & Ellis, D. (2015). An investigation into the impact of information behaviour on information failure: The Fukushima Daiichi nuclear power disaster. *International Journal of Information Management, 35*(1), 57–63. https://doi.org/10.1016/j.ijinfomgt.2014.10.002

The Fukushima Nuclear Accident Independent Investigation Commission. (2012). *The National Diet of Japan*. Retrieved February 4, 2019, from https://www.nirs.org/wp-content/uploads/fukushima/naiic_report.pdf

Tran, H. M., & Schönwälder, J. (2007). Fault Representation in Case-Based Reasoning. In A. Clemm, L. Z. Granville, & R. Stadler (Eds.), *Managing Virtualization of Networks and Services. DSOM 2007. Lecture Notes in Computer Science* (Vol. 4785, pp. 50–61). https://doi.org/10.1007/978-3-540-75694-1_5

Triantaphyllou, E. (2000). *Multi-Criteria Decision Making Methods: A Comparative Study*. Dordrecht, The Netherlands: Kluwer Academic Publishers (now Springer). https://doi.org/10.1007/978-1-4757-3157-6

UNDRR. (2017). UNDRR Terminology. Retrieved May 10, 2020, from https://www.undrr.org/terminology

van Borkulo, E., Scholten, H. J., Zlatanova, S., & van den Brink, A. (2005). Decision Making in Response and Relief Phases. In *Geo-information for Disaster Management, First International Symposium on Geo-information for Disaster Management* (pp. 47–54). Delft, Netherlands.

van Hee, K. M., Serebrenik, A., Sidorova, N., Voorhoeve, M., & van der Werf, J. M. E. M. (2007). Modelling with History-Dependent Petri Nets. In G. Alonso, P. Dadam, & M. Rosemann (Eds.), *Proceedings of the 5th International Conference on Business Process Management (BPM 2007), Lecture Notes in Computer Science* (*Vol. 4714*, pp. 320–327). Springer, Berlin, Heidelberg. https://doi.org/10.1007/978-3-540-75183-0_23

van Notten, P. W. F., Rotmans, J., van Asselt, M. B. A., & Rothman, D. S. (2003). An updated scenario typology. *Futures, 35*(5), 423–443. https://doi.org/10.1016/S0016-3287(02)00090-3

Veloso, M. M., & Carbonell, J. G. (1993). Derivational Analogy in PRODIGY: Automating Case Acquisition, Storage, and Utilization. *Machine Learning, 10*, 249–278. https://doi.org/10.1023/A:1022686910523

Vernez, D., Buchs, D., & Pierrehumbert, G. (2003). Perspectives in the use of coloured Petri nets for risk analysis and accident modelling. *Safety Science, 41*(5), 445–463. https://doi.org/10.1016/S0925-7535(01)00078-9

Wada, T., Tomiya, A., Enomoto, M., Sato, T., Morishita, D., Izumi, S., … Kawata, G. (2016). Radiological impact of the nuclear power plant accident on freshwater fish in Fukushima: An overview of monitoring results. *Journal of Environmental Radioactivity, 151, Pt.1*, 144–155. https://doi.org/10.1016/j.jenvrad.2015.09.017

Walter, H., Gering, F., Arnold, K., Gerich, B., Heinrich, G., & Welte, U. (2016). *RODOS-based Simulation of Potential Accident Scenarios for Emergency Response Management in the Vicinity of Nuclear Power Plants*. Bundesamt für Strahlenschutz.

Wang, F., & Huang, Q.-Y. (2010). The importance of spatial-temporal issues for case-based reasoning in disaster management. In *18th International Conference on Geoinformatics* (pp. 1–5). Beijing, China: IEEE. https://doi.org/10.1109/GEOINFORMATICS.2010.5567639

Wang, J., Tepfenhart, W., & Rosca, D. (2009). Emergency Response Workflow Resource Requirements Modeling and Analysis. *IEEE Transactions on Systems, Man, and Cybernetics, Part C (Applications and Reviews), 39*(3), 270–283. https://doi.org/10.1109/tsmcc.2009.2009125

Wang, X. Z., & Yeung, D. S. (2000). Using fuzzy integral to modeling case based reasoning with feature interaction. In *SMC 2000 Conference Proceedings. 2000 IEEE International Conference on Systems, Man and Cybernetics. "Cybernetics Evolving to Systems, Humans, Organizations, and their Complex Interactions"* (Vol. 5, pp. 3660–3665). https://doi.org/10.1109/ICSMC.2000.886578

Weber, B. G., & Ontanón, S. (2010). Using Automated Replay Annotation for Case-Based Planning in Games. In *Proceedings of the 18th International Conference on Case-Based Reasoning (ICCBR'10)* (pp. 15–24). Alessandria, Italy.

Weidlich, M., Dijkman, R., & Mendling, J. (2010). The ICoP framework: Identification of correspondences between process models. In B. Pernici (Ed.), *Advanced Information Systems Engineering. CAiSE 2010. Lecture Notes in Computer Science* (Vol. 6051, pp. 483–498). Springer, Berlin, Heidelberg. https://doi.org/10.1007/978-3-642-13094-6_37

Wettschereck, D., & Aha, D. W. (1995). Weighting features. In M. Veloso & A. Aamodt (Eds.), *CaseBased Reasoning Research and Development* (pp. 347–358). Springer, Berlin, Heidelberg. https://doi.org/10.1007/3-540-60598-3_31

Wilke, W., Vollrath, I., Althoff, K.-D., & Bergmann, R. (1997). A Framework for Learning Adaptation Knowledge Based on Knowledge Light Approaches. In *Proceedings of the Fifth German Workshop on Case-Based Reasoning* (pp. 235--242).

Wilson, D. R., & Martinez, T. R. (1997). Improved Heterogeneous Distance Functions. *Journal of Artificial Intelligence Research, 6*, 1–34. https://doi.org/10.1613/jair.346

Woleński, J. (2004). Polish Logic. *Logic Journal of IGPL, 12*(5), 399–428. https://doi.org/10.1093/jigpal/12.5.399

Wu, D., Li, J., & Liang, Y. (2013). Linear combination of multiple case-based reasoning with optimized weight for software effort estimation. *The Journal of Supercomputing, 64*, 898–918. https://doi.org/10.1007/s11227-010-0525-9

Xu, X., Wang, K., Ma, W., & Lin, J. (2010). Improving the Reliability of Case-Based Reasoning Systems. *International Journal of Computational Intelligence Systems, 3*(3), 256–265. https://doi.org/10.2991/ijcis.2010.3.3.1

Yan, A., Shao, H., & Guo, Z. (2014). Weight optimization for case-based reasoning using membrane computing. *Information Sciences, 287*, 109–120. https://doi.org/10.1016/j.ins.2014.07.043

Yan, A., & Wang, D. (2015). Expert Systems with Applications Trustworthiness evaluation and retrieval-based revision method for case-based reasoning classifiers. *Expert Systems with Applications, 42*(21), 8006–8013. https://doi.org/10.1016/j.eswa.2015.06.027

Yan, L., Jinsong, B., Xiaofeng, H., & Ye, J. (2009). A heuristic project scheduling approach for quick response to maritime disaster rescue. *International Journal of Project Management, 27*(6), 620–628. https://doi.org/10.1016/j.ijproman.2008.10.001

Yang, B.-S., Kwon Jeong, S., Oh, Y.-M., & Tan, A. C. C. (2004). Case-based reasoning system with Petri nets for induction motor fault diagnosis. *Expert Systems with Applications, 27*(2), 301–311. https://doi.org/10.1016/j.eswa.2004.02.004

Yumashev, D., & Johnson, P. (2017). Flexible decision making in the wake of large scale nuclear emergencies: Long-term response. *European Journal of Operational Research, 261*(1), 368–389. https://doi.org/10.1016/j.ejor.2017.01.054

Zadeh, L. a. (1965). Fuzzy sets. *Information and Control, 8*(3), 338–353. https://doi.org/10.1016/S0019-9958(65)90241-X

Zeevaert, T., Bousher, A., Brendler, V., Hedemann Jensen, P., & Nordlinder, S. (2001). Evaluation and ranking of restoration strategies for radioactively contaminated sites. *Journal of Environmental Radioactivity, 56*(1-2), 33–50. https://doi.org/10.1016/S0265-931X(01)00046-7

Zhang, L., Coenen, F., & Leng, P. (2002). Formalising optimal feature weight setting in case based diagnosis as linear programming problems. *Knowledge-Based Systems, 15*(7), 391–398. https://doi.org/10.1016/S0950-7051(02)00023-0

Zhao, J., Cui, L., Zhao, L., Qiu, T., & Chen, B. (2009). Learning HAZOP expert system by case-based reasoning and ontology. *Computers & Chemical Engineering, 33*(1), 371–378. https://doi.org/10.1016/j.compchemeng.2008.10.006

Zhong, M., Shi, C., Fu, T., He, L., & Shi, J. (2010). Study in performance analysis of China Urban Emergency Response System based on Petri net. *Safety Science, 48*(6), 755–762. https://doi.org/10.1016/j.ssci.2010.02.017

Zhou, J. (2013). Petri net modeling for the emergency response to chemical accidents. *Journal of Loss Prevention in the Process Industries, 26*(4), 766–770. https://doi.org/10.1016/j.jlp.2013.02.002

Zhou, J., & Reniers, G. (2016). Petri-net based modeling and queuing analysis for resource-oriented cooperation of emergency response actions. *Process Safety and Environmental Protection, 102*, 567–576. https://doi.org/10.1016/j.psep.2016.05.013

Zhou, X., & Wang, F. (2014). A spatial awareness case-based reasoning approach for typhoon disaster management. In *Proceedings of the IEEE International Conference on Software Engineering and Service Sciences, ICSESS* (pp. 893–896). https://doi.org/10.1109/ICSESS.2014.6933709

Appendix A Sources for the Attribute Catalogue

Method of Risk Analysis for Civil Protection

Table A.1: Attributes to describe the reference area (Federal Office of Civil Protection and Disaster Assistance 2011, p. 24)

Category	Information
Man	Number of inhabitants Population density Number of households
Environment	Protected areas Agricultural land
Economy	Economic performance Business tax receipts
Supply	Infrastructures of water supply Infrastructures of electricity supply Infrastructures of gas supply Infrastructures of telecommunication
Immaterial	Cultural assets

Table A.2: Parameters to describe a scenario (Federal Office of Civil Protection and Disaster Assistance 2011, p. 26)

Parameter	
Hazard	Development
Scene of occurrence	Notice time for warning (refers to the expectancy of an event and the ability of the population and the public authority to prepare)
Spatial dimension	Who is affected?
Intensity	Reference incidents (refers to comparable events in the past)
Time	Further information (refers to preparedness of authorities, relief units and helpers, damage susceptibility and robustness of persons or elements)
Duration	

Table A.3: Impact parameters (Federal Office of Civil Protection and Disaster Assistance 2011, p. 30 f.)

Category	Damage parameter
Man	Fatalities Injured Persons in need longer than 14 days Persons in need up to 14 days
Environment	Impairment of protected area Impairment of water bodies Impairment of ground water Impairment of agricultural land
Economy	Physical damage Consequential damage Loss of economic performance Loss of economic profitability
Supply	Disruption of water supply Disruption of energy supply Disruption of gas supply Disruption of telecommunication
Immaterial	Impact on public order and safety Political implications Psychological implications Damage to cultural assets

Disaster Inventory System (DesInventar)

Table A.4: Basic effects of a disaster (DesInventar Project 2009, p. 19-22)

Basic Effects
Deaths
Loss value (local currency/US$ according to exchange rate on the date of the disaster)
Routes affected (length of transport networks destroyed and/or rendered unusable)
Other losses (e.g. religious buildings, monuments, architectural or cultural heritage buildings, theatres and public installations, public administrations buildings, vehicles or buses lost, bridges)
Missing
Crops and woods
Observations about the effects
Wounded, sick
Livestock
Affected
Educational centers

Basic Effects
Relocated
Health Sector
Homes affected
Evacuees
Victims (persons whose goods have been damaged directly associated with the event)
Homes destroyed
Qualitative fields (affected or not affected): Transport Communications Aid organization installations Agriculture and fishing Aqueduct Sewerage Education Energy Industry Health

Tactical Situation Object (TSO)

Table A.5: Data elements of Tactical Situation Object (CEN, 2009a, p. 15-24)

Element name	Definition
Id	Identifier of the event
Name	Name for the event
Main event id	Link to the main event
Category	Scenario that leads to the event
Actor	Type of endangered objects
Location type	Location where the event takes place
Environment	Context of the event
Scale	Severity of the event
Certainty	Percentage probability of occurrence of the event
Occurrence time	Date and time of the occurrence of the event which may be in future
Status	Status of the event (complete, in progress, not started, under control)
Risk assessment	Predicted evolution of the event (increasing, decreasing or stable)
Casualties	Actual or predicted casualties
Decontaminated	Number of casualties needing treatment against CBRN agents
Triage red	Number of casualties at the "red" priority level

Element name	Definition
Triage yellow	Number of casualties at the "yellow" priority level
Triage green	Number of casualties at the "green" priority level
Triage black	Number of casualties at the "black" priority level
Missing	Number of individuals reported or presumed missing
Displaced	Number of people who are moved due to the event
Evacuated	Number of individuals who undergoing the process of being moved
Geographical location	Geographical location of the event
Type of area	Type of area
Weather	Weather at the location
Cause	Accidental, deliberate, natural
Resource type	Description of the resource
Capability of resource	Main domains of capabilities and competencies of the resource
Characteristics of resource	Information about the main physical characteristics (height, weight, size etc.)
Name of resource	Name for the resource
Quantity of resource	Quantity of resource

Real-time On-line Decision Support System for Off-site Emergency Management in Europe (RODOS)

Table A.6: Input data of JRodos (Ehrhardt et al. 2002, p.28-44)

Fix data	Model parameter (customization to national conditions)
	Geographical data (information necessary for the presentation of results on maps and data relating to special objects, such as human settlements, transport networks etc.)
	Statistical data (for calculating consequences – population distribution, economic data to estimate costs, agricultural production data)
	Nuclear power plant data (type, description, inventory)
	Countermeasure data (frame conditions and planning fundamentals such as intervention levels, EU maximum levels of activity concentration of food and feed, planning sectors, evacuation routes and availability of transport vehicle)
Real-time data	Actual radiological and meteorological data obtained from fixed and mobile monitoring stations
Prognostic data	Source term, atmospheric dispersion and meteorological forecast data
Additional source term information	End of chain reaction
	Begin of release

	Release height
	Released thermal output
	Proportion of iodine
	Release of nuclides

Appendix B Attribute Catalogue

Table B.1: Attributes describing the event

Attribute	Description	Attribute type	Domain
accident type		symbolic	nuclear power plant accident explosion of radiological dispersal service radiological accident with fire
endangered objects	types of endangered objects taken from TSO remark: the taxonomy of endangered objects is very general and should be specified motivation: countermeasures are targeted at surfaces, production systems etc. that are likely to be/have been contaminated	symbolic	see TSO
	Suggestion: additional endangered objects	symbolic	see EURANOS handbooks
location type	describes the type of location where the event is taking place	symbolic	see TSO
environment	describes the general environment or context of the event	symbolic	see TSO
scale	describes the severity of the event	numeric	see TSO
certainty	provides a percentage probability of occurrence of the event	numeric	[0,1]
occurrence time	describes the date and time of the occurrence of the event This may refer to a future occurrence.	temporal	

Attribute	Description	Attribute type	Domain
risk assessment	states the predicted evolution of the event	symbolic	increasing decreasing stable
type of area	type of area	symbolic	see TSO
weather	describes the weather at the location	symbolic	see TSO
cause	cause of the event	symbolic	accidental deliberate natural
source term			
release height		numeric, meter	
release duration		numeric, hours	
time of release	categories for release time	symbolic	day night
dose		numeric, Sv	
exposure pathways		symbolic	inhalation ingestion skin external radiation soil external radiation cloud
shielding		symbolic	yes no
size of area	size of affected area	numeric, ha	
number of people affected	number of people affected	numeric	

Table B.2: Attributes describing the nuclear power plant

Attribute	Description	Attribute type	Domain
name		textual	
type		symbolic	
gross output		numeric, MW	

Attribute	Description	Attribute type	Domain
net output		numeric, MW	
number of blocks		numeric	
burnup		numeric, GWd/tHM	

Table B.3: Attributes describing radionuclides

Attribute	Description	Attribute type	Domain
symbol			
name		symbolic	see EURANOS handbooks
alpha		numeric, MeV	
alpha percentage		numeric	
beta		numeric , MeV	
beta percentage		numeric	
gamma		numeric, KeV	
gamma percentage		numeric	
dominant radiation type		symbolic	alpha beta gamma
radioactive half-life		numeric	

Table B.4: Attributes describing the location

Attribute	Description	Attribute type	Domain
population size		numeric	
population density	mean value per km^2	numeric	
number of households		numeric	

Attribute	Description	Attribute type	Domain
population distribution		symbolic	rural urban metropolitan
groups:			
school children	percentage of	numeric	[0,1]
religious groups	percentage of	numeric	[0,1]
patients	percentage of	numeric	[0,1]
prisoners	percentage of	numeric	[0,1]
tourists	percentage of	numeric	[0,1]
movements:			
commuters	percentage of	numeric	[0,1]
students	percentage of	numeric	[0,1]
holidaymakers	percentage of	numeric	[0,1]
time population spend outdoors	mean value of time population spend outdoors	numeric, hours	
accommodation available	number of availability of and provision of resources for accommodation/housing	numeric	
availability of transport	percentage of private car ownership	numeric	[0,1]
transport infrastructure			
roads	scale	symbolic	few many
railways	scale	symbolic	few many
protected areas	percentage of whole area	numeric	[0,1]
	information on areas	textual	
agricultural land	percentage of whole area	numeric	[0,1]
gross domestic product		numeric	
business tax receipts		numeric	

Attribute	Description	Attribute type	Domain
infrastructure of water supply			
infrastructure of electricity supply		numeric, hours	
infrastructure of gas supply			
infrastructure of telecommunication			
cultural assets			
hospital	number of	numeric	
school	number of	numeric	
rest home	number of	numeric	
kindergarten	number of	numeric	
prison	number of	numeric	
type of buildings			
construction method			
configuration		symbolic	multi-storey terraced semi-detached detached
location factors			
air exchange/ ventilation			
background dose rates		numeric, Sv	
experience	experience from other emergencies, acceptability of types of management	textual	

Two types of consequences or damages have to be regarded. The first type of damages result from the incident itself, which are potentially location-dependent damages. The second type of damages result from implemented measures, which are important to evaluate measures.

Table B.5: Attributes for describing consequences

Attribute	Description	Attribute type	Domain
fatalities	number of	numeric	
injured	number of	numeric	
decontaminated	number of	numeric	
displaced	number of	numeric	
impairment of protected areas	protected areas which are damaged due to the incident (protected areas, national parks, biosphere reservations, landscape protection areas, natural parks)	numeric, ha	
impairment of water bodies	living space in surface waters or in the sea which are damaged due to the incident (rivers, canals, brooks, lakes, ponds)	numeric, km/ha	
impairment of groundwater	ground water which is contaminated due to the incident	numeric, ha	
impairment of agricultural land	agricultural land which is damaged due to the incident	numeric, ha	
	decrease in biodiversity		
	loss of plants and shrubs		
	risk of soil erosion		
	partial or full loss of soil fertility		
	landscape changes		
	contamination of soil due to chemicals used for tie-down option		
	disrepair of restricted areas		
physical damage/ direct costs:	sum of the replacement value of the direct material damage	numeric, monetary value	
cost of protection measures		numeric, monetary value	

Attribute	Description	Attribute type	Domain
labour		numeric, monetary value	
loss of production		numeric, monetary value	
consumables and equipment necessary for options		numeric, monetary value	
communication, support, transportation and the need to verify laboratory analyses or screening techniques for quality assurance		numeric, monetary value	
consequential damage/indirect costs:	includes: impacts on soil structure, fertility, risk of erosion, reduction or loss of tourism, relocation costs or business closures etc.	numeric, monetary value	
loss of economic performance		numeric, monetary value	
loss of economic profitability	business tax losses due to the incident	numeric, monetary value	
disruption of water supply	duration	numeric, hours	
disruption of water supply, people affected	number of	numeric	
disruption of energy supply	duration	numeric, hours	
disruption of energy supply, people affected	number of	numeric	
disruption of gas supply	duration	numeric, hours	
disruption of gas supply, people affected	number of	numeric	

Attribute	Description	Attribute type	Domain
disruption of telecommunication	duration	numeric, hours	
disruption of telecommunication, people affected	number of	numeric	
impact on public order and safety	extent of the consequences of the incident on public safety (e. g. public protests, violence against persons/objects)	textual	
political implications	extent of the consequences of the incident on the political-administrative sector (e. g. call for state actions, public calls for resignations)	textual	
psychological implications/ social impacts	extent of the loss of trust in public authorities (e.g. government, administration)	textual	
damage to cultural assets	cultural assets according to the Hague Convention which is damaged due to the incident number and degree of damage	numeric	
with/without implementation of a strategy		symbolic	with without

The EURANOS handbook for contaminated inhabited areas provides 48 recovery and 11 pre-release emergency measures whereat they can be implemented in the early or medium-long phase. The handbook for food production systems provide 58 measures and the handbook for drinking water further 10 measures. For each measure a datasheet exists. The handbooks include a detailed description for each attribute.

Table B.6: Attributes describing measures

Attribute	Description	Attribute type	Domain
name		symbolic	see EURANOS handbooks
objective		textual	
other benefits		textual	

Attribute	Description	Attribute type	Domain
management option description		textual	
target		textual	
targeted radionuclides		textual	
scale of application		textual	
exposure pathway pre intervention		textual	
time of application		textual	
legal constraints		textual	
environmental/ technical constraints		textual	
effectiveness		textual	
for inhabited areas:			
reduction in contamination on the surface		textual	
reduction in surface dose rates		textual	
reduction in resuspension		textual	
technical factors influencing effectiveness		textual	
social factors influencing effectiveness		textual	
required specific equipment		textual	
required ancillary equipment		textual	
required utilities and infrastructure		textual	
required consumables		textual	
required skills		textual	
required safety precautions		textual	
other feasibility limitations		textual	
amount and type of waste		textual	
possible transport, treatment and storage routes for waste		textual	
factors influencing waste issues		textual	
averted doses		textual	
factors influencing averted doses		textual	

Attribute	Description	Attribute type	Domain
additional doses		textual	
incremental dose		textual	
operator time for implementing the option		textual	
factors influencing costs		textual	
cost of equipment		textual	
cost of consumables		textual	
compensation costs		textual	
waste costs		textual	
assumptions influencing intervention costs		textual	
communication needs		textual	
environmental impact		textual	
social impact		textual	
ethical considerations		textual	
agricultural impact		textual	
other side effects		textual	
(FARMING Network) stakeholder opinion		textual	
practical experience		textual	
comments		textual	

Table B.7: Example taxonomy of the domain of the attribute 'location type' (CEN, 2009b, p. 23 f.)

Higher levels	Code	Definition	Additional description
	COAST	Coastal area	The land next to the sea, seashore
	INW	Inland waterway	A body of water, such as a river, canal or lake. It may be navigable if it is deep and wide enough for a vessel to pass and there are no obstructions
	NAT	Natural/rural	Natural/rural environment environment
	OSEA	Open Sea	Open Sea
	OTH	Other	Other
	PRIVAT		The location of the event is a private property, which may mean that the access to the location may require the authorization of the owner

Higher levels	Code	Definition	Additional description
	RAIL	Rail infra-structure	Rail infrastructure
	ROAD	Road infra-structure	Smoothed or paved surface, made for travelling by motor & other vehicles
	UDGN	Under-ground	Underground location
	URB	Urban area	Urban area location
/COAST	BNK	Beach/bank	Boundary between land and water
/COAST	CLF	Cliff	Either the incident is on the cliff face, or on a narrow strip between the cliff and water
/COAST	CSTW	Coastal Water	Sea, but possible navigation hazards between the open sea and the land
/COAST	EST	Estuary	Open water, but with navigation hazards dependent on the tide Tidal waters at the mouth of a river, or Fjord
/COAST	FEN	Fen	Boat access probably required wetland with open water
/INW	BOG	Marsh	Access difficult wetland with little open water
/INW	CAN	Canal water-way	Navigable waterway, potentially with waterside access Artificial waterway
/INW	ICELK	Iced lake	Lake, or pond covered by ice
/INW	LKE	Lake	Lake or pond, including loch and inland sea
/INW	RIV	River	Crossing limited to bridges or by boat River, greater than 5m
/NAT	CRP	Crop	Arable farmland
/NAT	GRS	Grassland	Pasture and open grassland, including parkland
/NAT	HFR	High forest	Characterised by dense woodland, with trees typically over 20 m Vehicular access by road only.
/NAT	HLS	Hillside	Hilly areas with limited road access
/NAT	HMT	High Moun-tain	Mountain above the area accessible by vehicle
/NAT	LMT	Mountain side	Mountainous areas with limited road access
/NAT	SSSI	Sites of scien-tific interest	Sites designated of special Scientific Interest (SSSI)

Higher levels	Code	Definition	Additional description
/OSEA	OFF	Sea Platform	Installation is offshore, including oil and gas platforms, associated accommodation platforms Also piers.
/OTH	CUT	Cutting	Limited access from the side, may be fire hazard A road or railway or canal below ground level
/OTH	ELV	Elevated Section	No access from the sides A road or railway or canal elevated above the normal ground level by a bridge or viaduct
/OTH	EMB	Embanked Section	Limited access from the side, may be fire hazard A road or railway or canal elevated by embankment
/OTH	LFR	Woodland	Characterised by open woodland Little vehicular access off road
/OTH	SRB	Scrub	Characterised by bushes and occasional trees Potential limited vehicular access
/PRIVAT	OWNRSC	Site with own rescue team	Private property belonging to an organization that owns a private rescue team (for example, an industrial site with an internal fire service)
/RAIL	TRK	Railway track	Railway track restricts access from the sides and difficult to drive along A standard gauge railway track
/ROAD	1RD	One-way Road	Road with single direction of travel, limiting the access direction A one-way road (not part of a dual carriageway), including slip roads on interchanges
/ROAD	DCA	Dual Carriageway	Dual carriageway, including motorway or autobahn so that the approach must be from an appropriate direction A road divided into two, such that crossing sides is not practical
/ROAD	NOR	Open Ground	Area with no road or path, but may be accessible in part to most vehicles An area which a road vehicle may be able to cross, but without any road or track
/ROAD	PTH	Path	Footpath A route unsuitable for road vehicles
/ROAD	RRD	Restricted Road	Road not suitable for all vehicles, e.g. due to low bridge A road with a notified restriction on traffic movement, such as a height restriction, a weight restriction, etc.

Higher levels	Code	Definition	Additional description
/ROAD	SRD	Side Road	Minor road which may restrict access to large vehicles, or traffic flow or prevent vehicles turning A road which is restricted by its width, or in urban areas, by parked cars, such that traffic in one direction must allow traffic in the other to pass
/ROAD	TRK	Trackway	Off-road, but a hard surface for vehicles An unmade-up road which traversable by light vehicles
/UDGN	MIN	Mine	Underground working, possibly disused
/UDGN	TUN	Tunnel	Tunnel A road, railway or canal in a tunnel
/UDGN	UND	Underground building	Underground building / commercial / industrial area
/URB	ASR	Assembly area	An assembly or a recreational area
/URB	HOSP	Hospital	Health institution (hospital, elderly house, etc.)
/URB	IND	Industrial area	Industrial area
/URB	MALL	Mall	The location of the event is a commercial centre
/URB	OFF	Office area	Office area
/URB	PRK	Park place	Park place
/URB	RES	Residential area	Residential area (house, residential dwelling, etc.)
/URB	STRT	Street	Public area (street for example)

Appendix C Evaluation Form for Impact Assessment

Please determine values for x and y.

MAN

Classification

	fatalities			injured		
disastrous		>	x		>	x
significant	x	-	y	x	-	y
moderate	x	-	y	x	-	y
minor	x	-	y	x	-	y
insignificant		≤	x		≤	x

REMARKS

ENVIRONMENT

Classification

	impairment of protected area	impairment of water bodies	impairment of ground water	impairment of agricultural land
disastrous	long term > x ha or temporarily > x ha	river > x km or lake > x ha or sea > x ha	> x ha	long term > x ha or temporarily > x ha
significant	long term > x - y ha or temporarily > x - y ha	river > x km or lake > x ha or sea > x ha	x - y ha	long term > x - y ha or temporarily > x - y ha
moderate	long term > x - y ha or temporarily > x - y ha	river > x km or lake > x ha or sea > x ha	x - y ha	long term > x - y ha or temporarily > x - y ha
minor	long term > x - y ha or temporarily > x - y ha	river > x km or lake > x ha or sea > x ha	x - y ha	long term > x - y ha or temporarily > x - y ha
insignificant	long term ≤ x ha or temporarily ≤ x ha	river ≤ x km or lake ≤ x ha or sea ≤ x ha	≤ x ha	long term ≤ x ha or temporarily ≤ x ha

REMARKS

ECONOMY

Classification

	physical damage			consequential damage			loss of economic performance			loss of economic profitability		
disastrous		>	x		>	x		>	x		>	x
significant	x	-	y	x	-	y	x	-	y	x	-	y
moderate	x	-	y	x	-	y	x	-	y	x	-	y
minor	x	-	y	x	-	y	x	-	y	x	-	y
insignificant		≤	x		≤	x		≤	x		≤	x

REMARKS

SUPPLY

Classification

	disruption of water supply	disruption of energy supply	disruption of gas supply	disruption of telecommunication
disastrous	> x persons for > x hours/days	> x persons for > x hours/days	> x persons for > x hours/days	> x persons for > x hours/days
significant	x - y persons for x - y hours/days	x - y persons for x - y hours/days	x - y persons for x - y hours/days	x - y persons for x - y hours/days
moderate	x - y persons for x - y hours/days	x - y persons for x - y hours/days	x - y persons for x - y hours/days	x - y persons for x - y hours/days
minor	x - y persons for x - y hours/days	x - y persons for x - y hours/days	x - y persons for x - y hours/days	x - y persons for x - y hours/days
insignificant	≤ x persons for ≤ x hours/days	≤ x persons for ≤ x hours/days	≤ x persons for ≤ x hours/days	≤ x persons for ≤ x hours/days

REMARKS

IMMATERIEL

Classification

	impact on public order and safety		political Implications		psychological Implications		damage to cultural assets	
disastrous	Extent		Extent		Extent		Extent	
significant	Extent		Extent		Extent		Extent	
moderate	Extent		Extent		Extent		Extent	
minor	Extent		Extent		Extent		Extent	
insignificant	Extent		Extent		Extent		Extent	

REMARKS

Appendix D Evaluation of the Attribute Catalogue

Event	attribute	pre-release	release	transition	long-term post-accident	notes
	accident type	4	4	4	4	
	endangered objects	4	4	4	4	merge to one attribute 'target' and update the taxonomy
	additional endangered objects	4	4	4	4	
	location type	4	4	4	4	merge with 'type of area' and update domain
	environment	4	4	3	3	change attribute into 'other environmental hazards';
	scale	4	4	4	4	INES
	certainty	4	3	0	0	certainty = probability of release; differences due to definition problems
	occurrence time	4	4	2	1	merge attribute with 'time of release' and offer categories (day/night; season etc.)
	risk assessment	4	4	2	2	
	type of area	3	4	4	4	delete
	weather	4	4	2	0	weather at release; update domain
	cause	3	3	1	0	
	source term	4	4	4	4	

Event attribute	pre-release	release	transition	long-term post-accident	notes
release height	4	4	2	0	
release duration	4	4	2	0	
time of release	4	4	0	0	delete
dose	4	4	4	4	
exposure pathways	4	4	4	4	
shielding	4	4	2	0	
size of area	4	4	4	4	
number of people affected	4	4	4	4	
dispersal process type	2	4	3	3	add; type of process leading to the release; fire, explosion
accident scenario type					add

Nuclear power plant attribute	pre-release	release	transition	long-term post-accident	notes
name					
type	4	4	0	0	
gross output	3	3	0	0	
net output	3	2	2	0	
number of blocks	3	3	0	0	
burnup	4	4	1	0	
additional attributes to describe a nuclear power plant					
inventory	4	4	1	1	add; in Bq
thermal Power	4	4	0	0	add

Location	attribute	pre-release	release	transition	long-term post-accident	notes
	population size	4	4	4	4	delete; same as affected people
	population density	4	4	4	4	per km^2
	number of households	4	4	4	4	per km^2
	population distribution	4	4	4	4	
	groups:					
	school children	4	4	4	4	in taxonomy of targets: children
	religious groups	0	0	2	2	delete
	patients	4	4	2	1	specification of percentage directly with targets
	prisoners	2	2	2	1	delete
	tourists	3	3	2	1	Integrate in the taxonomy of targets
	movements:					
	commuters	2	2	2	2	delete
	students	0	0	0	0	delete
	holidaymakers	2	2	0	2	delete
	time population spend outdoors	3	4	3	2	
	accommodation available	4	4	4	3	
	availability of transport	4	4	3	0	
	transport infrastructure:					
	roads	4	4	2	0	implicitly in population distribution

Location attribute	pre-release	release	transition	long-term post-accident	notes
					(urban, rural…)
railways	4	4	2	0	in taxonomy of endangered objects; delete
protected areas	3	4	3	4	
textual descr	4	4	4	4	
agricultural land	4	4	4	4	compare to land use, already included in taxonomy of targets
gross domestic product	2	3	3	3	
business tax receipts	0	2	3	3	delete
infrastructure of water supply	4	4	4	3	possible specifications: number of people relying on it; cubic meter (unknown importance for the population); risk to be contaminated [0,1];
infrastructure of electricity supply	2	4	4	3	
infrastructure of gas supply	1	3	3	2	

Location	attribute	pre-release	release	transi-tion	long-term post-accident	notes
	infrastructure of telecommunication	4	4	3	2	possible specification: speed of connection can give an insight about what type of information might be received; higher bandwidths allow sharing photos and videos from the incident site; low bandwidths allow basic SOS and 112 calls which can affect strategies for management
	cultural assets	2	2	3	4	delete; implicitly included in taxonomy of targets
	hospital	4	4	4	2	in taxonomy of targets
	school	4	4	4	4	in taxonomy of targets
	rest home	4	4	2	2	elderly is in taxonomy of targets
	kindergarten	4	4	4	4	in taxonomy of targets
	prison	2	2	2	1	delete
	type of buildings					in taxonomy of targets
	construction method	3	3	4	2	

Location	attribute	pre-release	release	transition	long-term post-accident	notes
	configuration	3	4	3	2	delete
	location factors	4	4	3	4	possible specifications: distance from the source; vicinity to natural objects (river, mounting); type of housing system (regular, chaotic)
	air exchange / ventilation	4	4	1	1	possible specifications: air exchanges per hour; presence/absence; type (forced/ natural)
	background dose rates	3	3	3	4	
	experience	4	4	4	4	categories: experienced, less experienced, no experience

Radionuclide	attribute	pre-release	release	transition	long-term post-accident	notes
	symbol	4	4	4	4	
	name	4	4	4	4	
	alpha	4	4	4	4	
	alpha percentage	4	4	4	4	
	beta	4	4	4	4	
	beta percentage	4	4	4	4	
	gamma	4	4	4	4	
	gamma percentage	4	4	4	4	

Radionuclide	attribute	pre-release	release	transition	long-term post-accident	notes
	dominant radiation type	4	4	4	4	
	radioactive half-life	4	4	4	4	
	additional attributes to describe a radionuclide					
	bioavailability					add
	mobility eg KD					add
	volatilisation					add
	physicochemical forms					add; can be very important in early phase as some contaminants will give inhalation dose and some not (due to e.g. aerosol size), and also in later time phases (governing the migration of some contaminants)

Consequence	attribute	pre-release	release	transition	long-term post-accident	notes
	fatalities	0	4	2	2	
	injured	0	4	2	1	
	decontaminated	0	4	3	1	

Conse-quence	attribute	pre-release	release	transi-tion	long-term post-accident	notes
	displaced	0	4	4	4	specify dis-placed (evac-uated, relo-cated or sheltered)
	impairment of pro-tected areas	0	3	4	4	
	impairment of water bodies	0	4	4	4	
	impairment of groundwater	0	4	4	4	specify groundwater because some locations use ground water for drinking water - others use surface waters or lake waters
	impairment of agri-cultural land	0	4	4	4	
	physical damage / direct costs:	0	4	4	3	
	cost of protection measures	0	4	4	3	delete; in-cluded in description of a measure
	labour	0	4	3	4	delete; in-cluded in de-scription of a measure
	loss of production	0	4	3	4	
	consumables and equipment necessary for options	0	4	3	4	delete; in-cluded in de-scription of a measure

Consequence	attribute	pre-release	release	transition	long-term post-accident	notes
	communication, support, transportation and the need to verify laboratory analyses or screening techniques for quality assurance	0	4	3	4	delete; included in description of a measure
	consequential damage /indirect costs:	0	4	3	4	
	loss of economic performance	0	2	3	3	
	loss of economic profitability	0	2	3	3	
	disruption of water supply	0	4	4	4	
	disruption of water supply, people affected	0	3	4	4	
	disruption of energy supply	0	4	4	3	
	disruption of energy supply, people affected	0	4	4	3	
	disruption of gas supply	0	3	3	2	
	disruption of gas supply, people affected	0	3	3	2	
	disruption of telecommunication	0	4	4	2	
	disruption of telecommunication, people affected	0	4	4	2	
	impact on public order and safety	0	4	3	3	categories: no impact, some negative impact, severe impact
	political implications	0	3	3	3	merge this attribute with

Conse-quence	attribute	pre-release	release	transi-tion	long-term post-accident	notes
						impact on public order an safety
	psychological implica-tions /social impacts	0	4	4	4	categories: no impact, some negative impact, severe impacts
	damage to cultural assets	0	3	3	2	merge this at-tribute with damage to cultural assets

Appendix E Hierarchy of Targets

Hierachy of targets, developed during the PREPARE project by Anne Nisbet.

1. **Inhabited Areas**
    a. Buildings
        i. Residential
            1. Multi-story
                a. External surfaces
                    i. Roofs
                    ii. Walls
                    iii. Gutters and downpipes
                b. Internal surfaces
                c. Precious objects
            2. Semi detached
            3. Detached
            4. Mobile homes and tents
        ii. Non residential
            1. Schools
            2. Hospital
            3. Offices
            4. Shops
            5. Recreational
            6. Cultural structures
        iii. Industrial
        iv. Infrastructure
            1. Roads
            2. Rail

3. Airports
4. Ports
5. Underground
6. Sewage and water treatment
7. Power generation

v. Transport

1. Cars, buses, motorbikes
2. Overland and Underground trains
3. Airplane
4. Ships, boats and submarines

2. Open Spaces

a. Parks and sports grounds

b. Countryside

i. Wild animals

1. Game

ii. Wild plants

1. Mushrooms and berries
2. Herbs

iii. Sites of special scientific interest

c. Beaches

d. Mountains

3. Water environment

a. Drinking water supplies

i. Reservoirs

ii. Surface water

iii. Ground water

iv. Rainwater

b. Inland waterways
    i. Rivers
        1. Aquatic food
    ii. Canals
c. Marine
    i. Coastal water
        1. Aquatic food
    ii. Deep sea
        1. Aquatic food

4. **Woods and Forests**
    a. Woods
    b. Forests

5. **Agricultural areas**
    a. Crop growing
        i. Cereals
        ii. Vegetables
        iii. Fruit
        iv. Fodder
        v. Industrial crops
    b. Livestock
        i. Beef cattle
            1. Meat
        ii. Dairy cows
            1. Milk
            2. Other dairy produce
        iii. Sheep
            1. Meat

2. Milk
3. Wool

iv. Goats

1. Meat
2. Milk

v. Pigs

1. Meat

vi. Chickens

1. Meat
2. Eggs

c. Horticulture

6. People

a. Adults

i. Pregnant women
ii. Elderly
iii. Hospital patients
iv. Nursing home patients

b. Adolescents

c. Children

d. Babies